DODGE Pickups

History and Restoration Guide 1918-1971

Don Bunn and Tom Brownell

MBI Publishing Company

First published in 1991 by MBI Publishing Company, PO Box 1, 729 Prospect Avenue, Osceola, WI 54020-0001 USA

The information in this book is true and complete to the best of our knowledge. All recommendations are made without any guarantee on the part of the author or Publisher, who also disclaim any liability incurred in connection with the use of this data or specific details.

We recognize that some words, model names and designations, for example, mentioned herein are the property of the trademark holder. We use them for identification purposes only. This is not an official publication.

MBI Publishing Company books are also available at discounts in bulk quantity for industrial or sales-promotional use. For details write to Special Sales Manager at Motorbooks International Wholesalers & Distributors, 729 Prospect Avenue, PO Box 1, Osceola, WI 54020-0001 USA.

Library of Congress Cataloging-in-Publication Data

Brownell, Tom.
    Dodge pickups : history and restoration guide, 1918–1971
    Tom Brownell, Don Bunn.
        p. cm.
    ISBN 0-87938-491-3
    1. Dodge trucks—History. 2. Dodge trucks—Conservation and restoration. I. Bunn, Don. II. Title.
TL230.5.D63B76   1991
629.28'73—dc20   90-48364

On the cover: The fabulous two-tone 1957 Dodge Sweptside, owned by Bill Warren, combined automotive styling with a truck's capabilities. *Bud Juneau, courtesy of Collectible Automobile*

On the title page: Artist Greg Norman's rendering of the 1954 half-ton pickup owned by Dan Schaefer of St. Paul, Minnesota. The truck is a rare Truck-O-Matic-equipped Dodge pickup.

Printed in the United States of America

Contents

Acknowledgments

It would be impossible to write a book of this scope without the assistance of a number of able and dedicated friends. We are fortunate in that we have many trucker friends who contributed most generously. We would like to thank the following individuals for their invaluable assistance.

John Zentmyer, Power-Wagon authority, Los Angeles, CA.

Greg Norman, artist, Richfield, MN.

Ron Cenowa, hobbyist, Dodge truck collector, toy truck collector, Utica, MI.

Mary Borchard, Chrysler Photographic, retired, Detroit, MI.

Manfred Strobel, manager of Chrysler Photographic, Detroit, MI.

James Wren, Motor Vehicle Manufacturers Association (MVMA), Detroit, MI.

Dan Kirchner, MVMA, Detroit, MI.

Paul McLaughlin, author, hobbyist, photographer, Albuquerque, NM.

Elliott Kahn, author, hobbyist, photographer, Clearwater Beach, FL.

Lanny Knutson, Plymouth Owners Club, Alberta, Canada.

Jim Benjaminson, Plymouth Owners Club, Cavalier, ND.

Steve Fish, Dodge truck dealer, Bloomington, MN.

Bruce Welle, Dodge truck dealer, Sauk Centre, MN.

Dick Copello, hobbyist, photographer, York, PA.

David Pollock, Dodge L-Six engines, Shawnigan Lake, British Columbia, Canada.

Dick Matott, Chazy, NY.

D. J. Smith, L'il Red Express, Detroit, MI.

Nancy Cox, Chrysler Historical Collection, Detroit, MI.

Bruce Thomas, Chrysler Historical Collection, Detroit, MI.

Bruce Horkey, pickup box restoration, Windom, MN.

Irv Burger, L-6 engine mechanic, Vadnais Heights, MN.

Special thanks go to Joel R. Miller for his dedication to making this the best possible Dodge truck book. Joel's writing, researching, editing, and proofing and his encouragement were of more value than words can express. The end result would not have been possible without him.

The following supplied information to help in compiling the paint code appendix: Lee A. Iacocca, L. W. Baker and Michael Aberlich of Chrysler Corporation, Bruce R. Thomas and staff of the Chrysler Historical Collection, Rick Pfenning of PPG Industries/Ditzler Automotive Finishes, Richard Perry and Rodger Hartley of the Dodge Brothers Club, and John S. White, Jr.

Unless otherwise noted, all photographs in this book are courtesy of Chrysler Photographic.

Introduction

Why a book on the light-duty trucks built by Chrysler? The answer is simple and obvious: none exists. Please notice we said Chrysler, not Dodge. Chrysler's Dodge Truck Division designed, engineered, and built corporate trucks, while corporate marketing decided what nameplates were affixed and how they were sold. Several excellent general reference books are available which cover Chrysler-built trucks, but this is the only book dedicated to Chrysler's light-duty trucks.

For all practical purposes, Dodge, Fargo, Plymouth, and DeSoto trucks are the same. It is true that they did vary slightly in trim details and sometimes even in mechanical specifications, but generally speaking they were identical.

A rough rule of thumb is that Dodge and Plymouth trucks were sold in the United States, Dodge and Fargo trucks were sold in Canada and DeSoto, Fargo and Dodge trucks were exported. Dodge, Fargo, Plymouth, and DeSoto trucks were built in the United States. Dodge, Fargo, and DeSoto trucks were built in Canada. In the early years the trucks built in Canada were sold in Canada. In recent years trucks built in Canada were sold in both the United States and Canada.

A second question the reader may have is, Why does the book deal primarily with the years 1933 to 1971? Chrysler purchased Dodge Brothers Inc. in June 1928. At that time, all Dodge Brothers-built trucks were badged as Graham Brothers, due to the relationship which had existed between the Graham brothers and Dodge. This relationship was dissolved shortly before Chrysler's purchase of Dodge Brothers. Chrysler immediately changed all truck name-

Dodge Truck styling model from October 18, 1955, revealed the modernistic lines that Dodge designers were working with.

This was a full-scale clay mockup, complete with chrome trim, doorhandles, bumpers, and production wheels and tires.

plates to Dodge Brothers because the Grahams were now a competitor; they had formed the Graham-Paige Company, a manufacturer of automobiles.

Between 1928 and 1933, Chrysler made a number of minor engineering and styling improvements to its truck line, but for the most part trucks continued without change. Finally, in 1933, Chrysler introduced the first trucks which were truly "Chryslerized," that is, trucks which Chrysler styled and engineered and trucks which were powered by Chrysler-built engines. The last year covered is 1971 because in 1972 Chrysler introduced an all-new Dodge truck which is the same basic full-sized truck as Dodge builds today.

You will find that this book is more than a history of Chrysler-built trucks. Indeed, it is a complete resource manual on collecting Chrysler-built light-duty trucks. The reader will find information on what to look for in a collector truck, how to repair and maintain it, its history, parts resources, clubs to help you find other owners, tech tips, restoration and rebuilding ideas, sources for literature and memorabilia, and several hundred photographs of Chrysler-built trucks.

Even if you don't own a collector truck, you will enjoy reading about and looking at photos of your favorite Chrysler-built light-duty trucks. Included are Pickups, Panels, Stakes, Canopies, Screens, Suburbans, Power-Wagons, Route-Vans, Sweptsides, Town Panels, Town Wagons, Custom Sports Specials, Vans, Compact Pickups, Campers, and Adventurers. Or, in other words, something for everybody. We trust you will find this book an excellent resource to help you own and enjoy your Chrysler-built trucks.

Don Bunn
Tom Brownell
1990

Original Dodge Truck dealer and service signs from the collection of Ron Cenowa.

Part I: History

Chapter 1

History of Dodge Trucks 1901–1932

A company often forges its reputation for building rough, tough and reliable products over years. Not so for Dodge. The Dodge Brothers name meant reliability from the start. Having already established reputations as master machinists when they opened their machine shop in Detroit in 1901, Horace and John

Dodge immediately attracted such history-making clients as Ransom E. Olds. When Olds launched his Curved Dash model in 1903, he turned to the Dodge Brothers for transmissions. Soon the Dodge Brothers shop was turning out mechanical assemblies for the bevy of fledgling auto makers clustering in the

The Dodge Brothers first commercial vehicles were ambulances that saw service with the American Expeditionary Force and Allies in World War I. These commercial models *began production on October 25, 1917. Dodge's reliability saved the lives of many wounded soldiers.*

The ambulance had a civilian counterpart which Dodge called the Screenside. This commercial model had a 1,000 lb. payload and was built on the 114 in. passenger-car chassis. The US Army also bought Screensides for use by the Signal, Ordnance and Quartermaster Corps. Shown here is a 1920 Dodge Screenside. Robert Quirk

Detroit area. But for a propitious link-up with a maverick inventor and tinkerer named Henry Ford, the Dodge Brothers role in automotive history might have been as a supplier of quality parts. The Ford connection would change the scope of the Dodge Brothers manufacturing operation and generate the capital to propel the parts supplier into a major automotive manufacturer.

Ford investors and suppliers

History knows Henry Ford as a mechanical genius who invented the moving assembly line. The fact is, the practical genius in the early years of the Ford Motor Company came from men like the metallurgist Harold Wills, production chief Charles Sorensen, and Ford's hard-driving accountant James Couzens. Without these men, Ford might well have frittered away his opportunity with his inveterate

Dodge was one of the first builders of woody wagons. The open sides and rear could be closed by lowering roll-up curtains not seen on this example. Shown here is a 1923 Dodge Suburban with body by Cantrell. The Suburban name would later be applied to Plymouth's popular all-metal station wagon.

tinkering, as indeed he had three years earlier with the Detroit Automobile Company, Ford's first manufacturing venture. As backers of the new Ford enterprise, the Dodge Brothers' investment was not without risk. Perhaps to cover their bets, the Dodges arranged to supply engines and other components, in addition to holding stock. The combination clicked and it wasn't long before profits on the engine supply business and cascading equity in the Ford Motor Company had turned the Dodge brothers, as well as their senior partner, into multi-millionaires. Today, the Dodge mansion (Meadow Brook Hall, now part of Oakland University), built by John Dodge's widow Matilda, stands as a monument to the incredible wealth-generating power of the automotive industry.

By 1914, the Model T was a heady success and with 58.5 percent of the stock, Henry Ford decided to run the show. First he announced the $5 day. The stockholders recoiled; what company would give away its profits to the workers? To their surprise, the $5 day (which didn't go automatically to all Ford employees, but was parceled out to a select few) poured even more money into the Ford Motor Company coffers as workers could now buy the cars they made. Ford's next bold move was to announce that all

<table>
<tr><td>

Dodge Dependability

In the early years of this century, cars and light trucks were not all that dependable. Owners put up with mechanical problems, electrical problems, tire problems, problems of not starting and so on. When the Dodge Brothers introduced their new vehicle in 1915, it wrote the book on dependable service.

So impressed were owners of these quality Hamtramck-built vehicles that they began to use the word "dependability" when referring to Dodges—cars and trucks equally. This movement was initiated by Dodge owners themselves, not by marketing or advertising people working for the Dodge Brothers. Our dictionary tells us that the word "dependable" is an adjective which means "able to be relied on," and "dependability" is its noun form. Dodge without *its* dependability would be like Mack without its bulldog or Chevy without its bow-tie.

</td></tr>
</table>

stock dividends would be diverted to build a manufacturing plant on the Rouge River. This giant facility would be unique in manufacturing history. At one

An enclosed Panel model completed Dodge's commercial line. Note the open driver's area. This 1924 model has the flat cowl that carries the hood line and gives the appearance of a longer *engine compartment. Otherwise, few styling changes are visible from the first commercial models.*

end, giant furnaces melted raw iron ore into steel, while at the other finished cars rumbled out onto the street. Certainly any manufacturing business needed adequate facilities, but Ford's plans for the Rouge were outlandishly grandiose—or so the stockholders thought. The Dodge brothers brought suit against Ford claiming that as investors and risk-takers they were entitled to their fair share of the company's earnings. But Ford had his dreams—and his 58.5 percent of the stock.

Construction of the Rouge plant went forward, and the wily Henry Ford decided he would maneuver his partners into selling out. The Dodge stock profit was enormous. In sixteen years, their ten percent share of the Ford Motor Company had grown from an initial investment of $10,000 to a cash-out value of $25 million, plus dividends between 1903 and 1919 of

$9.5 million. Still, the buy-out left Henry Ford substantially ahead. At a price of $105 million, the Ford family wound up owning every scrap of Ford Motor Company, representing total corporation assets of $1 billion.

Pioneer Dodge automobiles

Wishing to cut loose from Henry Ford's shadow, the Dodges had opened their own automotive manufacturing business in 1914, building just one model, a touring car, painted black. In many ways, this first Dodge was but an upscale Model T with three-speed transmission and leather upholstery. It wasn't appearance that sold these cars; it was Dodge's established reputation for reliability. Although the first year's production total of 249 cars hardly approached a trickle compared to Ford's tor-

Maxwell, shown here as a 1924–25 express model, became part of the Dodge story through its role as a staging platform from which Walter P. Chrysler created the Chrysler Corporation. Note the somewhat crude attempt at an enclosed cab.

rent, over the next twelve months, Dodge production would rise to 45,000 units, ranking it number three among domestic auto makers.

While America watched the European war from the sidelines, it sent its own small expeditionary force to Mexico in pursuit of a border-raiding bandit named Pancho Villa. Dodge's reputation caught an Army procurement officer's eye, and a score of Dodge touring cars traveled south of the border with the troops. The Dodge Touring's only modification for war consisted of olive-drab paint.

The Mexican incursion proved to be a testing ground for many an officer who a few decades later would become America's military heroes. Among them was a cavalryman named George S. Patton. Seeing the Dodges nimbly moving with the troops, Patton commandeered a part of the Dodge fleet for the world's first-recorded motorized cavalry charge.

It's reported that Pancho Villa also used a Dodge to flee his pursuers, and was shot to death riding in it.

The dust had barely settled in the Mexican foray when American doughboys were boarding ships for France. With them in the cargo holds was a new Dodge commercial model fitted out as an ambulance. The commercial line had appeared in 1917 as 1918 models, in response to pleas from dealers and customers. Built on the 114 in. passenger-car chassis and using car mechanical parts throughout, the commercial line consisted of one model: a delivery truck with screened-in sides, which garnered the name Screenside, and found a ready market. The Screenside went to farmers and others wanting a light delivery truck with Dodge dependability. The US government also placed a number of orders for Screensides to be used by the Signal, Ordinance and Quartermaster corps.

In 1925, a group of New York banking interests purchased the Dodge Brothers Corporation for $146 million, the largest cash transaction in the nation's history. This was the last year for the Series Three commercial line. A three-quarter-ton Panel is seen here.

The ambulance put Dodge reliability to the test on the front lines in Europe.

In 1918, Dodge's civilian commercial line added a panel delivery, which was basically an enclosed Screenside. Dodge was also providing its rugged chassis to aftermarket body builders who fitted it with fire apparatus, station wagon conversions, semi-tractors setups and lengthened stake bodies. Through the 1920s, the Dodge commercial line expanded in offerings and models. In 1921, Dodge combined with Graham to market a heavier-duty truck line; like their earlier arrangement with Ford, part of the Dodge-Graham agreement was that Graham would purchase engines for its trucks from Dodge. The light-duty line also expanded with a variety of delivery and hearse models, plus station wagons, which Dodge called Suburbans, with bodies by Cantrell.

Still, emphasis in the light-duty line was on deliveries built on the passenger-car chassis. The familiar pickup truck would not appear until 1924.

While the 1920s brought optimism and expansion, the era of frivolity and frolic also brought tragedy to the Dodge family. John Dodge contracted pneumonia and succumbed to the disease in 1920. Horace died just eleven months later. In the founders' absence, Frederick Haynes assumed leadership and the company prospered.

Haynes was no newcomer to the Dodge operation. He had joined the Dodges prior to their connections with Ransom Olds and Henry Ford, when the machinists had plied their skills making bicycles. Haynes left his employ at Dodge to study engineering at Cornell University, then worked for a brief period for Franklin, the air-cooled-car manufacturer. In

Graham, which had been a Dodge affiliate since 1916, was absorbed into the growing Dodge empire in 1924. The Graham line provided heavier-duty commercial models for Dodge dealers. By 1928, the Graham line had expanded to include *light-duty models such as the half-ton Delivery seen here. In this sense, Graham and Dodge trucks were in competition with one another, and this would be the last year for the Graham name.*

1912, Haynes returned to Detroit and joined Dodge Brothers just as they were laying plans for their car line. Starting in manufacturing, Haynes quickly moved to management and by the time of the Dodge brothers' deaths, he had gained familiarity with the entire operation.

Haynes proved to be a wise choice for the Dodge helm. To weather the brief, but sharp, postwar recession, Haynes expanded the company's commercial line, and found a ready market. He had the same success with new, closed car models. By 1923, annual sales had reached a total of 179,505 units, nearly double the volume of the 1921 recession year. To increase production further, Haynes embarked on a $5 million plant expansion. Sales increased and profits for 1924 swelled to nearly $20 million.

Dodge buy-out

The Dodge operation was now ripe for plucking and in 1925, a group of New York bankers purchased the Dodge Brothers Company for what to that time was the largest cash deal in history, $146 million. General Motors had been among the bidders for the Dodge name, reputation and manufacturing facilities, and had Billy Durant still been at the General's helm, the emerging giant might have outbid the New York bankers. In one of its first moves, the new management took control of Graham truck manufacture. The Graham acquisition's only effect on the light-duty commercial line was the entry of a one-ton model called the G Boy.

Although Dodge continued to set sales records under the new management, just three years later, in 1928, Dodge ownership changed hands again. This time the Dodge name found itself with Walter P. Chrysler's recently formed Chrysler Corporation. The feat of Chrysler's buying Dodge was an accomplishment on the order of David's slaying of Goliath. Here was a true Horatio Alger triumph, for Chrysler (which had not yet spawned Plymouth or DeSoto)

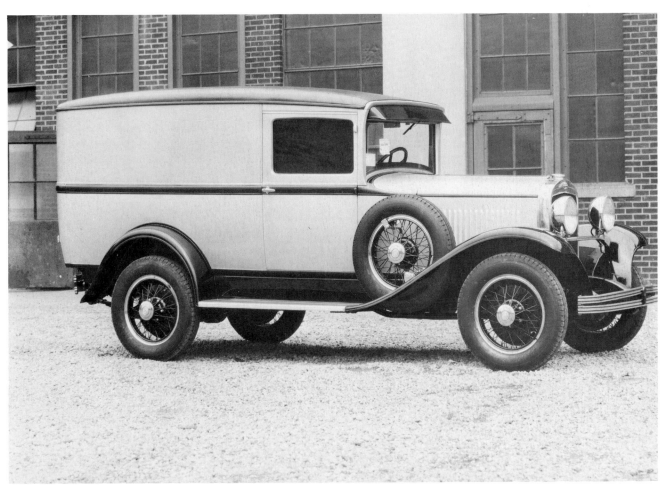

In 1928, the Chrysler Corporation launched a truck line under the Fargo name. Shortly after the creation of the Fargo commercial line, Chrysler bought the Dodge Brothers opera-tion and Fargo became unneeded competition to the already overlapping Dodge and Graham commercial lines. Seen here is a 1929 Fargo Packet Six half-ton Panel.

With the Depression shrinking car and truck sales, Chrysler dissolved its Fargo truck line in 1930. The name would re- *emerge in 1933 on Dodge trucks built for export. The Fargo example shown here is a 1929 express.*

Chrysler in Canada

Chrysler Corporation's presence in Canada is as old as the parent company. Walter Chrysler's great-great-grandfather was the first settler in what is now Chatham, Ontario. It has been said that Walter Chrysler, therefore, always had an affection for Canada, and chose to build a factory there the same year as he introduced the first car bearing his name in the United States. It's possible, however, that Walter Chrysler moved into Canada simply due to sound business planning.

Chrysler chose to start his Canadian company in Windsor, Ontario, a growing industrial city across the river from Detroit. Chrysler Canada began in 1924 as the Maxwell-Chrysler Company of Canada. Maxwell's Canadian roots actually stretch back to 1916 when its Canadian operation built a new car plant on Tecumseh Road East in Windsor. On June 17, 1925, only eleven days after the incorporation of Chrysler Corporation, Maxwell-Chrysler of Canada was reorganized and incorporated as the Chrysler Corporation of Canada, Limited.

In the early years, Chrysler built only cars in Canada. In 1928, when Chrysler purchased Dodge Brothers, it also acquired Dodge Brothers Canada and Graham Brothers Canada, a truck manufacturer. The first Canadian-built Dodge trucks rolled out of the Tecumseh Road plant in 1931. In the early years, interestingly enough, Chrysler Corporation of Canada built Dodge trucks ranging in size from half-ton all the way up to three-tons. Production figures for the earliest years were combined with US production figures, so only estimates can be made as to the total number of trucks built based on serial number charts. The best estimate is that 5,683 trucks

of all sizes were built between 1931 and 1935, the first year production records were maintained for both cars and trucks.

Up to 1937, all the engines used in building Canadian cars and trucks were shipped to Canada from Chrysler engine plants in the United States. On June 30, 1937, ground was broken for a new Windsor engine manufacturing plant, and production of Chrysler's L-head six-cylinder engines began the following year.

During World War II, Chrysler of Canada built 180,816 military trucks for service on all fronts.

Production of the first Canadian-built V-8 engines began in 1955 after the completion of a $29 million addition to the Windsor engine plant.

In 1963, the company's name was shortened to Chrysler Canada, Limited. The Pentastar corporate logo was adopted at this same time.

A historic agreement went into effect in 1965, joining the automotive industries of Canada and the United States together into a North American entity under the Canada-United States Automotive Trade Agreement, more commonly called the Autopact. This agreement permits duty-free trade in new motor vehicles between the two countries. Chrysler immediately began to ship large quantities of Canadian-built vehicles to the United States in exchange for models not built in Canada.

Prior to this agreement, Chrysler had built in Canada all the vehicles it sold in Canada. Before the agreement came into existence, Canadian-built vehicles were not exported to the United States. Over the years, this unique, bilateral trade agreement has worked beautifully to the mutual advantage of both countries.

By 1930, all of the Chrysler Corporation's trucks carried the Dodge nameplate. The truck line closely resembled the passenger-car line in styling. A half-ton Panel model is seen here.

totalled but one-fifth the assets and manufacturing capacity of Dodge. Walter P. had managed to put together a monumental stock and note payoff deal that put $170 million in the banker's pockets—a quick profit of $35 million.

Gobbling Dodge boosted Chrysler into the number-three slot among American manufacturers; by 1936, Chrysler would surpass Ford and assume the number-two rank it would occupy until 1952. The buy-out proved beneficial to both parties. Chrys-

In 1933, Dodge revived the Fargo name and applied it to Dodge trucks built in Detroit for export. Fargo had a sound of Wild West toughness and reliability that matched the Dodge reputation. This chassis-cab is awaiting shipment to some distant part of the world.

Fargo Trucks

Fargo Motor Corporation traces its origin all the way back to 1924 and the National Business Sales Division (NBSD) of Dodge Brothers. NBSD was organized for the purpose of marketing corporate vehicles to fleet buyers of Dodge commercial vehicles. Their purpose was to assist fleet owners by actually observing Dodge commercials while they were in use, to assist owners with maintenance information, and to gather data to assist in developing and designing future commercial vehicles to be added to Dodge's commercial line. Their goal was also to develop goodwill with owners to the mutual profit of both parties. The activities of the NBSD often led to the realization of the need for specialized marketing by the factory in order to sell large quantities of vehicles to fleet buyers.

Early in 1925, the NBSD took on responsibility for fleet sales of the entire Dodge line of both cars and trucks. NBSD's charter was twofold: to sell fleet accounts through Dodge Brothers dealers, who benefited from the sale, and to service fleet accounts after the sale was made. Chrysler Corporation in early 1926 had organized a National Fleet Sales Division under the supervision of Joe E. Fields. In midyear 1928, after Chrysler's purchase of Dodge Brothers, Fields realized the advantages of combining the two divisions to handle fleet sales for the entire corporation. At the same time, he adopted the policy prevalent in the industry of granting fleet buyers a discount.

Before purchasing Dodge Brothers, Chrysler had made the decision to organize a new and separate company, the Fargo Motor Corporation, through which the corporation would market commercial vehicles. Production began in August 1928 on the first Fargo, called the Clipper ED Series, a three-quarter-ton chassis with cowl; in September 1928, they added the Packet 4 EE Series, a half-ton chassis with cowl. The half-ton was priced at $545 list and the three-quarter-ton at $725. To either chassis-cowl could be added one of two bodies: a Panel at $250 or a Glass Side at $350. The Panel body was meant for commercial delivery work while the Glass Side was meant to be used for delivery and or passenger use. An optional item for the Glass Side was a "full-width crosswise seat"; by adding seats, the owner could create in effect a Suburban-type people and cargo hauler.

These first Fargo trucks, built from 1928 to 1930, were Chrysler trucks and not Dodge trucks. They were conceived, designed and engineered by Chrysler before its purchase of Dodge and did not share any parts with the Dodge trucks of 1928. As a matter of fact, these first Fargos were built with components from the Chrysler 65, DeSoto and Plymouth passenger cars. The Panel and Glass Side bodies were purchased from outside body manufacturers.

A new series of Packet half-ton and Clipper three-quarter-ton six-cylinder trucks was introduced in March 1929, and the one-ton Freighter was added in June. Body choices now expanded greatly with the addition of Canopy, Screen, Sedan, Pickup, Platform, Stake, Farm Box and Stock Rack. The addition of this wide variety of bodies showed the influence on Fargo trucks from Chrysler's purchase of Dodge Brothers. Dodge Brothers was already producing these bodies in their own plants making it a simple matter to mount them onto Fargo chassis. These models continued more or less unchanged up to November 1930, at which time production of Fargos ceased. Production total for all years was a total of 9,670 trucks, of which only thirty-nine were built in Canada, all others in Detroit.

In September 1931, Chrysler management merged the National Fleet Sales Division and the Fargo Motor Division into one corporation and Fargo Motor Corporation took over NFSD's activities. The functions of the Fargo Motor Corporation included promoting the sale of all Chrysler-built cars and trucks to fleets, including federal, state, county and local governments. Fargo was also active in developing specialized truck chassis and bodies to meet specific needs for private and government fleet users.

Beginning in 1933, with Fargo truck production in the United States, Fargos were exported throughout the world, but were not sold in Mexico. Production of Canadian Fargos began in 1936 and they were sold exclusively in Canada. DeSoto trucks, built in the United States only, were exported to Mexico, as well as to other parts of the world. For some unexplained reason, the name Fargo was not accepted in Mexico.

In the early 1930s, Chrysler's method of marketing was different in Canada than in the United States. In the United States, each division stood alone, while in Canada, because the market was smaller, Chrysler and Plymouth were paired, as were DeSoto and Dodge. Chrysler-Plymouth consequently was left without a truck to sell. Chrysler solved this problem by giving Chrysler-Plymouth dealers the Fargo truck line in 1936. In the beginning, Fargo built only half-, one-and-a-half-, and two-ton trucks, but by 1939 Fargo's line-up included trucks all the way up to four-tons.

Fargo trucks after 1933 were rebadged Dodges; however, there were some differences, notably in front-end sheet metal, nameplates and ornamentation. During the 1940s and 1950s, the Canadian plants used a different engine in the large-block L-six for all trucks up to two tons. By decreasing its bore and stroke, overall displacement was about equivalent to United States produced, light-duty Dodge trucks. Other than these differences, Fargos were, for all intents and purposes, the same vehicles. The careful observer will note that with the passage of time, distinctions between the two became fewer and fewer.

Fargo trucks are still in production to this day in various parts of the world, even though the Fargo nameplate was discontinued in Canada in 1972.

ler acquired Dodge's extensive dealer network, solid reputation and substantial manufacturing facility, while Dodge became recipient of Chrysler's sound engineering, which included the first downdraft carburetor to be installed on American-built engines (1929) and Floating Power (1933). Unlike GM (and Ford to a much lesser degree), at Chrysler, engineering was shared across the line. This highly practical approach made for the easy interchange of mechanical parts on cars and trucks from various family members of the Chrysler line that benefits Mopar collectors today.

Partly because of its niche in the Chrysler line, but also because of the Dodge truck reputation,

dealer network and buyer loyalty, Dodge was designated to carry the Corporation's commercial offerings. So esteemed was the Dodge name that Chrysler would continue to use the Dodge Brothers emblem on light trucks through 1935. Oddly, as important as the Dodge name was at home, for export and in Canada, Dodge trucks could also be seen carrying DeSoto and Fargo badges. For a short period from 1937–1941, slightly disguised Dodge pickups were also manufactured under the Plymouth name. This was more than simple badge engineering, however, as Plymouth trucks carried their own grille and the smaller Plymouth L–6 engine.

Walter P. Chrysler in his office. From this room the confident, competent executive commanded a manufacturing operation of gigantic proportions. The furniture seen in this setting is preserved in the Chrysler Historical Collection. The visitor and date of the photo are unknown.

Chapter 2

Glamour Era 1933–1935

The prime purpose of a truck is to carry as great a payload as possible with the utmost speed at the lowest cost per ton-mile. Thus, truck design did not change for change's sake, as was the common practice with passenger cars. Passenger-car buyers expected annual changes in style and in features which did not necessarily contribute to the vehicle's performance. A passenger-car buyer wanted the latest, most mod-

The 1933 Dodge Commercial Panel was the first of Dodge's famous double-level or humpback panels. Double-level Commercial Panels were built through 1938. The truck shown has the standard wire wheels; wood- and steel-spoke wheels were options. The Commercial Panel's wheelbase was 119 in. All other Commercials rode on a 111¼ in. wheelbase.

ern and up-to-date product, while the commercial buyer viewed a truck purchase as a business decision. His primary concern was in getting the most value for his dollar. For these reasons, trucks did not change dramatically from one year to the next. Instead, trucks witnessed a gradual evolution in styling, engineering, and in driver comfort and safety. As a matter of fact, there would not be a completely from-the-wheels-up new light truck from Dodge until 1961. Between 1933 and 1961, Dodge made major and significant changes to drivelines, chassis, cabs and styling, but in no single year did all of the above change to the point where we can say the new model was an "all-new" truck.

1933 HC Series

"Breathtaking beauty never before found in commercial vehicles," read the Dodge Commercial Cars sales literature for 1933. Still, most of the Dodge

trucks for the 1933 model year were not the all-new "Chryslerized" models of the Glamour Series. In fact, Dodge began the model year by carrying forward the 1932 models without change. By this time, these trucks were dated, as they had been around since the mid 1920s. Dodge phased in its new models beginning with the Commercial Sedan in December 1932. Although often referred to as a sedan delivery, Dodge officially called it a Commercial Sedan. The Commercial Sedan was a two-door sedan converted as a commercial vehicle by adding a sedan delivery-type rear door and by replacing the rear side windows with steel panels. The intent was to create a carlike, prestigious, light-delivery vehicle for retail merchants.

The Commercial Panel and Commercial Express pickup followed in January 1933. Although not introduced until well into the model year, Dodge still counted them as 1933 models. Today, 1933 pickups

The 1933 standard chassis with flat-faced cowl was Dodge's lowest-priced commercial vehicle selling for $340. The Commercial's double-drop, X-type frame was the same as used on

Dodge automobiles. The gas tank is nestled between the frame siderails at the extreme rear.

are rare because of the short production year. Once available, however, these glamorous new trucks sold well, allowing Dodge to register impressive sales gains over 1932.

All half-ton trucks, or Commercials, as Dodge liked to call them, were essentially passenger cars with truck bodies. The drivetrain, chassis, cab and front-end sheet metal were pure car. One-and-a-half-ton models were the next-larger-sized trucks available. These were true trucks in that they were built with a straight, ladder-type frame with heavy-duty components. The cabs of these larger trucks were the same as on Commercials, but the front fenders, bumpers, hoods and grilles had a big-truck look. Another major difference between then and now is that the largest-selling truck category was one-and-a-half-tonners, not one-ton and less as is true today. For example, in 1933, the category for one-and-a-half-ton captured 63.7 percent of the total truck market versus 27.8 percent for everything less than one-and-a-half-tons. Light-duty models did not take over the sales lead until the 1940s.

Engine and chassis

From the beginning, in 1933, Dodge truck engines were corporate automobile engines. Chrysler Corporation was always careful to merchandise engines according to its various car lines so that the larger and more expensive the car, the bigger its engine would be. For many years, the smallest corporate engine was used in Plymouths. Dodge shared the same basic block, but with a larger displacement achieved by a longer stroke. Plymouth and Dodge shared a 23 in. long block, commonly called the small-block. DeSoto and Chrysler shared a 25 in. block, called the big-block, but with different displacements—the smaller engine belonging to DeSoto, of course. All four engines down through the years saw service in Dodge trucks from half-ton to

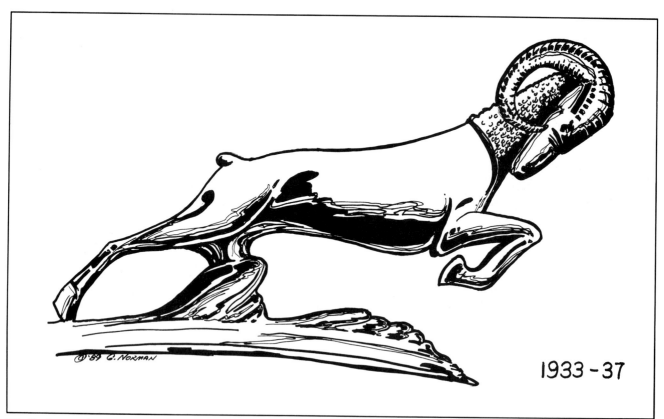

The Dodge ram hood ornament for 1933–1937 boasted classical, sweeping lines. Greg Norman

two-and-a-half tons. Dodge Truck Division, however, did have a huge L-6 engine which was used exclusively in three- and four-ton models. In 1933, Dodge used a large straight-eight engine in its largest trucks; this engine was dropped in 1935.

The 1933 small-block L-6 was an all-new corporate engine of 189.8 ci for Plymouth and 201.3 ci for Dodge. The Plymouth version was the engine chosen to power Dodge's Commercial Cars. Dodge Brothers built six-cylinder engines before the buy-out by Chrysler in 1928, but the 1933 L-6 was all new and developed by Chrysler. The new engine was a valve-in-block L-head design that featured insert rod and main bearings, insert valve seats, full-pressure lubrication, an oil filter, and a downdraft carburetor. Bore and stroke were 3⅛x4⅛ in., brake horsepower was 70 at 3600 rpm, net horsepower was 23.44, torque was

130 lb-ft at 1,200 rpm and the compression ratio was 5.5:1.

This engine remained essentially the same throughout the years. The only major change occurred in 1935 when full-length water jackets were added to provide cooling around the cylinder bores. On the original block casting, the water jackets stopped about halfway down the left side, leaving the cylinders to be exposed. The addition of full-length water jackets meant the starter motor had to be moved outboard on its axis about ¼ in. In order to install a 1935 engine into a 1933 or 1934 truck, one would have to either machine the bellhousing or use a later bellhousing. From 1935 on, the blocks were a bolt-for-bolt swap in the case of the small-block, a fact that kept many an old Dodge or Plymouth on the road. One has to be careful when purchasing an L-6 powered Dodge truck. Make sure you carefully check the engine number or you may later find that your

The chrome-plated radiator shell and headlights were standard equipment only on the Commercial Sedan. On all other Commercial models they were extra-cost equipment. This *vehicle's body is the same as the body used for a two-door sedan, except for its large sedan-delivery-type rear door and the steel panels which covered the rear side window openings.*

The Commercial Screen and the Commercial Canopy, shown here, employed a straight roof, unlike the double-level Commercial Panel. By adding screens at a cost of $12.50 to cover the open sides and double screen rear doors at $15, a Commercial Canopy became a Commercial Screen.

This 1933 station wagon with body by Cantrell was called a Suburban Sedan. With all seats installed, seven passengers could be accommodated; 6 ft. of cargo space was available when both backseats were removed.

truck has an engine from a newer Dodge or Plymouth car or even an industrial engine.

Early Dodge Commercials used a Willard 6–8 volt battery.

As was a common practice in those days on passenger cars, Dodge Commercials offered an automatic clutch and freewheeling unit as extra-cost equipment. A button mounted on the instrument panel controlled the automatic clutch and freewheeling units. When the button was completely in, both the clutch and freewheeling units were in operation. When the button was halfway out, the automatic clutch was locked out, but the freewheeling unit was still in operation. When the button was all the way out, both units were locked out.

Chrysler's passenger cars for 1933 touted Floating Power, and so did Dodge Commercial Cars. Floating Power engine mountings contributed to quieter, smoother and easier driving. Rubber engine mountings at the front and rear of the engine provided flexible, balanced supports that absorbed engine vibration and allowed a certain amount of natural engine movement.

Early Commercials rode on car chassis, and the new 1933 shared a chassis with the Dodge DP car. This chassis was of the double-drop, X-truss type, designed and braced so it resisted strain from every direction. It was strong enough for railroad bridge construction as all joints were securely riveted. A heavy, forward cross-member provided strength up front, and a combination gas tank shield and rear frame cross-member tied the rear together. As a safety measure, the 15 gallon gas tank was mounted between the frame members at the rear and was further protected by the shield.

Due to its passenger car heritage, the Commercial Car's front axle was constructed of a heat-treated, seamless-steel tube. King pins were carried in two large bronze bushings equipped with Zerk grease fittings. Steering was of the cross type with the steering gear itself of worm-and-sector design for easy steering. Steering gear ratio was 17:1 and the steering wheel diameter was a large and comfortable 17½ in.

Bodywork and interior

The new, streamlined, curved and softened styling introduced with the 1933 trucks was characterized by a slanted, V-type radiator grille that was slightly curved at the bottom. The windshield pillars sloped at the same angle as the radiator, which carried the attractive sloping lines from the bumper up to the roofline. As was common practice in those days, the doors were hinged at the rear, commonly called sui-

A well-accessorized 1933 Commercial Sedan. Its chrome-plated radiator, rear bumper, front bumper and headlights were standard equipment, but the front bumper guards, coach-type side-mounted lamps and right-side spotlight were options. Rear bumpers were standard equipment for Commercial Panels and Sedans only.

cide doors. Optional chrome-plated radiator shell and headlight buckets, along with the attractive leaping ram's head on the radiator cap, dressed up the trucks to make them the most attractive commercial vehicles available.

The smart-looking new Commercial Pickup cab was constructed of steel, but wood cross-bows reinforced the top and the cab was bolted to longitudinal hardwood sills. The cab was built as a unit, with sections joined together by welding and by nuts and bolts. The cab roof was of the French or inserted type, constructed of composite material over which a layer of cotton wadding was placed and then covered with heavy-duty weatherproof material. Special sealing composition held the fabric portion of the roof to steel portions, making it waterproof at the joints.

The seat cushion and back were of spring construction covered with a durable vinyl. The seat cushion was only 42½ in. wide, making it basically a two-man cab, although Dodge advertised it as a three-man cab. A tool compartment was located beneath the seat.

The standard paint scheme included front and rear fenders, running boards, splash aprons, headlight buckets and radiator shell in black, while the hood, cab, box and wheels were painted any standard paint color. Trucks could be ordered special from the factory, painted entirely in one color, if so desired.

The Commercial Pickup was of the two-unit type, that is, the cab was not built integrally with the box. Up to this time, Dodge pickup construction had been integral with no break between the cab and box. The floor of the box was made of corrugated steel with the sides, floor and cross sills securely welded together. The sides and flare boards were one piece with stake pockets provided. The full-width tailgate was also steel, supported by two adjustable chains. The box was small, measuring only 62¾ in. long by 45¾ in. wide and 15⅝ in. to the top of the flares. The tailgate was simple and plain; the Dodge name was neither embossed nor painted on.

Standard and optional equipment

Standard equipment for the Pickup included speedometer, oil pressure gauge, gas gauge, ammeter, heat indicator, ignition switch, choke, throttle, light switch with lighting dash lamp, cowl vent, front bumper, rubber-covered running boards, highbeam control switch, combination stop- and taillamp, five wire wheels with spare mounted in the right front fenderwell, horn, ventilating windshield, one windshield wiper, exterior rearview mirror and tool kit including grease gun. Both doors locked; the driver's from the inside and the passenger's from the outside.

Extra-cost optional equipment included chrome-plated front bumper, $7.50; chrome-plated rear bumper, $7.50; Duplate-laminated safety glass, $14; auxiliary seat for panel, $10; dual trumpet horns, $12.50; auxiliary windshield wiper, $4.50; metal tire cover, $5 each; interior sun visor, $2 each; freewheeling unit, $8; freewheeling and automatic clutch, $17.50; Duplate safety glass in windshield, $3.50; ornamental radiator cap, $2; tire lock, $1.20; coach-type lamps side-mounted for Commercial Sedan, $8; chrome-plated radiator shell, headlamps and hydraulic shock absorbers front and rear, designated as the Chassis Special Accessory Group, $15.

Specifications and prices

HC 111¼ in. wheelbase and HCL (L for long wheelbase, Commercial Panel only) 119 in. wheelbase Commercial Series, powered by an L–6 engine with 3⅛x4½ in. bore and stroke, 189.8 ci, advertised

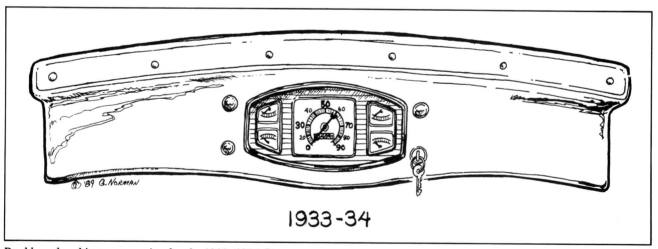

1933-34

Dashboard and instrumentation for the 1933–1934 Commercials were clustered to the center. Greg Norman

hp 70, three-speed transmission, 5.25x17 four-ply tires.

Commercial Pickup, $450.

Commercial Sedan, $555.

Commercial Panel, $540.

Production

Total truck production for the 1933 calendar year was 38,841. All trucks were built in Hamtramck, Michigan. No breakdown by model type is available. In 1933, Dodge built trucks from half-ton (Commercials) to four-ton capacities. The four-tonner was powered by a 385 ci eight.

Total output for 1933 represented an enormous increase over 1932 of 362 percent and market share soared 245 percent to 10.8 percent—Dodge's highest share since 1927. It appeared as if management had made the right moves when it restyled its Commercial and Standard (one-and-a-half- and two-ton) truck lines. Because heavy-duty trucks represented the smallest percentage of its total truck volume, Dodge management waited until the Second Series 1935 trucks to introduce new three-ton models. At the same time, management elected to discontinue all eight-cylinder four-ton models. From late 1935 until 1950, a three-ton was Dodge's largest standard offering; only the custom-built Airflow was rated at four-tons.

1934 KC Series

Businessmen and farmers agreed with Dodge that their Commercial Cars were the "handsomest delivery cars ever seen on any highway," as the brochures stated. Indeed, the sales recovery that began in 1933 leaped ahead in 1934 in spite of the severe depression. Continuing with a good thing begun in 1933, the 1934 pickup remained the same in appearance, but was mechanically improved.

As the 1933 new models were midyear introductions, most changes for 1934 also occurred well into the new model year. The only exception was that the new models—Commercial Canopy, Commercial Screenside and Westchester Suburban—were ready at the beginning of the model year. All other changes and improvements were phased in about January 1, 1934. The front axle changed to a beefy, drop-forged, I-beam type in place of the former tubular type. Engine size was increased to a bore and stroke of 3⅛x4⅜ in. or 201.3 ci. Compression ratio increased to 5.8:1, increasing torque to 136 lb-ft. The rear-axle ratio was reduced to 4.11:1 from 4.37:1. A new instrument panel was also added.

Introduced in late 1933, Dodge continued to build the K-20 Series, 131 in. wheelbase three-quarter- and one-ton models which were in fact K-30 one-and-a-half-ton trucks equipped with lighter

Dodge did build three-quarter- and one-ton trucks in the early thirties as seen in this 1934 K20X one-ton Screen. Three-quarter- and one-ton models were in reality 1½-ton trucks built with lighter springs and wheels. A K20 three-quarter-ton is the same as the one-tonner except it is equipped with wire wheels. The three-quarter- and one-ton's engine was the same 218 ci used in all 1½-ton trucks. Other bodies offered were Pickup, Panel and Canopy. Three-quarter- and one-ton trucks shared front end styling with 1½-tonners. The Screen was priced at only $830 picked up in Detroit.

springs and smaller wheels and tires. Pickup, Panel, Screenside and Canopy models were offered. This series styling matched that of the medium-duty one-and-a-half- and two-ton models.

Dodge Truck Division moved into an exclusive truck factory entirely segregating truck production from passenger-car production for the first time. Dodge Commercial Cars sold on average for $5 more than Chevrolet, $10 to $45 more than Ford, and $10 to $30 more than International. Good things always cost more.

Standard and optional equipment

The standard equipment list continued on the same as in 1933.

Extra-cost optional equipment included front and rear chrome-plated bumper, $7.50; Duplate safety glass throughout for Sedan, Panel and Pickup, $14; auxiliary seat for Panel or Canopy, $10; screen sides for Canopy only, $12.50; rear screen lift for Canopy, hinged at top, $14; double screen rear doors, $15; dual trumpet horns, $12.50; dual taillamps, $5; auxiliary windshield wiper, $4.50; metal tire cover, $5; interior sun visor, $2; freewheeling, $8; freewheeling and automatic clutch, $17.50; Duplex air cleaner, $5; Vortox air cleaner, $16; crankcase air intake ventilator, $3.50; Monarch governor, $8.50; Handy governor, $15; Duplate safety glass in windshield, $3.50; ornamental radiator cap, $2; tire lock, $1.20; coach-type lamps, side-mounted for Commercial Sedan, $8; chrome-plated radiator shell and headlamps, $5; shock absorbers, double-acting hydraulic, front and rear, $10; chrome-plated radiator shell, headlamps, hydraulic shocks, front and

1933–1938 Closed Deliveries

Dodge fielded the industry's most unique line of closed delivery vehicles throughout the Glamour Era. Due to the short model year in 1933, only two closed deliveries were offered.

Commercial Sedan

The Commercial Sedan was more car than truck because it employed a car's chassis, driveline and body. In fact, it was a regular Dodge two-door sedan, with a sedan delivery door cut into its rear. And instead of rear side windows, the areas were blanked out with sheet metal. Behind the driver's seat a 1/8 in. thick rubber mat covered the heavy plywood floor. The interior, including the rear door, was finished in plywood with a mahogany finish applied. A domelight illuminated the loading space. The driver's seat was both folding and adjustable; the companion seat was folding, removable and hinged to the floor. Headlining and door linings were made of imitation leather. Loading space was 52 in. long, 44¾ in. wide, and 37 in. high.

The Commercial Sedan could properly be called a Sedan Delivery, but Dodge never used that term; in fact, throughout its long history Dodge has never built a vehicle it called a Sedan Delivery. Because of how it was built, Dodge recommended it for only the lightest types of delivery work. It was ideal for the merchant who wanted a prestigious vehicle to deliver light merchandise door-to-door. Commercial Sedans were outfitted with chrome-plated radiator shells, headlights and rear bumper as standard equipment, and side-mounted coach lamps were an extra-cost option.

1933 Commercial Panel

The other unique closed delivery from Dodge in 1933 was the double-level or humpback Commercial Panel. Prior to 1933, before the introduction of a high-styled passenger-car-type Commercial, building a panel body with adequate loading space was easy. Engineers and designers simply ran the roofline up and back from the windshield header to the body's rear, which resulted in a high, boxlike truck with adequate load space. These bodies were constructed with a wooden top covered by weatherproof fabric. This same technique was tried with the new carlike front-end style, but it wouldn't work. Not enough load space could be designed in without compromising its style.

The modern front-end styling was at the same time an asset and a liability in terms of designing a panel body. Dodge designers tried at least six different variations and nothing worked. Remember that was long before the days of computer-aided-design (CAD); back then, design exercises entailed a great deal of manual labor using full-scale blackboards.

When Dodge designers realized they couldn't solve the problem using previous methods, they formulated an entirely new idea. They concluded the only solution was to put a step in the roof and smaller steps on each side of the body immediately behind the driver's compartment. This they would accomplish by using a combination of body dies, passenger-car dies for the front end and a new set for the truck body proper. What they concluded was a combination of the complete passenger-car body front end, including doors, along with an all-new panel body design with dimensions allowing reasonable load space. The new panel model boasted of an almost all-steel roof except for two areas. The first was a small weatherproofed fabric-covered section directly over the driver's compartment and the second and larger area was located over the cargo area.

Design problems were one thing, but production problems were yet another. Dodge engineers' biggest problem was in getting the stampings correct where the roof panels joined together. The first change was to make the radius slightly greater where the two roof panels joined to permit drawing the metal to the correct shape without its tearing and cracking. In actual production, liquid metal was used to smooth and complete the joints, which then had to be carefully ground down, first, with a rough grinder, and finally, touched up with a fine grinder.

The Dodge design team started on this project in the fall of 1931 and the first production models rolled off the line in January of 1933. That figures to be only fifteen to sixteen months from the time the idea was conceived to actual production.

What an achievement! The beautiful results speak for themselves. Remember too, Dodge built two series of panels: the 119 in. wheelbase Commercial Panel rated at a half ton and the 131 in. wheelbase Panel rated at one-and-a-half tons.

All Commercial Panels are highly sought after by collectors. The older the model, the more valuable it will be.

1934 Dual Purpose Sedan

This was a busy year at Dodge in terms of new commercials. The first, called a Dual Purpose Sedan, was a variant of the Commercial Sedan. It was a standard Commercial Sedan which could be converted into a two-door passenger sedan. In commercial use, removable steel signs, lettered like body panels, were placed behind the rear side glass panels. To convert to passenger use, an upholstered rear seat could be inserted through the large rear door. The rear door window could be opened with a standard window crank, and the entire interior was lined with upholstery fabric to provide the feel and comfort of an automobile.

1934 Commercial Canopy and Screen

The second introduction was the Commercial Canopy. Its roof construction consisted of longitudinal hardwood stringers with hardwood crossbows covered with padding and weatherproofed fabric. Its floor was constructed of 7/8 in. hardwood boards much like Dodge pickups would use from 1939 on. Side panels were built using a hardwood frame and then covered with metal. Wooden flareboards were bound with angle iron and strongly braced to carry the weight of the roof. The end gate was metal with inside chains, hooks and eye fasteners. The loading space was enclosed with heavy rollup, waterproof curtains. A Commercial Screen model was also offered. The Screen was essentially rear, designated as the Chassis Special Accessory Group, $15.

Specifications and prices

KC 111¼ in. wheelbase and KCL 119 in. wheelbase Commercial Series, powered by an L–6 engine, 3⅛x4⅜ in. bore and stroke, 201.3 ci, advertised at 70 hp, three-speed transmission, 5.25x17 four-ply tires.

Commercial Pickup, $480
Commercial Sedan, $595
Commercial Panel, $595
Commercial Canopy, $590
Commercial Screenside, $610
Commercial Dual Purpose Sedan, $780
Commercial Westchester Suburban, $745

Production

In this, the second year, but first full production year, of the glamorous Commercial Series, calendar year production again rose sharply from 38,841 to 68,469 units—a 176 percent improvement. Market share edged up to 11.4 percent for the third-best penetration in company history. Adding a Commercial Canopy, Screenside and Westchester Suburban contributed greatly to achieving remarkable production totals. All trucks were built in Hamtramck, Michigan.

1935 KC Series

Dodge was consistent during the Glamour Years and 1935 was no exception, as all changes and improvements again came late in the model year.

For the first time major changes were made in the Glamour Year trucks with the introduction of the 1935 Second Series. The most important improvement was a new, all-steel cab (no more fabric insert in the roof) with front-hinged doors. However, Dodge engineering released the new cab only for the Commercial Pickup and for all medium- and heavy-duty models. It is interesting to note that even though introduced late in the model year, the new cab was mated with the previous cab's hood and grille. The new cab went on to serve Dodge through the 1938 model year, and was the same cab used by Plymouth for their 1937 and 1938 pickups.

Wood in the new cab was limited to only three areas: the two front lower corners where it was bolted to the frame, and an area of approximately 2 by 3 ft. covering the transmission. The cab's right side was mounted on springs while the left was not.

In addition to the new cab, other appearance changes included 17 in., steel artillery wheels in place of wire wheels and new larger hubcaps, restyled with the name Dodge pressed in and painted. The optional

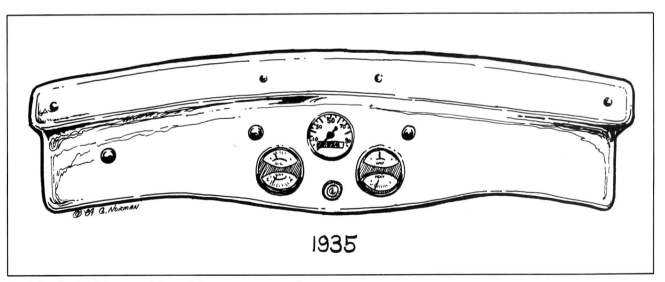

Dash for the 1935 Commercials used three gauges centered on the board. Greg Norman

A first-series 1935 Commercial Pickup. Second-series 1935 trucks featured front-hinged doors. The bumper was also new for 1935. Previous bumpers stepped back to the left and right from the center section. Note the interesting sunburst pattern painted on its wooden wheels.

The Commercial Panel was one of three light-duty Dodge trucks purchased by the US Army in 1935. These Army trucks differed from their civilian counterparts in only minor ways—the heavy grille guard, paint color, bumper and front tow hooks. All military models were also equipped with the steel spoke wheels and hubcaps of Second-Series trucks.

This low camera angle in combination with the high arched canvas covering the box causes the box to look out of proportion; actually, at only 5 ft. 2 in. long, it was small. Military *models were not equipped with the Dodge ram radiator cap ornament.*

wheel size was a 20 in. steel disk designed to provide additional clearance for rough roads.

A new bumper, smoother in style, with attractive, tapered ends, provided even more beauty to the world's most glamorous truck.

The most significant engineering improvement was the addition of full-length water jackets to the engine block in order to provide more adequate cooling to insure uniform expansion of the cylinder barrels, thus reducing piston ring and cylinder wear. Clutch pedal linkage was made less complicated to aid in smoother clutch actuation. The mounting point for the emergency brake handle was relocated from the transmission to the frame. Rear axle ratios

The third Dodge truck purchased by the Army was the wooden-bodied Suburban. Snap-on window covers were also *standard on the civilian model. Crankup glass windows were an option only in the front doors.*

This is one rare truck, a Second-Series 1935 Commercial Pickup with 119 in. wheelbase and long box. Dodge was the first pickup builder to market long- and short-box models. Bill Cox of Vanceboro, North Carolina, owns this fully restored truck, which has been in his family since new.

changed again with 4.124:1 being standard and 3.7:1 optional.

An interesting historical note is that late in the model year, on the medium- and heavy-duty models only, the hood-side nameplate now read Dodge in place of Dodge Brothers. Commercial Cars never displayed a hood-side nameplate.

One other change of interest concerns the ram on the radiator cap. Prior to 1935, the ram was cast in one piece; in 1935 it was a two-piece casting, the head being separate from the body.

Probably the most significant change to be ushered in with the new cab was the fact that a customer could now choose between two lengths of pickup boxes. This is the first time a half-ton pickup was available in the customer's choice of a long box or short box. The long box model was built on the 119 in. wheelbase chassis with a 70¾ in. box, versus the original 62¾ in. box.

In the 1935 model year, Dodge built its first four-ton Airflow, a streamlined behemoth with handsome good looks to delight every truck lover. This was also the final year for the 1920s vintage three- and four-ton heavy-duty trucks powered by an eight-cylinder engine. The Airflow would be the only four-ton Dodge-built truck until the B–2 Series of October 1949. Late in the model year, an entirely new three-ton chassis cab made its debut. It used the same new cab as the late 1935 pickup and was powered by a rugged 310 ci L–6. The new 1935 models were unveiled on October 1, 1934.

Many think Dodge did not build military trucks until World War II. This is not true, as Dodge actu-ally built is first military truck in 1934 (not counting those built by the Dodge Brothers Corporation for use in World War I), its first one-and-a-half-ton 4x4 in 1935, and also in that year, a number of military trucks based on the Commercial Series. Included were a Pickup, Sedan and Suburban. Production by type is not known, only that the total for all types exceeded 5,000.

Standard and optional equipment

The standard equipment list was the same as for 1933.

Extra-cost optional equipment included an accessory group consisting of dual trumpet horns, dual taillamps and auxiliary windshield wiper, $20; oil bath air cleaner, $2.50; Vortox air cleaner with standard breather cap, $17.50; Vortox air cleaner with Vortox breather cap, $19.50; chrome front bumper, $6; chrome rear bumper, $7; crankcase ventilator with carburetor air intake, $3.50; governor, $7.50; coach-type lamps for Commercial Sedan or Panel, $8; tire lock, $1.20; ornamental radiator cap, $2; chrome-plated radiator shell and headlamps, $7.50; long-arm rearview mirror, $2.50; Duplate safety glass in windshield, $5; Duplate throughout for Sedan, Panel or Pickup, $14; auxiliary seat for Panel, $10; single-acting hydraulic shocks for front and rear, $10; interior sun visor, $2; metal tire cover, $6.50; auxiliary windshield wiper, $4; chrome-plated radiator shell and headlamps, and hydraulic shocks, front and rear, $17.50.

Specifications and prices

KC 111¼ in. wheelbase and KCL 119 in. wheelbase Commercial Series, powered by an L–6 engine, 3⅛x4⅜ in. bore and stroke, 201.3 ci, advertised 70 hp, three-speed transmission, 5.25x17 four-ply tires.

Commercial Pickup, $480
Commercial Sedan, $595
Commercial Canopy, $590
Commercial Screenside, $610
Commercial Dual Purpose Sedan, $780
Commercial Westchester Suburban, $715
Commercial Pickup 119 in., NA
Commercial Panel 119 in., $595

Production

Production in this last calendar year of the Glamour Series leaped ahead by 122 percent to 83,701, but market share remained constant at 11.4 percent as total industry production rose 121 percent.

This is the first year Dodge truck export sales can be identified. They totaled 12,957. Dodge (that is, Dodge truck under Chrysler's ownership) began exporting trucks as early as 1929, but numbers are not available. This was also the first year Dodge trucks were assembled in Canada, with 1,500 being built this first year. This total is included in the total production number given above.

In order to better serve the entire truck market, during 1935, Dodge management opened a new plant in Los Angeles to produce cars and trucks. A total of 5,766 trucks came off the new assembly line the first year; this total is included in the production figure given above.

A family portrait of the entire Second-Series Dodge truck line for 1935 shows that all models but the Commercial Panel were built with the new front-hinged door cab. The style difference, other than the doors, is most noticeable in the shape of the new windshield and by the height of the door windows. The Stake model closest to the Commercial Panel is a one-and-a-half-tonner, the other stake is a two-ton. The black beauty on the far left is the new, Second-Series three-tonner. Except for the four-ton Airflow, a three-ton model was the largest truck Dodge built until 1950.

Chapter 3

Fore-Point Era 1936–1938

1936 LC Series

Except for the cab, engine and driveline, the 1936 LC Series, announced in November 1935, was an all-new truck. Dodge called the new model a major engineering advancement. Fore-Point related to the moving of the engine, cab and body forward 8 in. on the chassis to provide better load distribution by shifting additional weight to the front axle for better balance. This dramatically changed the pickup's appearance by moving the grille forward ahead of the front fenders, giving the truck modern styling.

For the first time, Dodge Commercials sat on a truck-type ladder frame with straight rails and five husky cross-members. (The Commercial Sedan was an exception as it continued to be built on an automobile X-type frame.) The wheelbase was now 116 in. and one length served all half-tonners. The gas tank was moved from the rear of the frame to a well-protected position inside the left frame rail below the driver's seat. The gas tank on all light-duty Dodge trucks remained in this location until 1961, when it was moved inside the cab behind the seat.

Dodge engineers and designers did their work well as the new Commercials were strikingly good looking. The modern grille was topped off by an extremely attractive bighorn ram hood ornament. (The hood ornament, which came into use with the 1933 model year, was also called a Rocky Mountain

The 1936 Plymouth P1 Sedan Delivery. Except for minor sheet metal and trim differences, it was basically the same vehicle as the Dodge Commercial Sedan. However, Dodge never used the term Sedan Delivery, and always named this body type a Commercial Sedan.

New Fore-Point style is evident in this 1936 Suburban Sedan. Its front axle was moved forward so that the peak of the grille *now extended beyond the front fenders. The new design helped to give Dodge Commercials a modern appearance.*

sheep.) Torpedo-shaped headlamps and narrow, horizontal, hood louvers accentuated the length of the hood and gave an impression of fleetness. Full-skirted front fenders with heavy, embossed beading around the edge extended across the running boards to produce a striking new beauty in commercial cars.

The pickup box, also restyled, was now 72 in. long—longer than even the long box of 1935. The box continued with all-steel construction and a heavy corrugated floor welded to both sides and cross sills, binding the whole box into one durable unit. For the first time on Dodge pickups, the flareboard edges were rolled to promote extra sturdiness. Stake

pockets were cleverly designed into the brackets which supported the side panels so that their vertical height matched that of the box's side panel.

Because the cab was new in late 1935, it continued without change. The seat was adjustable forward and backward to three positions, with a 3 in. adjustment. The seatback moved with the seat cushion. Cab interior was fully lined and trimmed, presenting a finished and pleasing appearance. A toolbox was provided on the floor behind the seatback, and the windshield opened for ventilation. Standard equipment consisted of cowl vent, windshield wiper and exterior rearview mirror.

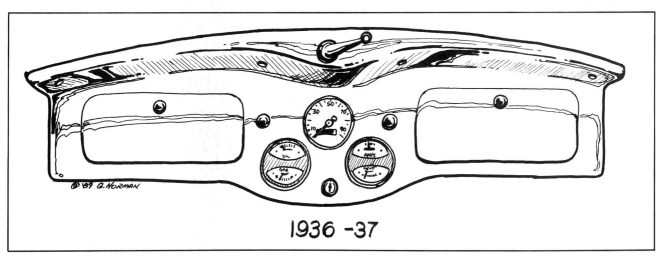

1936 -37

Dashboards changed again for 1936–1937 with the addition of gloveboxes. Greg Norman

33

Dodge Truck print advertising throughout the 1930s was geared toward selling economy. Better gas mileage than the competition delivered was one heavily promoted theme. Better gas mileage was a subtle stab at Ford's V–8 with its two extra cylinders.

Standard and optional equipment

Standard equipment included ammeter, speedometer, fuel gauge, oil-pressure gauge, engine temperature indicator and glove compartment. Choke, hand throttle, light switch and ignition switch on instrument panel. Floor-operated headlamp dimmer.

Extra-cost optional equipment included an oil bath air cleaner, $2.40; Vortox air cleaner with standard cap, $17.50; Vortox air cleaner with Vortox breather cap, $19.50; front chrome bumper, $6; rear chrome bumper, $7; crankcase ventilator with connection to carburetor air intake, $3.50; Handy governor, $10; Liebing governor, $5; tire lock, $1.20; oil filter, $2.75; chrome-plated radiator shell and headlamps, $7.50; long-arm rearview mirror, stationary type, $1; adjustable type, $2.50; safety glass in windshield, $4; safety glass throughout for Pickup, Panel, Canopy or Screenside, $10; single-acting shocks, front and rear, $10; auxiliary seat for Panel, Screenside or Canopy, $10; interior sun visor, $2; metal tire

Passenger-car styling is also seen on this 1936 Dodge Pickup owned by Angelo Holden. By 1936, Dodge was beginning to recover from the worst of the Depression. Advertised as "Beauty Winners" these handsome trucks appear to be just what the ad slogan suggested.

The one-color paint job on this handsome 1936 Commercial Pickup is unusual. The standard paint scheme was to paint fenders and splash aprons black while the cab and box were a second color. Light paint colors were also unusual for this time period as it seems most buyers preferred dark blue, green or black. This truck is either painted Prairie Gray, the only light color Dodge offered in 1936, or possibly a special fleet color.

The 1936 Dual Purpose Sedan differed from the Commercial Sedan in that it was equipped with a removeable rear seat and rear side windows. Removing the rear seat and installing steel blank-out plates quickly converted the Dual-Purpose Sedan from the family sedan to a light delivery truck.

The double-level Commercial Panel returned in 1936, but now with handsome, beaver-tail rear styling. The rear bottom of the Panel body slopes outward while the embossing on the body side panels sweeps over the rear fenders and around the rear of the body to create the beaver-tail look.

cover, $6.50; auxiliary windshield wiper, $4; Special Chassis Accessory group, including chrome-plated radiator shell and headlamps, front and rear shocks, $17.50.

Specifications and prices

All LC Commercials used one wheelbase length of 116 in., an L–6 engine with 3⅛x4⅜ in. bore and stroke, 201.3 ci, advertised 70 hp, three-speed transmission, 6.00x16 four-ply tires.

Commercial Pickup, $550
Commercial Sedan, $755
Commercial Panel, $640
Commercial Canopy, $650
Commercial Screenside, $670
Westchester Suburban, $770

Production

Consumers said yes to the Fore-Point Commercials as production soared to 109,392, an increase of 31 percent. Likewise, market share rose to its highest level ever of 13.4 percent. Of the total, 2,764 trucks were built in Canada and 8,599 in California. This is the first year production figures were kept by weight class, but no breakdown by body type is available. Figures are for United States calendar year production and do not include Canada. Half-ton total was 57,226; three-quarter-ton was 804 and one-ton was 1,595.

1937 MC and MD series

With a new engine, new models, new exterior styling and new cab interior styling, Dodge continued its aggressive marketing in 1937. Exterior restyling of the Commercial Series was minimal, limited to the grille and sides of the hood. The grille opening for 1937 was the same as in 1936, except the

This well-preserved 1936 LC Commercial Pickup belongs to Russel Liechty of Goshen, Indiana. Wooden side boards were added by the owner.

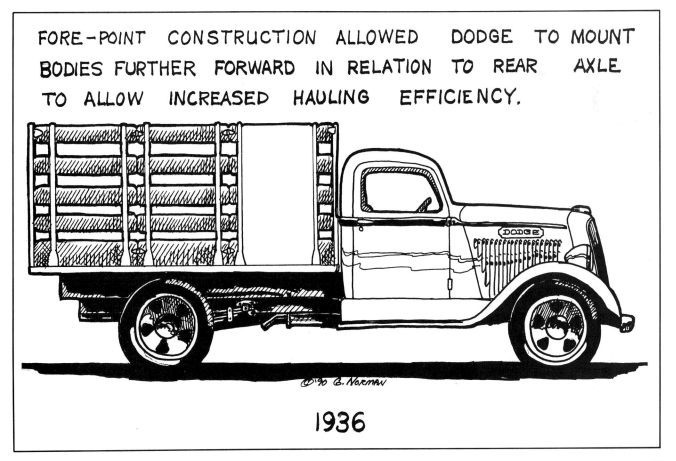

This 218 ci engine and three-speed transmission are from a 1937 MD Series three-quarter to one-ton pickup. Except for minor changes the outward appearance of this power unit is typical of all Dodge light-duty trucks built between 1935 and 1960.

The easiest way to differentiate a 1937 Dodge Commercial from a 1936 is by looking at its grille. Grille bars on 1937 models run horizontally; in 1936 they run vertically. The windows in these Commercial Panel's bodies were not standard, and the steel disk wheels were the first ever on a Dodge Commercial. At last Dodge moved away from the traditional, wire-and-wood spokes. The three-piece bumper guards and attractive chrome-plated radiator shell were extra-cost options. The panel on the far left is a one-and-a-half-ton.

grille bars changed from running vertically to horizontally. Hood restyling amounted to removing two small horizontal chrome strips over the cooling louvers, leaving just one large chrome strip down the middle.

A more modern, High Safety dash highlighted the cab interior. All knobs and controls were set flush because Dodge engineers wanted to prevent injuries resulting from projections on the dashboard. The entire cab was trimmed in an attractive gray material and the dashboard was painted gray enamel. The dash layout now consisted of two large round elements, one on either side of the midpoint of the dash. One was the speedometer and the other housed the ammeter, fuel gauge, oil pressure and temperature gauges. A Dodge nameplate ran vertically between the two round elements. On the right, a much larger glovebox balanced the dash layout and also carried a Dodge nameplate.

The new engine was the same L-6 small-block as before, but now with 3⅞x4⅟₁₆ in. bore and stroke giving 218.06 ci and developing 75 hp at 3000 rpm.

New entries for 1937 were the MD Series, including the MD-15 120 in. wheelbase three-quarter-ton and the MD-20 136 in. wheelbase one-ton. A 7 ft. pickup was offered on the 120 in. wheelbase chassis and a 9 ft. pickup was offered on the 136 in. wheelbase chassis. Transmission was a heavy-duty three-speed with optional four-speed available. These new three-quarter- and one-ton models differed from the previous three-quarter- and one-tonners in that the new models looked like heavier versions of the Commercial models, that is, much like current three-quarter- and one-ton pickups, not like lighter versions of a one-and-a-half-ton truck.

The standard color scheme was to paint the radiator shell, headlights and brackets, fenders, running boards and splash shields black; and the cab, hood, wheels and body any standard color. A complete single-color paint scheme could be ordered at extra charge.

The MD Series were the first Dodge pickups to have a spare tire carrier underslung at rear of the frame. Commercial Cars continued to store spares in front fenderwells.

This was the first year for a Plymouth pickup. Another interesting development was that this was the first year Dodge called its lightest pickup a "pickup." However, they continued to use the terms pickup and express interchangeably up until the 1950s—and even with the exciting, high-performance Little Red Express of 1978 and 1979!

Standard and optional equipment

Standard equipment remained the same as 1936.

Optional extra-cost equipment included oil bath air cleaner, $3.75; chrome-plated rear bumper (Panel

This outstanding 1937 three-quarter-ton pickup is owned by John Mosquera of Staten Island, New York. Its 120 in. wheelbase chassis carries a 7 ft. box.

only), $8.50; bumper guards, front and rear, per pair, $1.50; Leibing governor, $5; Monarch governor, $7.50; Handy governor, $10; dual horns, $7.50; side-mounted coach lamps for Panel and Sedan, $8; tire lock, $2.50; oil filter, $3.25; painted sheet metal to match standard body colors, included radiator shell, headlamps and brackets, fenders and splash shields, $7.50; long-arm rearview mirror, stationary type, $1.50; adjustable type, $2.50; safety glass in front doors, Westchester Suburban, $15; safety glass in front doors and front and rear-quarter sections, Westchester Suburban, $110; auxiliary seat for Panel, Canopy and Screen (standard on Sedan), $10; double-acting shocks hydraulic aeroplane type, front, $4.75, rear, $4.75; sun visor, interior, $2; metal tire cover, $6.50; four-speed transmission instead of standard three-speed, $25; and auxiliary windshield wiper, $4.

Specifications and prices

All MC Commercials used the 116 in. wheelbase and were powered by an L-6 engine with 3⅜x4⅟₁₆ in. bore and stroke, 218.06 ci, and advertised 75 hp. A three-speed transmission transmitted power to 6.00x16 four-ply tires.

The MD 120 in. wheelbase and MD 136 in. wheelbase three-quarter- and one-ton models had the same specifications as above, except 7.00x16 six-ply front and 7.50x16 six-ply rear tires.

MC Series
Commercial Pickup, $540
Commercial Sedan, $670

Here at the end of the assembly line we see one-and-a-half-ton chassis cabs on the right and in the middle and a Commercial Pickup ready to come off the left line. The 1938 models were the last trucks built in this plant as a new truck plant began building trucks with the 1939 models.

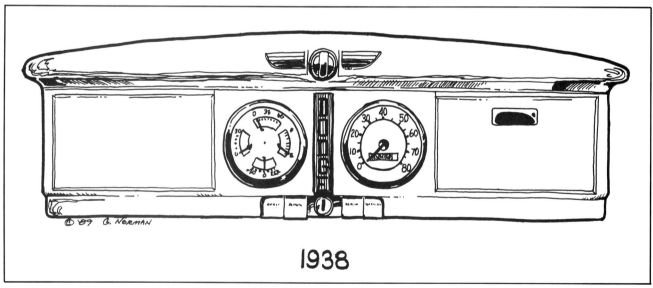

Dashboards were updated for 1938 with a modernistic look.
Greg Norman

Commercial Panel, $625
Commercial Canopy, $640
Commercial Screenside, $660
Westchester Suburban, $755
MD 120 in. Series
Pickup, $685
Stake, $685
Platform, $655
MD 136 in. Series
Pickup, $700
Panel, $800
Canopy, $765
Screenside, $785
Stake, $705
Platform, $675

Production

Calendar-year production totalled 121,917, an increase of 11.4 percent. Market share, however, fell half a percent because total industry production increased 15.8 percent. Included in the production numbers are 7,409 trucks built in California and 5,383 built in Canada; all the rest were built in Hamtramck, Michigan. By weight class, United States production only, calendar-year figures 59,663 half-ton, 5,060 three-quarter- and 8,574 one-ton.

1938 RC and RD Series

This was a quiet year at Dodge Truck Division as management marked time while getting ready for a fully restyled truck line in 1939, which would be built in an all-new truck plant in Warren, Michigan.

The only significant change in 1938 was a new front-end appearance. A more attractive grille gave Dodge trucks a smarter look for 1938. The new grille's center section featured vertical chrome bars set off by contrasting stripes painted body color. Flanking on either side were gleaming, horizontal chrome bars which swept from the grille's center and back on either side to form a pointed prow. Dodge stamped its emblem on the apron under the grille.

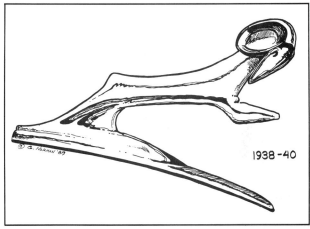

The Dodge ram hood ornament was refined for 1938–1940 trucks to an art deco look. Greg Norman

An attractive 1938 Dodge three-quarter- to one-ton, 136 in. wheelbase, 9 ft. Panel. Its owner insisted on a prestigious delivery vehicle, as seen by its two-sided whitewalls, chrome grille and headlights, disk wheels, and smart two-tone paint, which was in keeping with his exclusive merchandise.

This original-condition 1938 RD 136 in. wheelbase one-ton pickup with 9 ft. box is owned by Stephen Tobin of San Luis Obispo, California.

New hood louvers accentuated the length of the hood, sweeping from front to back.

In each of the three Fore-Point Era years, Dodge truck styling mirrored that of the Dodge passenger cars. This practice would continue for one more year, but after that, Dodge truck and car styling were never again similar, the Rampage car-type pickup of the early 1980s excepted.

Other than the above appearance changes, the only other changes included increasing the radiator core thickness for three-quarter- and one-ton models from three to 3⁵⁄₁₆ in. and making safety glass standard for all cabs and bodies.

The only new model for 1938 was a heavy-duty three-ton COE with cab by Montpelier Manufacturing Company. The four-ton custom-built Airflow continued to be built as well.

Standard and optional equipment

Standard equipment included ammeter, speedometer, fuel gauge, oil pressure gauge, engine temperature indicator and glovebox. Choke, hand-

Dodge Truck Collectibles

Many hobbyists enjoy collecting items related to their vehicle interest. Collectibles take many forms, including apparel such as hats and jackets, badges, models, sales literature, signs and sometimes even sheet metal parts such as a grille or tailgate that have been restored just for display. For some, collectibles are a way to extend the prospecting pleasure of scouring flea markets for items of interest after the rebuilding and restoring phase has ended. Collectibles bring one's old truck hobby interest out of the garage and into everyday life.

Dodge hats and jackets, available from parts vendors, make a statement about your collector interest. Clubs, such as the LCVA and Plymouth Owners Club, also sell apparel and bumper stickers that announce the wearer as a truck collector and Dodge or Plymouth devotee.

The radiator emblems of earlier Dodge trucks and nameplates from later models make attention-getting collectibles when attached to a mounting board and displayed in one's shop or den. Badges can often be purchased at flea markets or can be gathered at junkyards.

Dealer sales and service signs have become popular display items, often hanging in a collector's garage and sometimes in informal areas of the home. Original signs can occasionally be purchased from long-standing Dodge dealers, but better opportunities for purchase can be found at swap meets and auctions. Replicas in smaller scale of dealer signs are available from parts vendors such as Roberts Motor Parts.

Original Dodge Truck dealer and service signs from Ron Cenowa's collection.

Toy truck collecting is also a fun side of the hobby. This is a 1939–1940 Turner Toy Dodge dump truck from Ron Cenowa's collection.

throttle, light switch with red warning signal to show when bright lights are on, ignition switch on panel, foot-operated headlamp dimmer, vacuum windshield wiper, chrome front bumper, chrome rear bumper on Sedan, one bucket seat in Sedan, Panel, Screenside and Canopy, metal running boards, spare tire and tube, and safety glass throughout cabs and bodies.

Extra-cost optional equipment included oil bath air cleaner, $3.75; Vortox cleaner with standard breather cap, $17.50; Vortox with Vortox breather cap, $19.50; bumper guards, front and rear, per pair, $1.50; Chassis Accessory Group, chrome-plated radiator shell and headlights, double-acting hydraulic shocks, front and rear, $18.25; Leibing governor, $5; Monarch governor, $5; Handy governor, $10; chrome-plated headlamps, $2.75; dual horns, $7.50; side-mounted coach lamps for Panel and Sedan, $8.50; oil filter, $3.25; painted sheet metal to match standard body colors, included radiator shell, headlamps and brackets, fenders and splash shields, $5; full-width partition behind driver's seat for Canopy and Screenside, $15; chrome-plated radiator shell, $6; long-arm rearview mirror, stationary type, $1.50, adjustable type, $2.50; auxiliary seat for Sedan, Panel, Canopy and Screenside, $10; double-acting hydraulic shocks aeroplane type, front and rear, $4.75; interior sun visor, $2; spare tire carrier mounted in front fenderwell with lock (instead of underslung at rear), $3.50; four-speed transmission (instead of three-speed), $25; chrome-plated windshield frame, $3; and auxiliary windshield wiper, $4.

Specifications and prices

RC Commercial models continued to use a 116 in. wheelbase, were powered by an L-6 engine of 3⅜x4¼ in. bore and stroke for 218.06 ci, with adver-

tised 75 hp. Power transferred through a three-speed transmission to 6.00x16 four-ply tires.

The RD 120 in. wheelbase and RD 136 in. wheelbase three-quarter- and one-ton models specifications remained the same as RC, except 7.00x16 six-ply front and 7.50x16 six-ply rear tires.

RC Series
Commercial Pickup, $600
Commercial Sedan, $710
Commercial Panel, $695
Commercial Canopy, $690
Commercial Screenside, $710
RD 120 in. Series
Pickup, $725
Stake, $758
Platform, $725
RD 136 in. Series
Pickup, $776
Panel, $885
Canopy, $858
Screenside, $878
Stake, $809
Platform, $776

Production

This was a hard year for Dodge Truck Division because after five consecutive years of production increases, the bottom fell out and production plummeted 56 percent, all the way down to 53,613. Market share fell to 10.1 percent from 12.9 percent in 1937. Total industry production was also hard hit, falling 44 percent. Included in the 1938 total are 2,563 units built in California and 3,871 in Canada. All others were built in Hamtramck, Michigan. By weight class, United States only, calendar-year production amounted to 20,777 half-ton, 1,692 three-quarter-ton and 4,069 one-tonners.

Dodge's entire 1938 truck lineup from left to right: Commercial Pickup, Commercial Panel, three-quarter- to one-ton Pickup, three-quarter- to one-ton Panel, one-and-a-half-ton Pickup, one-and-a-half-ton Panel, one-and-a-half-ton Stake, two-ton Stake, three-ton Chassis Cab and custom-built four-ton Airflow Tanker.

Chapter 4

Job-Rated Era 1939–1947

1939 TC and TD Series

In 1939, streamlining was the buzzword used to describe a newly restyled car or truck as streamlined was in—in a big way. Trains were streamlined, as were boats, cars and even big trucks. Labatt's famous tractor-trailer beer trucks, for example, had a tractor as smooth and streamlined as an egg, with even the tractor's rear duals almost completely enclosed with a teardrop-shaped fairing. Remember too, that Dodge still built its heavy-duty Airflow in 1939. Building on its reputation, begun in 1933, for styling America's best-looking "Delivery Equipment," Dodge continued in 1939 by offering an all-new truck which was "streamlined from bumper to bumper."

Dodge's "up-to-the-minute," attractive new trucks were at the same time rugged and smart. Beginning with a sharp, pointed grille, which looked fully capable of slicing through the air, all other styling lines flowed from front to back, giving a sense of aerodynamics and speed. The grille's opening lines curved back on the right and left from the center, with long simple hood-side louvers continuing the flowing theme, and the raised speed lines at the back of both front and rear with full-skirted fenders cutting through the air. Deeply crowned front fenders provided a resting place for the headlights, which were positioned midway between the crowns and the hood sides. The sloped, two-piece V-type windshield

The non-vented steel disk wheels on this 133 in. wheelbase one-ton Pickup were used only on one-ton models; half- and three-quarter-ton models featured vented steel disk wheels.

The one-ton pickup with its 9 ft. box carried a maximum GVW of 6,000 lb.

added to the wind-splitting look, as did the teardrop-shaped headlight buckets. Even the forward leaping bighorn ram hood ornament imparted a sense of movement. In total, the new styling presented a sense of grace and action.

For the first time, all Dodge trucks shared the same front-end styling treatment with the half-ton models looking the same as the heavy-duty, three-ton models. It was not until 1946 that the three-ton model's front end was restyled to give it a brawny, heavy-truck look.

Unfortunately, Dodge designers did not hit the nail squarely on the head with their initial front-end style treatment. Chrome trim pieces placed low on the grille flowed back and up giving a mixed impression of decoration and aerodynamics. In 1940, Dodge designers corrected these contradicting lines and by 1941 the style was finalized to remain the same through 1947.

The 1939–1947 Job-Rated Era Dodge trucks are the most popular of all Dodge series with collectors. Prewar models are least commonly seen, the 1946–1947 models are the most common.

Engine and chassis

A major engineering change that ushered in the 1939 models was the revamped engine lineup. For the previous two years, a single engine powered the entire pickup line. It was an L–6, to be sure, of 218.06 ci, with bore and stroke of 3⅜x4¹⁄₁₆ in. This engine posed a problem in that it was in use only in light-duty Dodge trucks. Plymouth was powered by a 201.3 ci, 3⅛x4⅜ in. L–6 while Dodge cars used a 217.8 ci, 3¼x4⅜ in. L–6. Dodge engineering solved the problem of an extra block by dropping the 218.06,

For the first time since 1932, Dodge's 1939 half-ton Panel was of conventional design. Aluminum painted bumpers continued through 1947, except for late 1942 and early post World War II production. Bumpers in 1939 were changed to the heavy-duty, channel-steel type. Prior to 1939, light-duty Dodge trucks were equipped with spring-type, chrome-plated bumpers.

45

and substituting two available engines that were already in production, which simplified manufacturing, and parts inventory and reduced corporate costs. It was all so logical as now the only difference between the "Plymouth" and the "Dodge" engines was a $\frac{1}{8}$ in. bore diameter. While reducing the displacement of the half-ton pickup's engine may seem illogical, the situation was corrected in three years.

Other engine modifications included an increase in the carburetor bore size from $1\frac{1}{4}$ to $1\frac{1}{2}$ in. Dodge now fitted Auto-Lite spark plugs in place of the former Champions. A manually operated manifold heat control valve replaced the hot spot manifold.

For better cooling, the radiator core's frontal area was increased from 360 to 466 sq. in., although the core thickness was reduced from $3\frac{5}{16}$ to 3 in. The radiator fill cap was now placed under the hood.

The well-designed 1939 instrument panel did not change through 1947. Dodge cabs were always well-insulated with cardboard-type lining as seen on this half-ton Panel's fire- *wall, cowl sides, windshield header and roof. Soft linings gave Dodge cabs an inviting, warm, non-metallic look and feel which drivers appreciated.*

In addition to the new engine lineup, other engineering changes were made as well. On the chassis, the maximum gross vehicle weight for the three-quarter-ton was reduced from 5,200 to 5,000 lb. A new hypoid rear axle had replaced the spiral bevel axle on the three-quarter-ton, limiting capacity from 4,500 to 3,500 lb. Front spring length on the three-quarter-ton increased from 36 to 39 in. The three-quarter-ton, 136 in. wheelbase model was discontinued, and the one-ton wheelbase was shortened from 136 to 133 in. Rear wheel treads were, on the other hand, widened; the half-ton was increased from 57⅞ to 60 in., the three-quarter-ton from 59 to 60⁵⁄₃₂ in., and the one-ton from 59 to 61 in.

The braking power for all trucks was upgraded, with new brake linings that were molded versus being woven. The total area of the brake linings on the three-quarter-ton were reduced, however, from 188 to 154 sq. in., but increased on the one-ton from 188 to 190 sq. in. Parking brake lining on the three-quarter-ton was increased from 6x2 to 7x2 in.

Other changes included the spare tire carrier moved on the half-ton from the fenderwell to being underslung at the rear. The power takeoff access was also removed from the three-speed transmissions.

Fuel tanks increased from 15 to 18 gallons on half-tonners and from 16 to 18 gallons on three-quarter- and one-tonners.

Bodywork and interior

The new Dodge cab took a giant leap forward in terms of driver comfort and safety. Driver vision was considerably improved, due to a higher seat and additional glass area. A 4⅛ in. wider seat, which was adjustable forward and backward up to 3 in., afforded greater comfort. Attractive, durable, blue vinyl upholstery, hardboard headliner, door and dash liners contributed to a warm, inviting and attractive cab interior. Upholstery in trucks for the years 1939 and 1940 was blue; for 1941 and later, upholstery was brown. The new, larger, two-piece V-type windshield was of the ventilating type, swinging open at the turn of a handle located at the top center of the dash. An enlarged cowl vent provided additional ventilation. A toolbox was provided on the floor behind the seat.

Continuing with the safety-type dash introduced in 1937, the High Safety 1939 dash was restyled for better safety, convenience and better vision. The speedometer and gauges were now grouped at the left, in front of the driver. Control

This November 10, 1938, photo was taken inside Dodge's new, modern truck plant. It was a state of the art facility with acres of roof glass which created a well-lighted and pleasant place to work.

47

For 1939, Dodge completely restyled its truck line, giving all models—small to large—a distinct truck appearance. To many, these are the most handsomely styled of all Dodge trucks. The first models were introduced as the TC Series. Postwar models were called the WC Series as seen here.

buttons were recessed at the bottom center of the panel and a large glovebox was on the right. The dash was painted body color.

A new hood ornament, resembling that of the Glamour Years, but modernized and slightly heavier in scale, replaced the former radiator cap ornament now that the radiator cap was hidden below the hood.

For the first time in Dodge history, a complete range of pickups was offered, from the handsome half-ton, to a three-quarter-ton, a one-ton, and a one-and-a-half-ton. The one-and-a-half-tonner was a heavier version of the 9 ft. one-ton 133 in. wheelbase. All pickup box floors were now constructed of ¹³⁄₁₆ in. oak lumber joined by steel skid strips to provide great strength. Floors were painted black, regardless of box color.

Standard paint schemes on light-duty trucks changed little from 1933. The lower grille, front and rear fenders, running boards and headlights remained black; the hood, cab, box and wheels were cab color. The front bumper was painted aluminum.

An historical event of interest is that, for the first time, DeSoto and Plymouth trucks were sold at export. Both of these were really badge-engineered Dodge trucks. Two other interesting historical events for Chrysler Corporation occurred in this model year. First, on October 22, 1938, Dodge Truck Division entered the diesel truck field with a 331 ci diesel. Second, on December 6, 1938, Chrysler introduced

the industry's first fluid coupling between clutch and transmission called Fluid Drive. Ten years later Fluid Drive was made available in light-duty trucks.

Standard and optional equipment

Standard equipment included shock absorbers front and rear, spare tire and tube, front bumper, rear bumper on panels, radiator ornament, safety glass in all cabs and bodies, horn, combination stop and taillight, license plate brackets, tool kit, speedometer, fuel and pressure gauges, ammeter, engine temperature indicator, choke, hand throttle, light switch with high beam indicator light, ignition switch, package compartment, cowl ventilator, headlight dimmer, vacuum wiper, and one bucket seat in Panel, Canopy and Screenside models.

Extra-cost optional equipment included oil bath air cleaner, $3.25; Vortox air cleaner with standard breather cap, $17.50; Vortox air cleaner with Vortox breather cap, $19.50; rear bumper, $6; 25 amp. generator for slow-speed operation, $27.50; Leibing governor, $5; Monarch governor, $5; Handy governor, $10; chrome-plated headlamps, $2.75; side-mounted coach-type lamps for Panel, $8.50; oil filter, $3.25; full-width partition behind driver's seat, Canopy and Screenside, $15; long-arm rearview mirror, stationary type, $1.50; adjustable type, $2.50; auxiliary seat for Panel, Canopy or Screenside, $10; interior sun visor, $2; auxiliary taillight, $4; four-speed transmission, $17.50; chrome-plated windshield frame, $3; auxiliary vacuum wiper, $4; and dual electric wipers, $8.

Specifications and prices

TC half-ton, 116 in. wheelbase, powered by an L-6 engine, 3⅛x4⅜ in. bore and stroke, 201.3 ci, advertised 70 hp, three-speed transmission, 6.00x16 four-ply tires.

TD-15 three-quarter-ton, 120 in. wheelbase, powered by an L-6 engine, 3¼x4⅜ in. bore and stroke, 217.8 ci, advertised 77 hp, three-speed transmission, TA-15 six-ply tires.

TD-20 one-ton 120 in. wheelbase and TD-21 133 in. wheelbase. Same specifications as TD-15 except 7.00x16 six-ply front and 7.50x16 six-ply rear tires.

TC half-ton Series
Pickup, $590
Panel, $680
Canopy, $690
Screenside, $710
TD-15 three-quarter-ton Series
Pickup, $670
Stake, $705
Platform, $680
TD-20 one-ton Series
Pickup, $715

Stake, $750
Platform, $725
TD–21 one-ton Series
Pickup, $765
Panel, $855
Canopy, $840
Screenside, $860
Stake, $790
Platform, $760

Production summary

Dodge truck production recovered quite nicely in 1939 from the 1938 disaster, with a healthy 57 percent increase, topping off at 89,364 for the calendar year. Because total industry production increased only 42.8 percent, Dodge gained market share up to 11.8 percent. Of total production, 5,704 were built in Canada and 3,403 in Los Angeles. Total built by weight class, United States only, for the calendar year was 34,458 half-ton, 3,029 three-quarter-ton and 6,587 one-ton.

1940 VC and VD Series

As so often happens after a major new product introduction, the following year tends to be quiet, and such was the situation in 1940.

The only real change was the redesign of the grille. Dodge designers eliminated the conflicting-lines look by moving the chrome trim higher up on the grille. VC pickups are highly prized by collectors

due to this especially attractive and distinctive grille. They are easily identified by the horizontal breaks in the detail trim of the grille, and because of a change to sealed-beam headlights with tiny parking lights perched atop the headlight buckets.

While both engines continued as introduced in 1939, power output was boosted through redesigned camshafts. Brake horsepower on the 201 ci increased from 70 to 79 and torque increased from 148 to 154 lb-ft. For the 218 ci, brake horsepower rose from 77 to 82 and torque increased to 166 from 158 lb-ft.

Other mechanical changes included a fuel-line filter added at the carburetor, a floating-type oil pump intake and screen, and a new 35 amp generator.

Over the coming years, the GVW would be increased almost annually; for 1940, the half-ton GVW was raised from 4,000 to 4,200 lb., and the one-tons from 6,000 to 6,400 lb. A hypoid rear axle was also introduced for the one-ton, and the half-ton's wheel-attaching bolts were made in right- and left-hand threads.

Dodge pickups of these years were painted with wear- and weather-resisting Hi-Bake enamels. Cabs, bodies and all sheet metal were thoroughly protected against rust by Bonderizing, a special treatment which formed a coating over the metal to stop the formation of rust.

Three significant events occurred in 1940. On June 6, Chrysler opened a new engineering and

In terms of sheer numbers, Job-Rated Era Dodge trucks are the all-time favorites with Dodge collectors. The 1940 model's distinctive front-end style makes it unique and interesting, but not many 1939 and 1940 models are in the hands of collectors due to the fact that prewar production was limited and trucks were given hard use during the war years.

Dodge City: Warren, Michigan

Production began on Dodge's Job-Rated 1939 truck models on October 10, 1938, at an exclusive, new truck factory. Located in Warren, Michigan, a Detroit suburb, and built to provide "streamlined" truck production, this ultra-modern manufacturing facility was the pride of Chrysler Corporation

Sitting on a 50 acre site, with 658,222 sq. ft. under roof, and containing almost seven miles of production lines, conveyors and assembly lines, it was the final word in efficient truck manufacturing. The factory contained over 5 acres of glass to provide "daylight" working conditions. Dodge management counted on this new plant, with its clean, well-lit, well-layed-out interior, to enable its dedicated labor force to build the industry's highest-quality trucks.

Although considerably changed and expanded over the years, the Dodge Truck Division's Warren plant, renamed Dodge City in 1987, builds all Dodge trucks to this day on the same site, Ramchargers, vans and minivans excepted.

research building; a state-of-the-art facility equipped with all the latest equipment and furnishings. Sadly, Walter P. Chrysler died on August 18. Finally, Chrysler plants were shut down from October 9, 1939, to late in November by a labor dispute at a time when sales were in high gear and factories couldn't meet demand. The rumblings of war around the world made America nervous that it eventually would become involved, and that civilian auto production would be halted. Hitler's Blitzkrieg, the Lightning War to conquer Europe, touched off a tremendous vehicle demand here at home with the result that the entire auto industry continued to roll in high gear throughout 1940.

Standard and optional equipment

Sealed-beam headlights, 35 amp generator, shock absorbers front and rear, spare wheel tire and tube, front bumper, rear bumper on Panel models, long running boards, and rear fenders, radiator ornament, safety glass in all cabs and bodies, horn, combination stop and taillight, license brackets, tool

A 1940 Montpelier one-ton Forward Control delivery. Montpelier also built one-and-a-half- to three-ton cab-over-engine cabs for Dodge from 1937 to 1940, at which time Dodge *began building its own cab-overs. Montpelier was also an important supplier of Forward Control bodies to Dodge.*

50

kit, speedometer, fuel and oil gauges, ammeter, engine temperature indicator, choke, hand throttle, light switch with high beam indicator light, ignition switch, package compartment, cowl ventilator, headlight dimmer switch, and vacuum wiper. Panel, Canopy and Screenside models had one bucket seat only.

Extra-cost optional equipment included oil bath air cleaner, $2.50; Vortox air cleaner with standard breather cap, $17.50; Vortox air cleaner with Vortox breather cap, $19.50; airfoam seat cushion and seat back, $10; rear bumper, $6; domelight in cab, $3.50; 32 amp generator for slow-speed operation, $14; governor, $5; chrome-plated headlights, $3.50; heater and defroster, $25; dual horns, $7.50; coach-type side-mounted lamp for Panel, $8.50; regular oil filter, $3.25; De Luxe cartridge oil filter, $5; fenders, radiator shell, headlamps and running boards painted to match body color, $5; full-width, full-height partition behind driver's seat, Canopy or Screenside, $25; grille guard, $7.50; inside rearview mirror, $1; long-arm rearview mirror, stationary type, left side, $1.50, right side, $2.50, adjustable-type, long-arm mirror, left side, $2.50, right side $3.50; auxiliary seat for Panel, Canopy or Screenside, $12; interior sun visor,

$2; auxiliary taillamp, $2.50; tow hooks, front only, pair, $4; four-speed transmission, $17.50; chrome-plated windshield frame, $3; auxiliary vacuum, windshield wiper, $4; dual electric wipers, $13.

A 1940 half-ton Pickup owned by Ron Cenowa of Utica, Michigan. This truck is in original, like-new condition with only 34,000 total miles. Ron purchased it from its original farmer owner in this condition, except for detailing.

This 1940 one-ton Delivery with body by the DeKalb Wagon Company is an interesting example of prewar streamlining.

By 1941, Dodge's Job-Rated Era styling was set. It did not change through 1947, except that after the war the chrome bars on the lower grille did not return. Headlights on the 1941 models were moved outboard to the fender's centerline, parking lights were cowl-mounted and the leaping ram hood ornament disappeared. In 1941, two-tone paint schemes were a no-cost option as was a one-tone paint job as seen on this Pickup. Unless specified otherwise, the standard paint scheme painted all fenders black regardless of cab color.

Specifications and prices

All specifications remained the same as 1939 except advertised horsepower was now 70 hp for half-ton models and 82 hp for three-quarter and one-ton.

VC half-ton Series
Pickup, $590
Panel, $680
Canopy, $690
Screenside, $710
VD–15 three-quarter-ton Series
Pickup, $670
Stake, $705
Platform, $680
VD–20 one-ton Series
Pickup, $715
Stake, $750
Platform, $725
VD–21 one-ton Series
Pickup, $765
Panel, $855
Canopy, $840
Screenside, $860
Stake, $790
Platform, $760

Production

The outbreak of war in Europe had a positive effect on truck sales, and production jumped up 31.6 percent to 117,588 total. Of this total, 7,790 were built in Canada and 4,860 in Los Angeles. Market share improved by 11 percent, up to 13.1 percent. Calendar-year production, United States only, by

A 1941 Plymouth Commercial moved down the line immediately ahead of a half-ton military 4x4.

weight class was 49,712 half-ton, 4,514 three-quarter-ton and 7,523 one-ton. Dodge built 10,107 half-ton and 23 one-ton military trucks this year versus only 1,138 in 1939.

1941 WC and WD Series

This was another year of minor refinements and improvements both in appearance and engineering. Several appearance changes were made which continued for the balance of the Job-Rated Era. The most dramatic change, and one that receives mixed reviews from Dodge collectors, was the placement of the headlights outboard to pockets positioned on the crown of the fenders. Many Dodge lovers criticize this change as creating a bug-eyed look. Another appearance change which finalized the style was new chrome trim on the grille; this style was now set and remained unchanged through 1947. Parking lights moved from atop the headlights to the cowl. The only appearance change which did not survive beyond 1942 was the chrome strips added above the four horizontal louvers between the grille's center and the front fenders. Chrome-plated Dodge nameplates were added to the sides of the hood.

Another appearance change, which was limited to light-duty models only, was a two-tone paint scheme offered at no extra cost. Whereas the standard paint scheme had been to paint the lower grille, headlights, fenders and running boards black with the cab, hood, wheels and box painted body color, now the buyer could order a truck with his choice of any of seven standard paint colors on those parts formerly painted black and any other color for the balance. Or, without additional cost, the buyer could have his pickup painted all-over in one of the seven standard colors. This change results in a big break for the restorer, as you have a wide variety of original paint scheme as long as you stay with the seven standard colors.

Since 1933, Dodge trucks had featured an attractive, chrome-plated Rocky Mountain sheep or bighorn hood ornament. This ornament became synonymous with Dodge toughness as it stood poised on its rear legs in the classic hard-charging, head-butting posture. In 1941, the 1930s style fighting ram disappeared and was replaced by a 1940s modern stylized ornament. More than forty years later, in the early 1980s, the classic ram hood ornament returned to grace the front of all Dodge pickups, a welcomed return.

The last exterior appearance change for 1941 was a redesigned front bumper. Where previously the bumper had been basically straight, it was now contoured to follow the shape of the grille. This change added considerably to the truck's front appearance.

For the first time since the Job-Rated Series began, Dodge improved the cab interior. Both the

Canopies were not limited to fruit and vegetable peddlers. The Grimaldi Plumbing Company bought a 1941 Panel and a 1941 Canopy to perform the same tasks. Tradesmen appreciated being able to reach inside the Canopy's body from over its sides, which is not that different from the side-opening pickup toppers many tradesmen use today.

The Burlington, Iowa, Fire Department took delivery of this one-ton, open-cab fire truck on June 24, 1941.

seat and back cushions were redesigned by using double-cone coil springs, heavier construction, and thicker padding between springs and upholstery covering. Even the upholstery color was changed from the original blue to Morocco brown. All other cab interior trim was also changed to brown, resulting in

On June 18, 1941, Dr. N. C. Heron took delivery of a new half-ton panel. His nineteen-year-old 1922 Dodge Commercial Panel looks as good as his new Panel. What does a doctor need with a Panel? Maybe he was a veterinarian. Super sleuth Joel Miller researched this matter and uncovered the fact that Dr. Heron was "involved in the manufacture of pharmaceuticals and used his Dodge Panels to pick up needed chemicals and to deliver the finished products around the local area."

an attractive, luxurious cab. And, for the first time in Dodge history, a DeLuxe cab interior package was offered for added luxury.

Engineering improvements included more horsepower and torque squeezed from the engines without increasing displacement but by changing to new higher-lift cams. The half-ton was now rated at 82.5 hp and 160 lb-ft; the three-quarter-ton and one-ton were 85 hp and 170 lb-ft. In addition, the oil bath air cleaner was made standard, and a new three-speed synchro-shift transmission was available for all light-duties.

On the chassis, a full-floating-type rear axle was made standard for one-ton models. Dual rear wheels and 20 in. wheels were optional for the one-tons.

In the cab, redesigned bucket seats with higher backs, heavier padding and springs were placed in Panels and Canopies. The seats tilted and were adjustable forward and backward.

Standard and optional equipment

Standard equipment included sealed-beam headlights, two-tone color combinations, 35 amp generator, oil bath air cleaner, shocks front and rear, spare wheel, tire and tube, front bumper, rear bumper on Panel models, long running boards and rear fenders, radiator ornament, safety glass in all cabs and bodies, horn, combination stop and tail-lamp, license brackets, tool kit, speedometer, fuel and oil pressure gauges, ammeter, engine temperature indicator, choke, hand throttle, light switch with high beam indicator light, ignition switch, package compartment, cowl ventilator, high beam switch, vacuum wiper and one bucket seat in Panel, Canopy and Screenside models.

Extra-cost optional equipment included Vortox air cleaner with standard breather cap, $17.50; Vortox air cleaner with Vortox breather cap, $19.50; airfoam seat cushion and back, $10; 119 amp battery, $2.50; rear bumper, $6; DeLuxe cab equipment, consisting of brown, genuine leather upholstery, airfoam seat and back cushions, armrest on left door, electric wiper (in place of vacuum), domelight, one interior sun visor and chrome windshield frame, $25; domelight in cab, $2.50; 32 amp generator for slow-speed operations, $8; glove compartment door lock, $1.50; Handy governor, $5; chrome-plated headlights and parking lights, $3.50; heater and defroster, $25; dual horns, $5; coach-type lights, cowl-mounted for Panel, $8.50; regular oil filter, $3.25, replaceable type oil filter, $6; fenders and lower radiator grille painted standard colors (running boards, headlights and parking lights black, no charge; partition full-width,

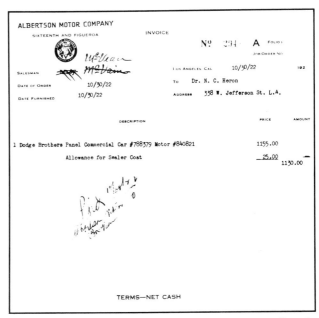

The invoice from Albertson Motor Company recording the sale to Dr. Heron of his 1923 Dodge is dated October 30, 1922. The "Delivered in Detroit" price on the 1941 Panel was $730. If nothing else, the Great Depression of the 1930s served to shrink prices.

The William Green & Son Grocery company on August 28, 1941, took delivery of three new 1941 half-ton Pickups equipped with an aftermarket canopy conversion. The two- *tone paint job seen on these trucks was a no-charge option in 1941.*

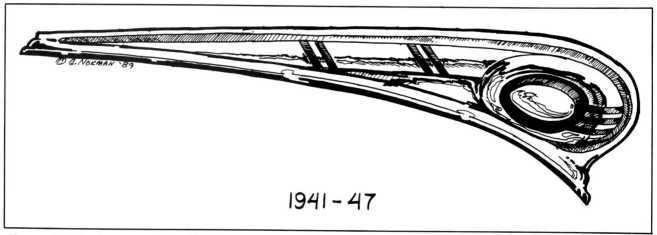

1941 - 47

The ram head hood ornament for 1941–1947 was more orna-ment than ram. The style was angular and modernistic. Greg Norman

full-height behind driver's seat for Canopy and Screenside, $20; partition full-width and height with full-width seat for Canopy and Screenside, $25; grille guards, $7.50; inside rearview mirror, $1; short-arm rearview mirror, right side, $1.50, left side, $2.50; long-arm adjustable type, left side, $2.50, right side, $3; auxiliary seat for Panel, Canopy and Screenside, $12; auxiliary seat, adjustable type, for Panel, Can-opy and Screenside, $14.50; interior sun visor, $2; auxiliary taillamp, $2.50; two tow hooks front only, $4; four-speed transmission, $17.50; chrome-plated windshield frame, $3; dual electric wipers, $13, and single electric wiper for DeLuxe cabs, $8.

Specifications and prices

WC half-ton 116 in. wheelbase, powered by an L–6 engine 3⅛x4⅜ in. bore and stroke, 201 ci, adver-tised 82.5 hp. Three-speed transmission, 6.00x16 four-ply tires.

A 1941 half-ton Panel owned by Ron Cenowa of Utica, Michigan. The panel is in original condition with only 23,000 miles. This truck's first owner was a mortician, which accounts for its few miles.

WD–15 three-quarter-ton, 120 in. wheelbase, powered by an L–6 engine 3¼x4⅜ in. bore and stroke, 218 ci, advertised 85 hp. Three-speed trans-mission, TA–15 six-ply tires.

WD–20 120 in. wheelbase and WD–21 133 in. wheelbase one-ton, all specifications the same as WD–15 except 6.50x16 six-ply tires front and 7.00x16 six-ply rears.

WC half-ton Series
Pickup, $630
Panel, $730
Canopy, $740
Screenside, $760
WD–15 three-quarter-ton Series
Pickup, $705
Stake, $740
Platform, $715
WD–20 one-ton Series
Pickup, $770
Stake, $805
Platform, $780
WD–21 one-ton-Series
Pickup, $800
Panel, $890
Canopy, $895
Screenside, $915
Stake, $825
Platform, $805

Production

Military orders fueled another big rise in cal-endar-year production, topping off at 166,602, a 41.7 percent increase, but market share held steady at 13.1 percent. Of the total, 12,376 were built in Canada, 7,164 in Los Angeles, plus 54,235 military trucks, all half-tons. Calendar-year production by weight class, United States only, was 88,903 half ton, 5,841 three-quarter-ton and 8,593 one-ton.

This was the last year for the Plymouth pickup until years later when the Plymouth nameplate was affixed to an imported truck.

1942 WC and WD Series

The 1941 models carried over without any appearance changes for 1942. The no-charge, two-tone color combinations on light-duty models also returned for 1942.

Since the spring of 1940, the industry, in general, and Dodge, in particular, began to prosper greatly with the flood of incoming orders for military trucks. Because Dodge built its first military 4x4 in 1934, it had established itself as the industry's 4x4 leader. In 1942, Dodge began producing its famous three-quarter-ton, T214 Series Army trucks. A total of 255,195 were built before peace was declared in 1945. In 1946, the T214 military chassis became the platform for the world famous civilian Power Wagon.

Because of a heavy commitment to military trucks, civilian trucks took a back seat in 1942. However, engine sizes and power changes increased substantially, as well as engine applications. Engine realignments came as a result of military needs. When the three-quarter-ton, T214 Series 4x4 military models replaced the former half-ton 4x4 military models, a more powerful engine was required. The base engine for half- and three-quarter-ton models increased to 218 ci (same as the 1941 one-ton) by increasing the bore by 1/8 in. and the next larger engine went to 230 ci, thanks to a 1/4 in. longer stroke. Many hundreds of thousands of 230s went into the T214 military workhorse, and after the war its civilian adaptation, the Power Wagon.

Other engine improvements included a compression ratio increase from 6.5:1 to 6.8:1 on the 218 ci engine and from 6.5:1 to 6.7:1 on the one-ton 230 ci engine. The intake port diameter was also increased

1939-1947 Closed Deliveries

In 1939, Dodge put into place a well-defined, logical model and nominal-size rating system. At long last the now-familiar half-, three-quarter-, one-, one-and-a-half-, two- and three-ton rating system was put in use. No longer was the prefix commercial used to identify the lightest-weight models. And no longer would trucks share components, except engines, or sheet metal parts with cars.

Complete cab and body models whether single units such as a panel or two units such as a pickup with cab and box were limited as to their total offering and predictable as to what models were offered in the various weight ratings.

Light-duty closed deliveries during the Job-Rated Era were limited, consisting of a half-ton Panel, Canopy and Screen. There were no three-quarter-ton closed models. The one-ton Panel, Canopy and Screen models were built on the 133 in. wheelbase chassis, not on the 120 in. chassis as previously shared with three-quarter-ton models.

In addition to these factory-built closed deliveries, Dodge also supplied chassis on which delivery bodies of all types from several specialty body manufacturers were mounted. These chassis were most commonly half-, three-quarter- or one-ton capacities, but one-and-a-half- and even two-ton deliveries were not uncommon. Three body builders who supplied quantities of bodies for Dodge chassis were Metropolitan, Boyertown Body Company and Montpelier.

Panel bodies were of rugged, long-lasting, welded, all-steel construction. The roof over the load compartment had an area which was waterproof fabric, rather than steel. The load compartment floor was constructed of 13/16 in. hardwood topped with protective steel skid strips. All mechanical components, dashboard and front-end sheet metal to back of the front doors were the same as all other models. One folding and adjustable bucket-type seat was provided for all closed deliveries, but a second seat could be ordered at extra cost.

The Canopy was a hybrid model, a combination Panel and Pickup. The body was the same as the panel to just back of the front doors. The load compartment consisted of a box which looked much like a pickup, including rolled-edge steel flares, a steel tailgate supported by chains and a 13/16 in. hardwood floor protected by steel skid strips. Two rear corner posts supported the top. Roll up, waterproof canvas curtains protected rear and side openings.

The top construction was a work of beauty. The top was basically a series of long, steam-bent, wooden strips which ran from the windshield header to the rear. This wooden frame was then covered with a heavy, durable, weatherproof fabric. A Canopy was, therefore, really a pickup with a canopy cover.

While considered a separate model, the Screen was a Canopy with screen sides which give the load some degree of security.

In 1939, a half-ton Panel sold for $680 and a Canopy for $690. It is amazing that Dodge could sell the obviously much more complex-to-manufacture Canopy for only $10 more.

The closed delivery model lineup remained unchanged through 1947.

Panels and Canopies did not sell in the quantities pickups did, and therefore are not as plentiful today. Panels are also not as highly sought after as Pickups by collectors. Canopies are now extremely rare and, therefore, highly desired for their uniqueness and beauty. Prices of Canopies should continue to escalate as more and more collectors seek them out.

from 1⁵⁄₁₆ to 1¹³⁄₁₆ in. for half-ton and three-quarter-ton models. Spark plugs changed from A7 to A5. The clutch housings on all light-duties were strengthened with reinforcing ribs. The fan diameter increased from 17 to 18 in. on the one-ton, and the radiator core was redesigned on all models with more water cells per square inch. Half-ton frames were strengthened with an increase in stock thickness.

On March 4, 1942, a "stop manufacturing" order was issued by the War Production Board to all civilian truck builders. Our Canadian allies followed suit ten days later. Civilian truck rationing began on March 9, 1942.

Standard and optional equipment

Standard equipment included speedometer, ammeter, oil pressure gauge, engine heat indicator, fuel gauge, choke, hand throttle, instrument panel light, locking ignition switch, headlight switch, beam control button, package compartment, cowl ventilator, cowl lights, combination stop and taillight, front bumper, radiator ornament, one vacuum wiper, safety glass, spare wheel, license plate brackets, tool kit, no-cost two-tone paint, underslung tire carrier, horn, long running boards, and rear fenders and rear bumpers on Panel models.

Extra-cost optional equipment included rear bumper, $7; airfoam seats, $12; DeLuxe cab equipment consisting of DeLuxe seat cushions and back in leather, armrest on left door, single electric wiper, domelight and single sun visor, $33; domelight, $3; glove compartment lock, $1.60; heater and defroster, $28; inside mirror, $1.50; short-arm mirror, right side, $1.50, long-arm, adjustable, left side, $2, right side, $3; full-width, full-height partition behind driver's seat for Canopy or Screenside, $22; full-width, full-height partition with full-width seat for Canopy or Screenside, $33; screen sides for Canopy bodies, $25; auxiliary seat for Panel, Screenside or Canopy, $21; adjustable auxiliary seat for Panel, Canopy or Screenside, $25; interior sun visor, $2.50; auxiliary vacuum wiper, $5; dual electric wipers, $14; coach lamps for Panel, $10; auxiliary taillamps, $4; automatic choke, $5; governor, $21; oil filter, $4; replaceable oil filter, $7; dual horns, $6; grille guard, $9; four-speed transmission, $20.

Specifications and prices

WC half-ton, 116 in. wheelbase, powered by an L-6 engine 3¼x4⅜ in. bore and stroke, 218 ci. advertised 95 hp; three-speed transmission, 6.00x16 four-ply tires.

WD-15 three-quarter-ton, 120 in. wheelbase, same specifications as WC except 6.50x16 six-ply tires front and 7.00x16 six-ply tires rear.

WD-20 120 in. wheelbase and WD-21 133 in. wheelbase one-ton, powered by an L-6 engine,

3¼x4⅜ in. bore and stroke, 230 ci, advertised 105 hp. Three-speed transmission, 650x16 six-ply front and 7.00x16 six-ply rear tires.

WC half-ton
Pickup, $780
Panel, $892
Canopy, $905
WD-15 three-quarter-ton Series
Pickup, $847
Stake, $890
Platform, $885
WD-20 one-ton Series
Pickup, $938
Stake, $978
Platform, $973
WD-21 one-ton Series
Pickup, $972
Panel, $1,071
Canopy, NA
Stake, $1,000
Platform, $995

Production

Although Dodge did not post a big production increase for the calendar year, at least a positive 0.2 percent was better than the rest of the industry, which recorded a drop of 13 percent for the year. For that reason, Dodge's total truck production for the year of 169,837 allowed them to post an all-time record high market share of 15.4 percent, an increase over 1941 of 17.6 percent. Of the total output, 41,665 were built in Canada and 2,420 in Los Angeles. Breakdown by weight class for the calendar year for United States only was 22,572 half-ton, 77,694 three-quarter-ton, and 1,138 one-ton. The government bought a total of 96,649 military trucks: 19,600 half-ton, 77,046 three-quarter-ton and three one-ton trucks.

1945–1947 WC and WD Series

Yes, Dodge civilian trucks did go into production in 1945. The beloved WC began to come off the line in April and was built continuously for the balance of the year. One one-ton was built in November and 139 more followed in December. Unfortunately, production figures are not available by body type, but it is suspected that only chassis-cab and pickups were built. Most of the 1945 production was concentrated on one and one-half-ton models and many of these were COEs. No civilian trucks were built in 1943, but already in 1944 a limited quantity of one-and-a-half-tonners deemed necessary for critical civilian use were produced.

No exterior or interior appearance changes were made on the 1945, 1946 or 1947 models. Numerous engineering changes that resulted from lessons learned producing military trucks immediately found their way into civilian trucks. Mechanical changes included a rotor-type oil pump and the oil dipstick was enclosed in a longer steel tube. Mushroom-type starter pedal pad was introduced.

The chassis GVW was increased on all models, with half-tons raised from 4,200 to 4,600 lb., three-quarter-tons from 5,000 to 5,200 lb., and one-tons from 6,400 to 7,000 lb. Axle capacity was increased for select models as well. Front axle capacity for half-tons was increased from 2,000 to 2,200 lb., and rear axle capacity for one-tons from 4,500 to 5,000 lb. The rear axle shaft diameter was increased on all light-duties, and a four-pinion differential was also new. For comfort, air-bound-type seats with a regulator valve were placed in all cabs.

Braking capabilities were improved with Cycle welded brake linings for all light-duties. The front brake on three-quarter-tons was increased from 10x2

The half-ton 1947 WC Pickup on the right is equipped with 20 in. wheels, while an identical Pickup on the left rides on standard 16 in. wheels.

On April 11, 1945, the first half-ton Pickup built since February 1942 moved down the line along with three-quarter-ton 4x4 military trucks. Most civilian trucks built in 1945 were one-and-a-half-ton chassis cabs. These trucks were sold only to buyers who could prove they contributed in an important way to the war effort. The grille, hubcaps, hood ornament and other trim items are painted to conserve chrome.

This 1947 one-ton Canopy is a rare truck. By 1947 (its last year), this bodystyle was a relic of the past. One-ton Canopies were not a high-volume model.

to 11x2 in., and safety-type wheel rims were added to half-tons.

Steering gear was upgraded for all light-duties with a Gemmer number 305 worm and roller replac-

When one studies the intricate and complex wooden roof structure made of steam bent stringers and cross-members, as seen on this 1947 half-ton Canopy, you wonder how Dodge could sell the Canopy model for only a few dollars more than the steel-roofed Panel.

ing the former number 120 worm and sector. This changed the ratio from 17:1 to 18:1.

Only one new light-duty model was introduced in 1946. This was the Power Wagon.

Two historical notes for 1946. Dodge opened a 369,000 sq. ft. addition to its Warren, Michigan, truck plant on March 1, 1946. On April 20, 1946, Dodge completed its contract with China to build 15,000 heavy-duty trucks, the T234 Burma Road trucks.

Specifications and prices

WC half-ton, 116 in. wheelbase, powered by an L-6 engine, 3¼x4⅜ in. bore and stroke, 218 ci, advertised 95 hp. Three-speed transmission, 6.00x16 four-ply tires.

WD-15 three-quarter-ton, 120 in. wheelbase, same specifications as the half-ton except TA-15 six-ply tires.

WD-20 120 in. wheelbase and WD-21 133 in. wheelbase one-ton, powered by an L-6 engine, 3¼x4⅝ in. bore and stroke, 230 ci, advertised 105 hp; 102 hp in 1947. Three-speed transmission, 6.50x16 six-ply front and 7.00x16 six-ply rear tires.

WC half-ton Series
Pickup, $989
Panel, $1,119

Canopy, $1,184
WD–15 three-quarter-ton Series
Pickup, $1,096
Stake, $1,166
Platform, $1,121
WD–20 one-ton Series
Pickup, $1,162
Stake, $1,232
Platform, $1,187
WD–21 one-ton Series
Pickup, $1,187
Canopy, $1,352
Stake, $1,272
Platform, $1,222

Production

In 1943, Dodge built 76,664 three-quarter-ton military trucks. In 1944, the number was almost the same: 63,118 three-quarter-ton military trucks and two three-quarter-ton export trucks. Things began to return to normal in 1945 as 54,783 trucks rolled off the assembly line; of these, 38,399 were three-quarter-ton military trucks, but also 16,240 civilian half-ton models and 144 one-ton civilian models. Dodge also built medium- and heavy-duty trucks during these years.

In 1946, the challenge was not one of how to sell trucks, but of how to get them to the dealers as the entire industry was plagued by material shortages and labor problems. In spite of the problems, Dodge posted a respectable total of 148,438, allowing it to garner the highest peacetime market share total of all time, 14.5 percent. Of the total 9,751 were built in

A 1946 WD21 one-ton Stake owned by Ron Cenowa of Utica, Michigan. This dual-rear-wheel, red-and-black beauty has been restored to factory specifications.

Los Angeles, 12,919 in Canada; none were military trucks. Light-duty production by weight class, United States only, was 45,512 half-ton, 3,835 three-quarter-ton and 17,399 one-ton.

For 1947, total production was up 23.9 percent to 183,865, but market share fell slightly to 13.8 percent because the industry total increased 30 percent. Of the total, 13,320 were built in Los Angeles, 17,378 in Canada; none were military trucks. Breakdown by weight class was 42,542 half-ton, 9,992 three-quarter-ton and 27,773 one-ton. Dodge lost truck production in October 1947 when all Chrysler Corporation production schedules were cut back approximately 40 percent due to steel shortages.

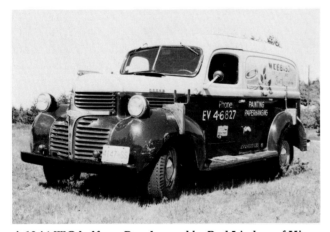

A 1946 WC half-ton Panel owned by Rod Lindsey of Victoria, British Columbia, Canada. It is a surprisingly well-preserved, original truck which could be restored or enjoyed as is. This truck has not been touched or changed in any way since Rod acquired it after its original owner worked it for 30 years.

A restored 1947 WC half-ton Pickup owned by Gary Herman of Merrill, Iowa. The original-equipment hand crank is shown in the crank hole just above the bumper. The bumper should be painted aluminum.

Chapter 5

Pilot-House Era 1948-1953

The Job-Rated years were good for Dodge. Sales and market share totals increased dramatically between 1939 and 1947, bolstered, of course, prior to World War II by a surging economy and in the postwar years by a pent-up demand for trucks to support a booming economy. Dodge profited too by the reputation it earned during the war for its tough, dependable, three-quarter- and one-and-a-half-ton, 4x4 military trucks. Dodge was not bashful about boasting of its war experience. For example, its 1947 sales catalog stated that, "Again in World War II . . . as in the first World War . . . Dodge-Built Army Vehicles strengthened the Dodge Reputation for Dependability." This was not an empty boast as tough Dodge army trucks proved themselves many times over during World War II and again after the war when its three-quarter-ton Army 4x4 became the world-famous one-ton Power Wagon in civilian life. Dodge-built army trucks must have been outstanding, because the Army came back in 1950 asking Dodge for more trucks to help fight the Korean War.

1948-1949 B-1 Series

After nine years of dependable service, the W Series was forced to give way to a more modern truck. Competition forced the issue as all major light-duty builders brought out new models at about the same time. The seller's market created by the war's pent-up demand was rapidly winding down, forcing truck builders to give truck users other reasons to buy.

Dodge's Pilot-House Safety Cab pickups came close to being all-new trucks from the wheels up. The only reason they weren't was due to the engines and transmissions, which were carried over unchanged. The two basic hallmarks of the Pilot-House era were driver comfort and an appealing style, which was not only modern, but revolutionary.

Bodywork and interior

Before beginning to design the first new truck since 1939, Dodge designers interviewed truck owners, operators and drivers in order to ascertain what the man behind the wheel wanted. The answers came back loud and clear—a truly comfortable cab. The

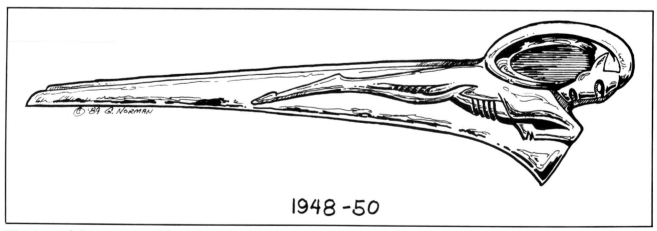

1948 -50

The shape of the ram emerged from the stylized hood ornament of the prewar trucks for the 1948-1950 era. Greg Norman

Pilot-House cab was higher, wider, longer, fully weatherproofed and provided excellent vision through its large, non-opening windshield. Its chair-height, comfortable, adjustable seat assured the driver a comfortable ride.

To reduce noise and vibration, the cab was mounted at four points on rubber insulators. Additional cab strength was built in by reducing the size of the floor opening to a small hole over the transmission. Because the engine was moved forward, the parking brake lever and shift lever could also be moved ahead (the shift lever was reshaped to clear the instrument panel), creating a clear floor space from door to door.

The larger, two-piece windshield with 18 in. high glass provided excellent vision. Wide defroster outlets formed in the windshield garnish moldings assured clear vision in cold weather. For the first time, the windshield wiper motor was located at the top center of the cowl below the windshield, with the windshield wiper switch placed on top of the instrument panel; in previous models, wiper motors were located in the header above the windshield. Standard equipment for light-duty trucks were dual vacuum wipers; dual electric wipers were available as an extra-cost option.

Entry and exit became much easier due to higher and wider doors positioned directly over the running boards. Side vision improved too, thanks to door window glass that was 2 in. wider than on 1947 models. A deluxe extra-cost feature, which also increased visibility, was the door vent windows without fixed center posts. Instead, the posts cranked down with the window. Cab rear-quarter windows completed all-around vision from inside the Pilot-House cab. Aiding driver and passenger comfort, a

Grille bars as seen this 1948 three-quarter-ton Stake and on all 1948–1950 light-duty trucks were stainless steel. On medium- and heavy-duty models, grille bars were painted body color. This truck is equipped with a DeLuxe cab as seen by its corner windows and vent windows.

wide cowl ventilator sent streams of cool air into the cab.

For the first time, the seat was mounted on a full-width, tubular frame, adjustable fore and aft on roller guides and held in place by a convenient latch directly below and centered in front of the seat frame. The seat height was a full 1½ in. higher from the floor than the WC's seat, bringing it more nearly to chair height for added driver comfort. The 57½ in. wide seat made for a true three-man cab. As with Dodge since the early 1930s, the cab roof, cab rear, door panels and areas below the dash were fully lined, giving a warmer, more comfortable feeling to the cab interior. The instrument panel and other cab interior metal was painted cab color. Seat upholstery was a dark brown leatherlike vinyl.

Three levels of cab trim were offered: standard, deluxe and custom. Deluxe equipment included vent wings in cab doors and cab rear-quarter windows.

Custom equipment included the above plus deluxe seat and back cushions, domelight, armrest on left door, dual interior sun visors and dual electric wipers. For all models, the steering wheel angle was flattened, and wheel grips were deepened for greater comfort and safety. All Pilot-House trucks up to the two-tons were equipped with an 18 in. steering wheel.

Dodge's quest for driver comfort, specifically a wider cab, resulted in a new style trend. The Pilot-House cabs boasted a wider, more massive truck appearance. A one-piece grille panel extending from fender to fender set the style theme. Front fender housings ran straight back from the grille panel and blended into the cab doors, creating a definite streamlined look. A slight flare accentuating the front fenderwell openings balanced the overall side styling by matching the radius of the rear fenders. The front-end styling of Fords or Chevrolets of this era con-

Beginning in 1948, the standard paint scheme for the Pickups Dodge called "Practical Pick-ups" was to paint the box and rear fenders black regardless of cab color. The three grille guards were extra-cost equipment. The cab shown is the Standard type without corner or vent windows. In 1948-1950,

the ram head hood ornament was standard equipment. Because of their short wheelbases, set-back front axles and cross-steering, Pilot-House Era Practical Pick-ups were highly maneuverable, fun and easy to drive, a fact that is appreciated to this day by Pilot-House Era collectors.

tinued to use a 1930s type, bolted-on front fender. Dodge thereby positioned itself as the truck industry's style leader.

Dodge chose not to fit an alligator-style hood onto its Pilot-House trucks; instead a side-opening hood was used. This allowed convenient access to the full length of the engine. A single locking handle in the center of the side panels actuated catches at each end of the hood side panels. Check straps restricted the hood opening, and props were provided to hold the side panels open. From the left side of the truck, the driver could easily and quickly check the oil, battery and radiator levels, and fan belt tension. The gas tank filler cap is also located on the left side.

Engines and chassis

Gas tanks on Pickups were redesigned to allow them to mount higher into the seat riser, giving an additional 2 in. of ground clearance. The fuel gauge was changed at the same time to an electro-magnetic type.

Engines for all Pickups remained the same as in 1947, but performance improved thanks to the use of a straight-through muffler which decreased back pressure. Other improvements included moving the coil from the firewall and mounting it onto the engine, a change which led to improved cold weather starting as the shorter coil lead offered less resistance and a hotter spark; a new splashproof distributor, with built-in resistors to prevent moisture shorting, and a vacuum and mechanical distributor advance were also new.

Model Numbers

Dodge used a number to designate the series and another letter to indicate load capacity on Pilot-House pickups. Thus, the first B designates B Series, the 1 designates the 1948 or 1949 model year (this number remained constant for two years indicating no change, little change, from year to year), the second B designates half-ton capacity. The model breakdown, then, is as follows:

B-1-B-108: half-ton, 108 in. wheelbase

B-1-C-116: three-quarter-ton, 116 in. wheelbase

B-1-D-116: one-ton, 116 in. wheelbase

B-1-D-126: one-ton, 126 in. wheelbase

B-1-PW-126: one-ton, 126 in. wheelbase Power Wagon

Trucks also used an engineering code; the letter prefix and three digits made up the first part of the truck's engine number. For example, T142–xxxx, indicates a 1948 half-ton, T144 is a three-quarter-ton, T146 a one-ton and T136 a Power Wagon. The Power Wagon's engineering code did not change during its entire existence. For this reason, a Power Wagon's engine number prefix is always T137, whether it's an early small-block 230 or a later big-block 251.

Engineering codes for other Pilot-House pickups are:

B-2: 1950 T172 half-ton, T174 three-quarter-ton, T176 one-ton

B-3: 1951–1952 T306 half-ton, T308 three-quarter-ton, T310 one-ton

B-4: 1953 engineering codes same as for B-3

Engine numbers are invaluable for determining if the engine in a Dodge truck is correct. Engine numbers are found stamped on a boss located at the front, top, left side of the block.

This 1949 Standard cab half-ton Panel was owned by Ross Roy, Incorporated, the advertising firm which did, and still does, much of Chrysler Corporation's advertising and market- *ing materials. The chrome wheel covers are an aftermarket item.*

Front springs on all pickups were lengthened to 42 in. to provide a better ride. Spring capacities were also increased to handle the heavier loads being placed on the front axle.

Cross steering was another new pickup feature. The drag link extended from the steering gear to the front axle steering arm on the opposite end of the axle. This arrangement permitted a 37 degree turning angle both right and left. Cross steering, along with shorter wheelbases and wider front treads, resulted in a smaller turning diameter and improved maneuverability.

Pilot-House pickups gave the first real evidence that designers and engineers were becoming concerned with driver comfort. This is most clearly seen in the accessories engineered into these trucks as extra equipment, including radios (the first ever in a Dodge truck), recirculating fresh-air heater systems, cigar lighter, ashtray, dual electric windshield wipers, armrests, domelight and vent windows.

The fresh-air heater system was another Dodge innovation. This simple and comparatively inexpensive accessory supplied fresh air to the cab under all climatic conditions, giving the driver a healthier, more comfortable and safer cab by eliminating window fogging and guaranteeing a constant supply of fresh air.

Other chassis modifications included increasing GVWs on half-ton models from 4,600 to 4,850 lb., three-quarter-ton from 5,200 to 5,500 lb. and one-

This 1948-1950 one-ton dual-wheel platform was spotted on the streets of Albuquerque, New Mexico, by Paul McLaughlin. This truck appears to have been restored. It does not look like a work truck, but evidently is used for daily transportation.

Ron Cenowa's 1949 Pilot-House half-ton Pickup. Everything on this 28,000 mile beauty is original, including tires and muffler. This truck was discovered on a Nebraska farm exactly as seen except for detailing.

A 1949 half-ton Panel converted to a people mover by the Special Equipment Group. This truck may be one of a kind or one of a fleet. The danger for a collector who finds a special truck like this one is to make the mistake of rejecting it as not being factory built because it is not listed in either the price list or sales brochures. The reality is that due to its uniqueness it is more desirable. In the event you do locate a Dodge truck which is "different," look it over carefully. If it seems to be a factory built unit, chances are good that it is authentic.

This original-condition 1948 one-ton Pickup belongs to Steven Tressel of Mira Loma, California. Its 9 ft. box is capable of handling oversized loads.

ton from 7,000 to 7,500 lb. Wheelbases on all pickups were shortened 8 in. by moving the front wheels back. Also, half- and three-quarter-ton front wheel tread was increased from 5¾ to 58⅝ in., and rear tread was increased from 60⅜ to 61¼ in. The one-ton's front axle I-beam size was increased. On one-ton models the brake lining was increased from 196.7 to 209 sq. in. Braking was improved on half- and three-quarter-ton pickups through the use of new dual-cylinder rear brakes. The one-ton's radiator core thickness was reduced from 3 to 2¾ in. All instruments were reengineered to be removeable from in front of the dash panel. For driver convenience, cabs were fitted with higher doors with hold-open checks and concealed lower hinges.

Standard and optional equipment

For the half-ton pickup, standard equipment included five 6.00x16 four-ply tires on disk wheels, double-acting shocks front and rear, one-pint oil bath air cleaner, underslung tire carrier, long running

---

A Revolutionary New Pickup Box

The first new idea in pickup boxes came from Dodge in 1948. As you would expect from Dodge, the idea was practical, rather than aesthetic. The new box was simply higher, wider and deeper than anyone had made before and was bigger than the competition would make for several more years. It offered more room, greater strength and improved appearance. For half-tons, the new body was ¾ in. wider; for three-quarter- and one-tons, it was 5¾ in. wider. Flareboards and tailgate were 5½ in. higher giving a whopping forty percent increase in capacity over the body on the half-ton W Series pickup it replaced. The body side panels were one piece, extending from top of flareboards to the running boards eliminating splash shields between the floor and running boards. The floor of the Dodge Pilot-House pickup's box was originally oak. For authenticity, the floor in your restoration should be painted black regardless of body paint color, not given a furniture-like natural wood finish. The new box was called simply the high-side box.

Dodge truck marketing immediately jumped on this new, larger pickup box and began to advertise and promote it heavily. It was clearly the largest pickup box available, and Dodge let it be known that if you had a large load to carry, you should buy a Dodge.

Newly restyled rear fenders came as part of the new high-side box package. The rear fenders were smaller as they were patterned after the simple cycle type which made them low, wide and sturdy, so that a driver could have more room to stand on the running board to access his load. To further ease loading and unloading, an easily installed, rear fender step plate was made an extra-cost option.

---

boards and rear fenders, front bumper (rear on panel only), 2,200 lb. capacity front axle, 3,300 lb. capacity rear axle, 900 lb. capacity front springs, 1,200 lb. capacity rear springs, 10 in. clutch, three-speed transmission, dual vacuum wipers, interior sun visor left side, and 4.4:1 rear axle ratio with 4.78:1 optional at no charge.

Extra-cost optional equipment for the half-ton pickup included one-quart oil bath air cleaner, $1.75; Deluxe cab equipment consisting of vent wings in cab door windows and cab rear-quarter windows, $25; Custom cab equipment consisting of above plus

This April 18, 1949, Country Gentleman *ad pitched Dodge trucks to farmers. Farming was a bigger industry 40 years ago than it is today, and therefore, represented an important truck market.*

Dodge Truck Radios

Before the advent of the Pilot-House Era trucks, a buyer could not purchase a factory-engineered radio installed in a Dodge truck. Radios were a dealer-installed accessory, as were car radios during this period of time. The MoPar radio, which was engineered for a 1948 to 1950 Dodge truck, is the same radio as used in Chrysler cars for the time period 1940 to 1948, a fact that makes them easy to find and affordable.

B-1 and B-2 radios

The MoPar truck radio features five push-buttons, an illuminated vertical dial, a tone control knob and a tuning knob. The MoPar radio fits into the dash by simply removing the knockout plate on the left side and then mounting the speaker behind the round grille located on the right side. Installation is quick and easy because the radio is self-contained except for its speaker.

B-3 and B-4 radios

As was true with radios for B-1 and B-2 Series trucks, radios were again a dealer-installed accessory for B-3 and B-4 Series trucks. The correct Mopar radio for a 1951 to 1953 Dodge truck is Model 610-T. This radio is a three-piece unit consisting of a power unit, control unit and speaker assembly.

Installation is a little more difficult with this model because of dealing with three pieces. The power unit goes in first and bolts to the firewall, the control unit fits behind the horizontal knockout plate and is supported by a mounting bracket that bolts to the steering column brace and the speaker assembly fits behind the grille beside the glovebox.

Not all 1951 to 1953 trucks left the factory with a radio knockout plate, and in that case you will have to devise a template and cut your own.

The radio for 1948-1950 Dodge trucks is the same as used on all Chrysler Corporation autos from 1940 to First-Series 1949. The radio shown is for a car. The truck radio is the same, except its speaker is smaller in diameter. One plastic control knob is missing. This type of radio is generally in good supply at swap meets at reasonable prices. Installation is quick and easy, too.

Instrument panel typical of 1948-1950 Pilot-House Era trucks. The radio knock-out plate is located on the left side and can be seen through the steering wheel. This is an early photo taken when the emergency brake lever was still floor-mounted. The plate on the windshield header contains operating instructions for the Air-O-Ride seat. Moving the lever to the left softened the ride and moving it to the right firmed it up.

deluxe seat cushion and seatback, domelight, armrest on left door, dual interior sun visors, dual electric wipers, $46; 11 in. clutch, $6.50; generator for high charging at low engine speed, $9.50; engine governor, $7; bumper guards (three to a set), $5; dual electric horns, $12; long mirror, left side, $2; long mirror, right side, $3; replaceable-element oil filter, $8.50; pickup body and rear fenders painted to match cab (Dodge Truck Red or Armour Yellow only), $5; rear fenders painted to match cab, any standard Dodge Truck color, $2.50; 750 lb. rear springs, no charge; auxiliary taillamp, $6; and four-speed transmission, $30.

Specifications and prices

B-108 half-ton, 108 in. wheelbase, powered by an L-6 engine, 3¼x4⅜ in. bore and stroke, 218 ci,

This rear view of a 1949 Route-Van chassis clearly shows its major mechanical components. The I-beam rear axle is a bit hidden in this view, but a close look shows it just below the rear frame cross-member. The two live rear axles are evident as is the off-center-mounted engine. The high kick-up in the frame by the rear axles helped provide a low flat cargo floor. The gas tank's location directly in front of the driver caused some drivers to be cautious.

Route-Van chassis with front sections were supplied to body builders for them to mount special bodies. This interior shot of a front section provides a clear view of the Pilot-House Era instruments, the hand brake located on the left of the steering wheel, the package shelf over the engine and the panaramic view through its oversized windshield.

advertised 95 hp, three-speed transmission, 6.00x16 four-ply tires.

C–116 three-quarter-ton, 116 in. wheelbase; all other specifications same as half-ton except TA–15 six-ply tires.

D–116 one-ton, 116 in. wheelbase, powered by an L–6 engine, 3¼x4⅝ in. bore and stroke, 230 ci, advertised 102 hp, three-speed transmission, 6.00x6 six-ply tires front and 7.00x16 six-ply rear tires.

D–126 one-ton, 126 in. wheelbase; all other specifications same as D–116.

B–108 half-ton Series
Pickup, $1,263
Panel, $1,448
C–116 three-quarter-ton Series
Pickup, $1,371
Stake, $1,430
Platform, $1,377
D–116 one-ton Series
Pickup, $1,435

Stake, $1,494
Platform, $1,441
D–126 one-ton Series
Pickup, $1,465
Stake, $1,539
Platform, $1,473

Production

Production inched up only slightly in 1948 by 4,429 units, to 188,294, in spite of the fact dealers had an exciting new product to sell. Market share fell one full point to 12.8 percent as total industry production increased 10.2 percent versus Dodge's 2.4 percent rise.

In 1949, production fell 20,470 units to 167,824, but market share bounced back to 13.6 percent, because even though Dodge sales fell 10.9 percent, industry total sales fell 16.1 percent.

Dodge Division opened a new plant in San Leandro, California, on May 4, 1948. Of the total production in 1948, 7,390 trucks were built in the

---

1948–1953 Closed Deliveries

There were many evolutionary changes in truck styling and engineering, but in 1948 there was instead an evolutionary change in economics and sociology affecting light-duty trucks. With the introduction of Dodge's Pilot-House trucks, the first two truck models Dodge ever built, the Canopy and Screenside, passed from the scene due to obsolescence. These two models had sprung up in an earlier era when many businesses, such as food retailers, were handling business in a far different manner.

It would be interesting to know actual production figures by model, but unfortunately they don't exist. When studying the existing historical data, such as advertisements, magazine articles, sales literature and photograph collections, a clear pattern emerges in which fewer Canopies and Screens are shown as they are replaced by pickups and other light-delivery trucks. In other words, trucks were being put to work delivering consumer goods and services from a retail store directly to the household's door.

It is true, however, that in the early years Canopies and Screens were also employed by tradesmen. And again, over the decades, there was a shift by tradesmen from Canopies and Screens to Pickups, Panels and Chassis Cabs fitted with speciality bodies of all types.

In the Pilot-House Era, Dodge marketed only one closed delivery, the half-ton Panel. It was essentially the same as the Panel it replaced, but updated in style and engineering. Due to its boxier overall style, it could actually hold a bigger load in its wider, higher and longer cargo area. The Pilot-House Panel did not change over its existence, except for the mechanical and engineering improvements as noted with the open-bodied trucks.

Route-Vans were built in a factory constructed specially for them. The Route-Van factory was located in the main Dodge truck manufacturing complex adjacent to the truck plant. During the Korean War, when Dodge again built 4x4 military trucks, they were built in the Route-Van factory. Notice that the fourth truck behind three Army trucks is a Route-Van.

Route-Van

The Route-Van may be the Pilot-House Era's least-remembered truck.

The Route-Van is a shining example of a great idea on paper, but the execution in taking it from paper to reality was sadly lacking. It was over-engineered and over-built to the point where its price did not allow it to compete effectively in the market. It also suffered from quality problems, one of which concerned structural body integrity. Due to a shortage of bracing and strengthening, its body and both side and rear doors rattled and squeaked. Another major design flaw was the location of its gas tank directly in front of the driver immediately beside the engine with the gas tank filler located at the front of the truck—what would have happened in the event of a front-end crash? It was also originally designed as a stand-drive truck, but Dodge discovered too late that Divco already had the rights to stand-drive sewn up.

Dodge management had such high hopes for the Route-Van they built a special plant adjacent to the main truck plant to build exclusively Route-Vans. Volume never justified this expense. Later on, when Dodge began to produce military 4x4s for the Korean War, they were built on the same line as Route-Vans. It is doubtful Dodge could have justified the cost of the Route-Van program even if they had been able to capture the lion's share of the market as that market in those days only amounted to 15,000–20,000 units per year.

Bodywork and interior

The primary design goal was to substantially reduce the truck floor's overall height. A low floor was important in reducing driver fatigue, and this was accomplished by using two rear axles. The load-supporting front axle was the usual, rugged I-beam type. The rear axle, which moved the load, was an important engineering advancement; it made possible a tremendous frame kick-up, which lowered the floor 10 in. closer to the ground than any other delivery truck. When the Route-Van was parked at the curb, stepping to the ground was only half the normal distance.

Dodge engineers set out to design a truck which would increase the driver's efficiency. The low floor height was only one of several unique and innovative

A short-wheelbase 1949 Route-Van in typical service delivering milk. The driver saved energy during his work day because of the low step and because he could exit through wide side doors without twisting and turning his way through.

solutions. Another was moving the engine far to the right side in order to provide more sitting and driving space for the driver, and to allow unobstructed access to the cargo area. The space over the engine was turned into a convenient package shelf. Extra-wide doors at the front and rear allowed the driver to walk straight in or out with arms full of packages without twisting or turning sideways.

The interior height at the center was 6 ft., 4 in., which provided plenty of headroom for most men to move around comfortably. In addition, the "non-slip" safety steel floor was flat, making it easy for the driver to "work" his load. Even though the Route-Van was unusually high inside, it had a low center of gravity, which gave the truck good stability and ride. The high, wide load space made it ideal for rack-type loading. Racks or shelves could be built on each side of its 6 ft. width and still leave a center aisle for the driver. For these reasons, the Route-Van was an ideal vehicle to convert into a mobile workshop, display or salesroom for any number of specialized applications.

Two types of driver's seats were available. The standard seat was pedestal mounted and adjustable 4 in. forward and backward and 3 in. vertically. The seatback could be folded down out of the way. The optional seat was mounted on a pipe, and the whole seat could be swung-away and the seatback folded down. A buyer could purchase a foam rubber seat cushion for the pedestal-mounted seat only.

Route-Van's windshield area totalled a generous 1,865 sq. in.; for comparison, the windshield area on a conventional Dodge truck cab measured 901 sq. in. The windshield wiper's linkage was of the pantograph type, with dual arms as commonly seen on buses. The driver's compartment was equipped with a large triangular vent window, located between the windshield and door. As an extra-cost option, a buyer could order a ventilating wing in these windows. Large windows in the side doors and two large windows in the rear doors gave the driver excellent visibility.

Routine servicing was accomplished either through an outside, front-opening hood or an inside, hinged engine cover. The front-opening hood gave access to the radiator, gas tank filter, oil level gauge and oil filler pipe. All other engine servicing was done through the inside engine cover.

Along with the innovative and unique two rear axle system, the other new and revolutionary development introduced in the Route-Van was Fluid Drive, which was not available on other light-duty Dodge trucks until 1950. A Route-Van with Fluid Drive was also equipped with an electro-hydraulic service brake holder system as a group option. This device worked on the rear wheel service brakes. The driver had only to flick a switch on the steering column cowl bracket to apply the service brakes as a parking brake. When he returned, he flicked the switch to off, kicked the brake pedal and drove away.

The combination of Fluid Drive and the electro-hydraulic brake system contributed greatly to driver efficiency. For example, the driver could shift into his driving gear when first starting out and not shift again for the balance of his route. Instead, he would set his electric switch upon stopping, letting the Fluid Drive "slippage" idle his engine, flick off the electric brake upon returning, and simply press the accelerator pedal to drive off. Fluid Drive provided nearly all the features of an automatic transmission—several years ahead of the industry. Fluid Drive lightened the driver's job, speeded up the delivery process and safeguarded his load from rough handling as the truck would never jerk due to faulty clutch operation, and reduced maintenance costs. If the Route-Van could have been stand-drive it might have been the ideal delivery truck.

Standard and optional equipment

Standard equipment for the 1949 Route-Van included three-speed transmission on DU models, four-speed transmission on EU models, 230 ci L-6 engine, 10 in. clutch on DU models and 11 in. clutch on EU models, front bumper, rear bumper with safety-tread plate, front shock absorbers, outside rearview mirror on left side, electric windshield wiper on left side, double-hinged, swinging-type rear doors, rear door hold-open device, sliding-type front doors, outside door locks on right side and rear doors, tail- and stoplight, one domelight in 7 ft. body, two domelights in 9½ ft. and 12½ ft. bodies, 1 in. thick roof insulation, body undercoating at vital points, and Air-O-Ride seat cushion, adjustable up and down, fore and aft.

Extra-cost optional equipment included Fluid Drive, auxiliary parking brake (hydraulic service brake holder), jackknife doors front and rear, 32 amp generator for high charging at low engine speed, body rub rails, four-speed transmission on DU models with Fluid Drive, ventilating wings, spare tire carrier, dual electric windshield wipers, replaceable-element oil filter, one-quart oil bath air cleaner, grille guards, rear shock absorbers, and right-hand rearview mirror.

Specifications and prices

B-1-DU one-ton, 102 in. wheelbase without Fluid Drive, with 7 ft. panel body, $2,395.

B-1-DUF one-ton, 102 in. wheelbase with Fluid Drive, with 7 ft. panel body, $2,450.

B-1-DU one-ton, 117 in. wheelbase without Fluid Drive, with 9½ ft. panel body, $2,480.

B-1-DUF one-ton, 117 in. wheelbase with Fluid Drive, with 9½ ft. panel body, $2,535.

B-1-EU one-and-a-half-ton, 142 in. wheelbase without Fluid Drive, with 12½ ft. panel body, $2,770.

B-1-DUF one-and-a-half-ton, 142 in. wheelbase with Fluid Drive, with 12½ ft. panel body, $2,825.

Production

Production figures for Route-Vans are not available but it's suspected that production was low as delivery trucks as a whole were not a significant part of the total truck business and quite a number of companies competed in this small market segment. The Route-Van's price also tended to dampen sales.

Route-Vans stayed in production, basically unchanged, through the 1955 model year.

new plant, 8,643 in the Los Angeles plant, 15,974 in Canada and the balance in Warren, Michigan. This was the last year for production at the Los Angeles plant. Calendar-year production by weight class, United States only, was 52,094 half-ton, 11,279 three-quarter-ton and 31,110 one-ton.

Production for 1949 was again concentrated in Warren, Michigan, with 140,296; 9,966 from San Leandro and 17,668 from Canada. Production in 1949 by weight class, United States only, was 66,270 half-ton, 18,407 three-quarter-ton and 26,052 one-ton.

Several labor disputes during 1948–1949 combined to force total production down. A strike from May 12 to June 7, 1948, shut down all Chrysler plants, walkouts at the Briggs and Budd Company on June 8 slowed production, and extreme heat the week of August 16 idled most Chrysler plants. Also, on November 15, the Route-Van was introduced as a 1949 model. To the relief of the entire industry, by 1949—for the first time since the war—auto and truck manufacturers could get as much steel as they needed.

"Hometown Motors, Inc," Dodge-Plymouth dealers used car lot in miniature, was a tool to instruct dealers on how to run a successful used car and truck department. A close examination of the "Ready to Run" used truck department located at the lower right reveals two Ford Bonus Built light-duty stakes, two Bonus Built panels, a Studebaker R Series pickup, two Chevrolet Advanced Design pickups, an International KB Series pickup and assorted Dodge Pilot-House Era Pickups and one-and-a-half-ton Stakes.

1950 B-2 Series

Even though the 1950 models retained the same appearance as 1948 and 1949, they were vastly improved trucks with numerous mechanical changes incorporated to make 1950 pickups last longer, operate more economically and handle easier.

Inside the 1950 pickup's cab, a steering-column-mounted, three-speed transmission shift lever replaced the former floor-mounted lever. Second, the hand brake lever was moved to under the dash panel and located about in its center; Dodge called it the Right Spot hand brake. The new hand brake was simply and quickly set by pulling straight out on its T-shaped handle. Releasing the hand brake required a half turn to the right; a return spring pulled the handle back to its original position. These two improvements cleared the floor of all obstructions, giving comfortable seating for three and making it easy for riders to slide across the seat from one side to the other.

Fluid Drive

The Fluid Drive semi-automatic transmission represented a major step forward in pickup driving. The first truck use was in Dodge's Route-Van in 1949, and it was a Dodge exclusive. Fluid Drive was introduced way back in 1939 in Chrysler autos and by 1950, Fluid Drive had proven itself in millions of miles in thousands of cars. On the trucks, Fluid Drive was a midyear introduction, available beginning in April 1950. Fluid Drive was simple in concept and trouble-free in operation. Its net effect was to offer Dodge pickups a semi-automatic transmission. As with the superior handling characteristics of Dodge Pilot-House pickups, one has to actually drive a Fluid Drive-equipped pickup to fully appreciate its benefits.

To drive a Fluid Drive truck, the driver disengages the clutch while starting the engine and engages the clutch to start out, with the option of starting in high gear, or if the truck is heavily loaded, the driver probably would make better time by upshifting from at least second gear. In either case, the driver could conceivably drive all day in city traffic without shifting (except into reverse). To stop, the driver has only to step on the brake. The truck will idle with the clutch engaged due to "slippage" in the Fluid Drive unit at low speeds. To resume, the driver takes his foot off the brake and accelerates up to speed. Fluid Drive was available in all pickups and with either three- or four-speed transmissions.

Fluid Drive was a popular option in every year it was offered and consequently, Fluid Drive-equipped pickups are now available in good supply. If you have a chance to buy a Fluid Drive-equipped pickup, by all means snap it up—you'll love it!

Low-side pickup box

None of the above changes were apparent from the outside, but one change for 1950 was all too apparent. That was a "new" low-side pickup box offered only on the half-ton model. Actually, this was the low-side box as used on Job-Rated pickups of 1939–1947. I think the low-side box was a step backwards as it made Dodge pickups look just like the other guys. The low-side pickup box now became the standard box, with the high-side box an extra cost option. Very few low-side boxes were sold, making them rare and somewhat of an oddity. Nevertheless, I don't consider them as desirable as high-side pickups.

Other engineering advances included increasing the one-ton pickup's GVW from 7,500 to 8,000 lb. by increasing its rear axle rating from 5,500 to 5,800 lb. and by replacing its 7/8 in. diamater tie rod with a 1 in. rod. The 10 in. clutch's spring pressure was increased to 1,504 from 1,395 lb. A 40 amp generator was made standard equipment. Auxiliary rear springs became an extra-cost item for one-ton pickups. The electrical system was completely redesigned including a new splash and dustproof distributor, a new high-output generator and neoprene-covered spark plug wires. A new camshaft in the 230 engine increased valve lift from .364 to .379 in.

Standard and optional equipment

Standard equipment for the half-ton pickup included five disk wheels, 6.00x16 four-ply tires, hydraulic shocks front and rear, one-pint oil bath air cleaner, underslung tire carrier, long running boards and rear fenders, front bumper, 320 watt 40 amp generator, short-arm left-side mirror, 3,200 lb. capacity front axle, 3,300 lb. capacity rear axle, 900 lb. capacity front springs, 1,200 lb. capacity rear springs, 10 in. clutch, three-speed transmission, dual vacuum wipers, left-side interior sun visor and rear axle ratios of 4.1:1 or 4.78:1.

Extra-cost optional equipment for the half-ton pickup included one-quart oil bath air cleaner, $1.75; 120 amp battery, $5; high-side or low-side pickup box, same price; rear bumper, $7; Deluxe cab equipment, $25; Custom cab equipment, $56; 11 in. clutch, $6.50; Fluid Drive, $38; electric fuel pump, $13; generator for high charging at low speeds, $9.50; governor, $7; grille guards (three to a set), $5; dual electric horns, $12; left-side, long-arm mirror, $2, right-side, long-arm mirror, $3; sealed-type oil filter, $4.75; replaceable oil filter, $8.50; pickup box and rear fenders painted to match cab in any standard Dodge Truck color, $5; 750 lb. capacity rear springs, no charge; auxiliary taillamp, $6; four-speed transmission, $30; dual electric wipers, $7.50.

Specifications and prices

All specifications for all models remained the same as 1948–1949 except advertised hp of the 218 ci engine increased to 95.

B-108 half-ton Series
Pickup, $1,213
Panel, $1,398
C-116 three-quarter-ton Series
Pickup, $1,331
Stake, $1,390
Platform, $1,337
D-116 one-ton Series
Pickup, $1,385
Stake, $1,444
Platform, $1,391
D-126 one-ton Series
Pickup, $1,415
Stake, $1,489
Platform, $1,423

Production

This year turned out to be a good sales year for the auto and truck industry because America's farm economy was good and farmers bought trucks, especially pickups. Sales were also bolstered by a scare buying wave following the outbreak of fighting in Korea.

A 1951 to 1953 half-ton, engine number T306. The rectangular-shaped boss located on the block immediately above the round frost plug is where you will find the engine number for all Dodge L-6s built between 1933 and 1960. This truck is equipped with a factory oil filter and rare dual horns. Notice that the oil dipstick is missing from its tube. Not visible in this photo, but located on the block in raised numbers below the distributor is the engine block's casting date. The casting date will help you determine if the engine in your truck is original, and will pinpoint its date of manufacture.

75

Unfortunately, Chrysler Corporation did not benefit as well as it could have due to a disasterous strike which closed all plants in February, March and April! During these three months, Dodge built only sixty-eight trucks and the four car divisions built a total of five cars! Furthermore, production in January was only about 50 percent of normal, and May, the first month back in business, was off by one third. All told, Dodge lost approximately 57,500 trucks to the strike.

Production for the calendar year topped off at 139,031, down 17.2 percent. Market share fell to under 10 percent for the first time since 1932! Of the total output, 9,471 were built in San Leandro, 16,877 in Canada and the balance in Warren, Michigan.

Production by weight classes, United States only, was 51,250 half-ton, 14,928 three-quarter-ton and 14,861 one-ton. Based on production schedules, it is estimated that 10,560 Panels were built, approximately 20 percent of half-ton production. This means

about 40,000 half-ton pickups rolled off the line. Route-Van production is estimated to be about 2,100.

Dodge built a number of trucks this year for the US Post Office, many of them Panels.

1951 B–3 Series

After three years without any change in appearance, the 1951 models changed greatly and incorporated several significant engineering improvements. Completely restyled front-end sheet metal made Dodge pickups even more pleasing in appearance, but there was no mistaking the distinctive Dodge characteristics. It was still, without a doubt, the front-end of a Dodge Job-Rated pickup.

The new grille consisted of two large, horizontal louvers with an attractive Job-Rated medallion in the center. Only in 1951 was the Job-Rated medallion chrome plated; the following two years it was painted aluminum. A distinctive Dodge nameplate was cen-

The instrument panel of 1951–1952 light-duty models was clean in style, functional and thoughtfully laid out. The rare factory ashtray and cigar lighter are located below the radio speaker grille. With the shift lever column-mounted, and the

Right-Spot parking brake handle located under the dash, the entire cab floor was unobstructed. The instrument panel on 1953 models looked the same except the chrome trim strip just above the control knobs was replaced by a Dodge nameplate.

tered directly above the grille. A new front bumper wrapped further around the fenders to give greater protection.

New 4 in. diameter parking lights met Society of Automotive Engineers (SAE) specifications, so (Class A) turn signals could be added if the buyer so chose.

For the first time since 1933, the famous Dodge ram hood ornament was no longer a standard feature. It could be purchased, however, as an extra-cost option.

Windshield wipers were improved by repositioning them to cover more useable glass area, and when not in use, they would lie in an out-of-the-way, horizontal position at the base of the windshield.

In order to add to driver comfort and convenience, several cab improvements were made. First, the instrument panel was redesigned. All instruments were now arranged in a cluster directly in front of the driver where they could be seen at a glance.

This 1951 half-ton Spring Special two-tone Pickup is as unusual and elegant as any 1951 Dodge pickup could be. The distinctive two-tone was a marketing tool used only in the spring to promote pickup business. The chrome grille bars and parking light housings were a factory installed extra-cost option only in 1951. Spring Special pickups are rare.

A 1951 half-ton Pickup with low-side box. It is obvious that the low-side box was an afterthought because its low height makes the cab's back panel embossing visible. The low-side box was the standard box and the high-side was available at extra cost. So few low-side boxes were sold they are a real oddity today.

Dial numbers were larger and light ivory in color to form a definite contrast to the green background.

Cab interior trim colors were now two-tone; the seat upholstery was a deep, rich brown vinyl, while light tan was used on roof, quarter panels and doors. Trim panels had always been a Dodge truck hallmark; drivers appreciated the feeling of warmness they added by eliminating the metallic coldness as found in competitive pickups.

A welcome cab change was the way Dodge engineers moved the steering wheel back and down, making a more comfortable driving stance. Also, Dodge designers upgraded the appearance of the steering wheel by adding an attractive, chrome-plated horn ring.

Two highly visible and welcome underhood improvements included eliminating the radiator-to-dash tie rods which always seem to be in the way when servicing the engine, and changing the location of the hood prop by fastening it to the dash, which moved it out of the way and made it easier to operate.

The low-side pickup box was now also standard on three-quarter- and one-ton pickups, and rear fenders were strengthened and improved by rolling a bead into their outside edge, thereby reinforcing the metal to prevent tearing.

Several engine improvements were instituted for 1951, some of which are visible and some not. First, compression ratio was increased to 7.0:1, which boosted the horsepower to 97 on the 218 engine and 103 on the 230. Molded rubber spark plug covers contributed to better efficiency in wet weather operation. The new spark plug was "hotter," which meant better engine operation at low speeds and less fouling of plugs. A new, narrow, low-friction fan belt replaced the old wide type. A 45 amp generator became standard equipment. The radiator bypass was removed from the top of the water pump and permanently built into the pump and cylinder block.

Other engineering refinements included a new four-speed transmission with synchros, which replaced a non-synchro type as optional equipment for all pickups. For better ride control Chrysler-made Oriflow shocks replaced Delco or Monroe shocks on all pickups. Type AR8A spark plugs replaced the former ASR type. The low-side box became standard for all pickups; the high-side box was available as extra equipment.

Standard and optional equipment

Standard equipment for the half-ton pickup included five disk wheels, 6.00x16 four-ply tires, hydraulic shocks front and rear, one-pint oil bath air cleaner, underslung tire carrier, long running boards and rear fenders, front bumper, 360 watt, 45 amp generator, 100 amp battery, short-arm left-side mirror, 2,200 lb. capacity front axle, 3,300 lb. capacity rear axle, 900 lb. capacity front springs, 1,000 lb. capacity rear springs, 10 in. clutch, three-speed transmission with lever on column, dual vacuum windshield wipers, interior sun visor, and rear axle ratios of 3.73:1, 4.1:1 or 4.78:1.

Extra-cost optional equipment for the half-ton pickup included one-quart oil bath air cleaner, $1.75; ashtray, $2; 120 amp battery, $5; high-side pickup box, $7; rear bumper, $8; Deluxe cab equipment, $30; Custom cab equipment, $30; 11 in. clutch, $7.50; domelight, $5; Fluid Drive, $38; electric fuel pump, $13; generator for high charging at low speeds, $9.50; engine governor, $7; grille guards (two to a set), $3.50; dual electric horns, $12; left-side long-arm rearview mirror, $2, right-side long-arm rearview mirror, $3; sealed-type oil filter, $5; replaceable oil filter, $9; pickup box and rear fenders painted to match cab, any standard Dodge Truck color, $5; airfoam padding seat cushion, $10; 1,200 lb. capacity rear springs, $2; auxiliary taillamp, $6; four-speed transmission, $50; dual electric wipers, $8; door vent wings, $15.

Specifications and prices

All specifications remained the same as 1948–1949, except advertised engine horsepower increased to 97 for the 218 and 103 for the 230.

B–108 half-ton Series
Pickup, $1,293
Panel, $1,493
C–116 three-quarter-ton Series
Pickup, $1,441
Stake, $1,515
Platform, $1,457
D–116 one-ton Series
Pickup, $1,500
Stake, $1,574
Platform, $1,516
D–126 one-ton Series
Pickup, $1,530
Stake, $1,619
Platform, $1,548

Production

This was a strange year for the auto industry due to the Korean War and the industry came under control of the National Production Authority. The NPA was tough on car builders but lenient with truck builders because civilian trucks contributed to the war effort. Production was regulated according to how the NPA doled out controlled materials, steel for example. Late in 1951, the NPA began to control truck building calculated upon a percentage-of-industry share determined by sales totals for the years 1947–1949. The NPA would determine how many total civilian trucks could be built per quarter for

Cab interior of a 1951–1952 half-ton panel. The right-side seat was an extra-cost option as was the ashtray below the radio speaker grille. Cab shown is equipped with the DeLuxe package as seen by the door vent windows and left-side armrest. Because of its unobstructed floor, the driver could easily exit and enter through the right door.

each of three weight categories: lights, mediums and heavies. Each builder was given a percentage of the total; for Dodge the shares were 13.44 lights, 12.23 mediums and 13.15 heavies.

Production in 1951 bounced back from the 1950 disaster to set an all-time record of 188,690 trucks. It was also the first year in history that total United States truck production topped 1.4 million units and the first time ever that combined United States and Canada production topped 1.5 million. Of the Dodge total, 14,081 were built in San Leandro, 20,830 in Canada and the balance in Warren, Michigan. Market share jumped to 12.2 percent, not a record, but a healthy number, almost three points above 1950. Production by weight class, United States only, was 58,992 half-ton, 26,865 three-quarter-ton and 22,152 one-ton.

Historical notes include resumption of military truck building with 11,246 three-quarter-ton 4x4s built in 1951. Remodeling of Dodge main production areas also began to prepare for manufacturing of V–8 engines. A new engine plant was opened in Trenton, Michigan, where two-and-a-half- to four-ton engines, along with industrial and marine engines, were machined.

1952 B-3 Series

The only appearance change between 1951 and 1952 was in the Job-Rated medallion, which was chrome plated in 1951 and painted aluminum in 1952.

Engineering improvements and changes for 1952 pickups included a new 4.1:1 rear-axle ratio on one-ton pickups in place of the former 4.3:1 ratio. For greater strength the rear axle shafts on half- and three-quarter-ton pickups was changed from ten to sixteen splines. The GVW on half-ton pickups was increased from 4,850 to 4,900 lb. A new Ball and Ball carburetor superseded the Bendix-Stromberg carburetor for one-ton pickups. Straight-bore front wheel cylinders replaced the stepped-type cylinders for all pickups.

Standard and optional equipment

Standard equipment for the half-ton pickup included five disk wheels, 6.00x16 four-ply tires, hydraulic shocks front and rear, one-pint oil bath air cleaner, underslung tire carrier, long running boards and rear fenders, front bumper, 360 watt, 45 amp generator, 100 amp battery, short rearview mirror on the left side, 2,200 lb. capacity front axle, 3,300 lb. capacity rear axle, 900 lb. front springs, 1,000 lb. rear springs, 10 in. clutch, three-speed transmission, dual vacuum wipers, left-side interior sun visor and rear axle ratio of 4.1:1.

Extra-cost optional equipment for the half-ton pickup included one-quart oil bath air cleaner, $1.47; ashtray, $1.53; high-side pickup box, $8.27; Deluxe cab equipment, $30.59; Custom cab equipment,

The author's restored 1952 half-ton Pickup posed in front of a restored World War II B-25 bomber at a nearby air museum. The front turn signals of the truck were mounted on the cowl, which is unusual, but they have been there since new.

Dennis Hall of Osoyoos, British Columbia, owns this original-condition 1952 Fargo half-ton. Note the Fargo nameplate above grille and on hood sides as well as the Fargo globe logo on the medallion located in the grille's center. This truck is equipped with its original big-block L-6, which has been bored and stroked to displace 218 ci.

$69.36; electric fuel pump, $13.96; generator for high charging at low engine speed, $10.38; engine governor, $7.17; grille guards (two per set), $4.44; dual electric horns, $12.42; left-side long-arm mirror, $2.10, right-side long-arm mirror, $3.23; replaceable-element oil filter, $9.27; pickup box and rear fenders painted to match cab, any standard Dodge Truck color, $6.44; airfoam padding on seat cushion, $9.52; 1,200 lb. rear springs, no charge; auxiliary taillamp, $6.63; Fluid Drive, $43.14; four-speed transmission $61.01.

Specifications and prices

No change from 1951.
B–108 half-ton Series
Pickup, $1,440
Panel, $1,650
C–116 three-quarter-ton Series
Pickup, $1,578
Stake, $1,646
Platform, $1,586
D–116 one-ton Series
Pickup, $1,637
Stake, $1,703
Platform, $1,643
D–126 one-ton Series
Pickup, $1,670
Stake, $1,755
Platform, $1,679

Production

This was the final year government regulations controlled availability of materials vital to the auto and truck industry. These government regulations dampened production to a point, but the heaviest blow to production was a steel strike, which greatly reduced third-quarter production. Dodge lost over 11,000 units to the strike, which prevented establishing an all-time production record. Production topped off at 179,099, 5.1 percent below 1951, but better than total industry production which fell 8.9 percent. This enabled Dodge to gain almost one point of market share, which rose to 13.1 percent, a market share high which would not be bested until 1976, the first year Dodge broke the magic 500,000 unit mark!

In 1952, Dodge built 20,650 trucks in Canada, 13,944 in San Leandro and the balance in Warren, Michigan. Production by weight class, United States only, was 52,172 half-ton, 40,563 three-quarter-ton and 20,279 one-ton. Military production was 26,143 three-quarter-ton (included in three-quarter-ton total).

1953 B–3 Series

This sixth and last year of the Pilot-House Era was unusual in that Dodge management opted to

This 1953 half-ton Pickup which belongs to Wayne Thomas of Spokane, Washington, is the only surviving Spring Special I am aware of. It has been in Wayne's family since his uncle purchased it in 1953. Shortly after his uncle bought this truck, it was involved in a front-end collision. The dealer who repaired it did not have a 1953 front clip on hand so instead installed a 1949 front clip!

The B Series continued with only minor styling revisions, seen most notably in the grille through 1953. The panel model shown here was a strong seller. Note the old-style phone number on the door.

make a number of changes to a truck which would be totally changed the following year. Normally, the last year of a series saw only minor cosmetic changes, if any at all.

Dodge advertised "Over Fifty Truck Improvements" for the 1953 line. These ranged from cosmetic appearance to major mechanical innovations, and included one new model, which in itself is an interesting story.

Truck-O-Matic

The most important innovation in respect to pickups was the introduction of an automatic transmission. Dodge's automatic, called Truck-O-Matic, was technically semi-automatic, as the clutch was retained. It was the corporation's M6 transmission, also used in DeSoto and Chrysler autos. It was used in conjunction with Fluid Drive and was available only in half- and three-quarter-ton trucks. The clutch was used for starting and shifting into either of

two ranges, high or low, or reverse. Once in high range the driver did not use the clutch again in normal driving.

Truck-O-Matic-equipped pickups have an emblem identifying that fact attached below the Dodge nameplates on each side of the hood. Truck-O-Matic was a $110 extra-cost option, so few pickups equipped with this feature found their way into the hands of buyers. For this reason, Truck-O-Matic-equipped pickups are extremely rare. If you find one, bring it home. Parts and service for the Truck-O-Matic transmission are still available; remember that many DeSoto and Chrysler cars equipped with the same transmission are currently in the hands of Mopar collectors.

New pickup

The new model for 1953 was a long 116 in. wheelbase half-ton pickup with the 7½-ft. box as used on three-quarter-ton pickups. Back in late 1935, Dodge had also offered two choices of wheelbase

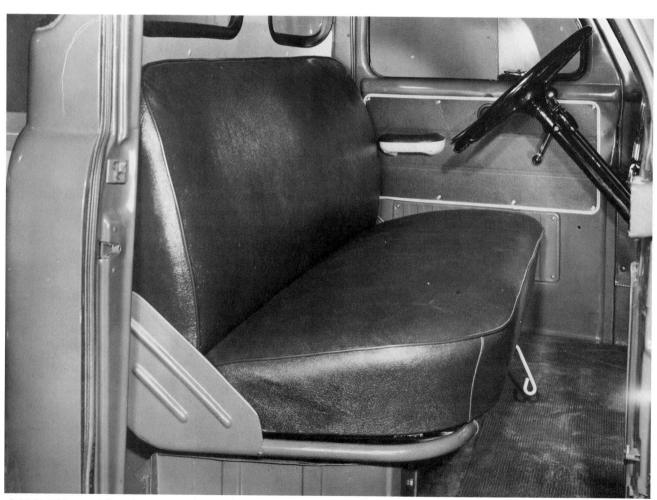

A 1953 Pickup cab interior. Cab shown is equipped with the Custom equipment package: corner windows, vent wings, armrests and two sun visors. The light-colored welting on the door panels is indicative of 1953. The lever below the seat adjusts the seat's backward and forward travel.

lengths. At that time this was a Dodge first, but the two-body option lasted only until the 1936 model year. In 1953, Dodge again set the pace in half-ton pickup options with the Big Three's first long-box, short-box option, a practice which remains to this day. Basically, the new model was aimed at those buyers who needed to haul long or bulky, but not heavy, loads. The 116 in. wheelbase half-ton was available only with a high-side box.

New rear fender

I have never been able to understand why Dodge management chose to introduce a new "streamlined" rear fender in 1953. They said it was to enhance the appearance of Dodge pickups. I disagree. The original, non-skirted rear fender had been specifically designed to balance the front and rear lines of Pilot-House pickups, now the new, longer, skirted "modern" fender ruined the Pilot-House pickup's distinctive and handsome lines, in my opinion. I think Dodge should have waited one more year to put this fender into production. As it turned out, this fender ran without change until 1985; one more year wouldn't have mattered.

Other appearance changes for 1953 included a redesigned Dodge nameplate on the front of the hood. Its stated purpose was to make the front of the truck look wider through the use of more widely spaced letters. For the first time since 1938, a Dodge nameplate was affixed to the instrument panel. A two-tone upholstery color scheme added to the cab's inviting good looks; the colors used were maroon and gray. Exterior changes included omitting striping from the grille molding, restyled hubcaps, and chrome-plated headlight and parking light rims. Dodge-Tint tinted glass for all glass areas was added to the list of extra cost options.

Engineering changes for 1953 included switching the pickup's floor construction from oak to yellow pine, welding the exhaust pipe to the muffler, increasing the Fluid Drive-equipped pickup's emergency brake size to 7x2 in. for greater holding power. The size of the fuel tank was increased to 17 gallons, and it was redesigned and relocated to provide clearance for the M6 automatic transmission. The 1,200 lb. rear spring was made standard equipment on half-ton pickups and the 1,000 lb. rear spring extra equipment. A high output heater became available at extra cost.

Standard and optional equipment

Standard equipment for the half-ton pickup included five disk wheels, 6.00x16 four-ply tires, hydraulic shocks front and rear, one-pint oil bath air cleaner, underslung tire carrier, long running boards and rear fenders, front bumper, 360 watt 45 amp generator, 100 amp battery, short-arm left-side mir-

ror, 2,200 lb. capacity front axle, 3,300 lb. capacity rear axle, 900 lb. capacity front springs, 1,200 lb. capacity rear springs, 10 in. clutch, three-speed transmission, dual vacuum wipers, left-side interior sun visor, and rear axle ratios of 4.1:1 and 4.78:1.

Extra-cost optional equipment for the half-ton pickup included one-quart oil bath air cleaner, $1.47; ashtray, $1.53; rear bumper, $8.25; Deluxe cab equipment, $29.75; Custom cab equipment, $56; electric fuel pump, $13.96; generator for high charging at low engine speeds, $10.38; Dodge-Tint glass, $12.30; engine governor, $7.17; grille guards (two per set), $4.44; dual electric horns, $12.42; left-side long-arm mirror, $2.10, right-side long-arm mirror, $3.23; replaceable-element oil filter, $9.27; pickup box and rear fenders painted to match cab, any standard Dodge Truck color, $6.44; airfoam padding seat cushion, $9.52; 1,000 lb. capacity rear springs, no charge; auxiliary taillamp, $6.63; Fluid Drive, $43.14; four-speed transmission, $61.01; Truck-O-Matic transmission, $110; rear-quarter windows for standard cab, $12.33.

Specifications and prices

No changes from 1952.
B–108 half-ton Series
Pickup, $1,344
Panel, $1,541
B–116 half-ton Series
Pickup, $1,379
C–116 three-quarter-ton Series
Pickup, $1,471
Stake, $1,528
Platform, $1,469
D–116 one-ton Series
Pickup, $1,536
Stake, $1,586
Platform, $1,527
D–126 one-ton Series
Pickup, $1,568
Stake, $1,638
Platform, $1,562

Production

This was a sad year for Dodge as its production fell 29.8 percent to 125,819 while the industry was off only 3.2 percent. Market share plummeted 27.5 percent to 9.5. Production in San Leandro was 8,122, Canada 17,214 and the balance in Warren, Michigan. Production by weight classes, United States only, was 36,409 half-ton, 29,924 three-quarter-ton and 13,152 one-ton. Military three-quarter-ton production was 20,207.

Dodge production took a sudden and dramatic downturn in 1953 because Dodge found itself caught in the crossfire of the sales leadership battle being waged between Ford and Chevrolet. Ford, in 1953,

Milk Wagon Fire Truck

By Joel R. Miller

The year was 1951. Multnomah County Fire District 13 in Rose City, an unincorporated community near Portland, Oregon, had just purchased Rescue 13, a shiny, new Dodge Route-Van. The volunteer fire department's dances and bake sales had at last raised enough money to buy the new rescue rig.

Rod Martin, a Portland Fire Bureau battalion chief, remembers the Dodge well. As a volunteer, and later as a paid firefighter, Chief Martin was assigned to Rescue 13 from 1960–1966. The firefighters nicknamed Rescue 13 the Milk Wagon because, frankly, it looked like the type of truck a dairy might have used.

One of the Chief's most vivid memories of the Milk Wagon was the night he and his partner were rushing to the scene of a fire. Flying down a hill, his co-pilot reminded him to turn at the next intersection. Hitting the corner a bit fast, the truck went up on two wheels and he thought they were going to roll over. Fortunately, the truck slammed back down onto all four and both men breathed a sigh of relief.

Chief Martin said the Dodge was always reliable. It carried first-aid gear, axes, shovels, ventilating fans, portable hydraulic jacks, saws, and the like. Due to the size and weight of the equipment, the truck was somewhat top-heavy. The Fluid Drive didn't make it speedy, either. Regardless, Rescue 13

always did its job admirably. With its siren wailing and lights blazing, the Milk Wagon faithfully served the department for twenty years.

In 1971, after being replaced by a new fire engine, Rescue 13 was transferred to Multnomah County Fire District 10's Toy & Joy Makers. Toy &

Multnomah County Fire District 13's 1951 Route-Van was officially called Rescue 13, but known as the Milk Wagon because it looked like a milk truck. The Milk Wagon served the Department dependably as a rescue rig for many years. It is now owned by Mike Gross, a firefighter from Portland, Oregon.

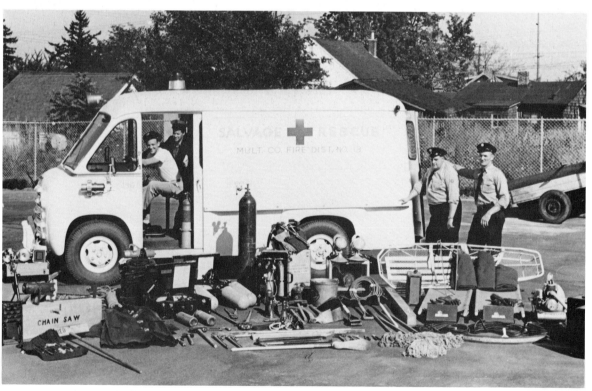

It's no wonder the Milk Wagon was so top-heavy! Multnomah County, Oregon, Fire District 13's Dodge Route-Van in the 1950s. It must have taken some kind of expert packing job to jam in that vast array of salvage and rescue equipment. Rescue 13 faithfully served the department for a quarter-century.

Joy volunteers make gifts of repaired toys to brighten the faces of less-fortunate children at Christmas time.

In the mid 1970s after years of dependable service, but badly needing an engine overhaul and front-end work, the Route-Van was retired. It was sold to a firefighter who planned to convert it into a motor home. Eventually, he had the engine rebuilt, but soon decided the old truck just wasn't right for his purposes.

In 1983, he sold the Dodge to Mike Gross who works as a dispatcher for the Portland Fire Bureau. Mike is working to find some front-end parts and get the old Milk Wagon back on the road.

A 1953 half-ton Pickup is easy to identify due to its restyled rear fender, wide-spaced letters in the Dodge nameplate, absence of striping on grille bars and restyled hubcaps. This truck has been painted one color, which was an extra-cost option as were its grille guards and rear bumper. After the Korean War ended, headlight and parking light rims were again chrome plated.

began to aggressively challenge Chevrolet for the number-one sales position for both cars and trucks. Their battle continued hot and heavy for the rest of the decade and, unfortunately, Dodge suffered because of it. Ford won the car leadership battle in both 1957 and 1959, but was unable to wrest the truck leadership position away until some years later.

Dodge fielded an excellent line of pickups, including the Big Three's first and only long-bed half-ton. Other product improvements and enhancements, including a semi-automatic transmission, tinted windows and comfortable interiors, made Dodge pickups an attractive buy. The reality of the situation, however, was that the domineering roles played by the industry's two giants caused the smaller players to suffer; the so-called independents found themselves in the same position as Dodge. Dodge may have fared even worse if they had not been as aggressive as they were in terms of introducing new products, new models and a host of engineering advancements.

Government restrictions on production came off in February giving a boost to light-duty sales. Light-duty trucks was the best-selling category and had been the most restricted by government controls. When controls expired, light-duty sales shot up, but not at Dodge!

Chapter 6

Functional Design Era 1954–1956

An October 5, 1953, full-sized clay of a cab-wide box proposal. The cab was the standard Functional Design Era cab. This box, which showed the shape of fenders formed into its side panels, was attractive. However, this box never went into production. Too bad it didn't, as it would have been well ahead of its time. The split rear bumper was also unique. It reminds one of Chevrolet's 1955 Cameo. Disregard the 1949 Michigan plate, this photo was dated October 5, 1953.

Dodge Truck management entered 1954 with an air of expectancy after chalking up two highly successful, back-to-back, model series. Still, Dodge faced stiff competition in 1954 as it embarked on a new truck era. Chevrolet continued with its successful Advanced Design models, only slightly changed from its introduction in 1947. Ford, on the other hand, brought out its second new truck since World War II in 1953. Ford's F–100 Series clearly was well ahead of the market, not only in styling, but also with its V–8 engine option and other engineering advancements. Consequently, Ford's F–100 Series represented formidable competition. Confronted by Ford's F–100, Dodge's high-angular Pilot-House styling had become obsolete overnight.

1954 C–1 Series

In 1948, the Pilot-House Dodge trucks had contributed numerous improvements to basic truck design. These included the shortest practical wheelbases for a given cab-to-rear axle dimension, wider-tread front axle with increased front wheel cut for smaller turning circles, and a full-width, comfortable, three-man cab.

Designer renderings of proposed Panel and Commuter models to be built from the same platform. There was nothing new or novel, of course, about using one platform to create two models—it had been standard industry practice since the teens. The small window behind the door was also not a new concept. Windows like this were standard equipment on most

Graham Brothers and Dodge Brothers trucks in the 1920s and early 1930s. At that time, they were called vestibule cabs. In appearance, they looked similar to today's Club Cab. The only feature that became reality was the wraparound windshield which went into production in midyear 1955. These drawings were dated March 29, 1954.

86

Functional Design trucks retained all of the Pilot-House design advancements, while adding a lower driving compartment, lower pickup loading height and lower hood height. Dodge design engineers reasoned that a low running board height, low cab floor height and low loading height would contribute to less driver fatigue and increased driver efficiency. The lower hood height permitted the driver to see the road closer to the front of the truck, another safety measure.

Bodywork and interior

All front-end sheet metal was new, simplicity and serviceability being the key design factors. A pyramidally shaped grille opening with two heavy, floating horizontal grille bars harmonized with the front fender and hood lines to offer a pleasing look without restricting airflow to the radiator. Standard paint finish for grille bars was body color.

Six-cylinder models sported a ram's-head medallion placed at the center of the hood just above the Dodge nameplate, while V–8 models displayed a V–8 emblem. On United States models, small, ornamental chrome chevrons, located between the headlights and parking lights, could be ordered as optional equipment along with the chrome moldings on the

center grille bar, but these came as standard equipment on export and Canadian models. The moldings on Dodge models were chrome, chrome striped with blue for Canadian Fargos, and chrome striped with red for export DeSotos. The Dodge Job-Rated motto in script letters appeared at the rear of each front fender.

Dodge had stubbornly refused to use model designations on light-duty trucks as made popular by Ford with its F–1, F–2 and so forth in 1948. But in 1954, Dodge weakened and began the use of model designations (F, G, H, and so on) on the front fenders of medium and heavy-duty models. Not until after the Functional Design Era ended would Dodge begin to identify light-duty models according to nominal ratings, that is D100, D200 and D300.

The standard paint scheme for half-ton pickups was to paint the box and rear fenders black, regardless of cab color. Painting the box and rear fenders cab color was an extra-cost option. Three-quarter- and one-ton pickups, painted any standard color, used a single-color scheme.

The Functional Design cab was completely new in construction and styling, inside and out, and used a minimum of extraneous ornamentation. The primary

A Standard cab 1954 half-ton Pickup with low-side box. A high-side box was available at extra cost. New-for-1954, one-piece curved windshield, rounded front and rear fenders and hood, and lower overall cab height combined to produce a pleasing contemporary appearance. Grille bars were painted cab color.

design objectives were comfort, safety, durability and appearance.

Dodge designers shaped exterior surfaces so as to present a smooth, well-rounded, pleasing appearance. Front fender lines extended through the cab doors and terminated just at the rear of the cab to accentuate the low appearance and provide distinct lines for two-tone paint schemes. The continuity of the front fender lines, in combination with the lowered hood lines, gave an impression of great length. But while the clean new lines, along with a gently curved one-piece windshield, and lower overall silhouette certainly provided a more modern look, the dated, three-piece, butterfly hood detracted from an otherwise pleasing style.

The redesigned and improved basic cab structure was now mostly a one-piece stamping which resulted in increased structural rigidity and improved sealing. Previously, the same structure consisted of many small detail parts that bolted to the basic structure. The new cab facilitated both production assembly and service. Cab mounting was on four rubber cushions, thus eliminating noisy metal-to-metal contacts between frame and cab. Cab sealing due to the new one-piece construction was also vastly improved.

For safety sake, all glass areas increased substantially, a Pickup cab's glass area totalled 2,115 sq. in. versus only 1,773 sq. in. previously.

The increase in the windshield glass area was achieved by use of a new one-piece, curved glass, set in a narrow rubber seal, and corner pillars of the smallest size possible. The lock-seam type of rubber seal eliminated interior windshield garnish moldings.

A late 1954 model-year entry was Dodge's first V-8 powered light-duty truck. Medium- and heavy-duty V-8s were ready at new model year time. The V-8 was an ohv engine, but not a Hemi, in spite of its Power-Dome name. Dodge pretested the light-duty V-8 at Bonneville Salt Flats and at its Chelsea, Michigan, proving grounds before its official introduction. The Bonneville speed runs and Chelsea high-speed endurance tests were more for public relations and advertising than for serious engineering evaluations.

Each cab door window was 2 in. higher and 3 in. longer. The 2 in. gain in height was obtained by lowering the window sill, which offered a more comfortable position to rest one's arm on the doorsill.

New seat and back cushion contours gave drivers a comfortable, correct knee position, back position and proper eye-level position. Seat cushion construction consisted of a two-stage-type spring designed to reduce rebound with heavy padding for a softer pillow. Upholstery was a two-tone high-quality vinyl of dark gray. The space under the seat was enclosed all around to provide a convenient place for tools and other equipment. The seat was adjustable on ball bearings, with 4 in. of travel. A new simpler, stronger, channel-type seat frame facilitated seat adjustment.

The standard windshield wiper was vacuum operated, but electric wipers could be ordered at extra cost. As a further aid to safety, the wiped area was increased by moving the wiper pivots toward the outer edge of the windshield.

The new instrument panel was a masterpiece of simplicity and utility. Two symmetrical oval shapes, one at each end of the panel, provided the mounting for instruments and the radio speaker. Positioning all controls in a line at the bottom edge of the instrument panel placed them within easy reach of the driver. A small step backward, the attractive chrome horn ring, which had been standard on Pilot-House pickups, was now an extra.

Another Dodge truck innovation was locating the glovebox in the center of the instrument panel, easily reached by the driver without stretching across the full width of the cab. An ashtray was an extra-cost option.

Pickup bodies carried over, except that the ground-to-floor height and running board-to-ground

Slide-open rear cab windows are not a recent innovation. Dodge experimented with sliding rear windows and pop-out corner windows in 1954. It's too bad Dodge did not put them into production.

height was reduced to facilitate handling loads, even from over the sides.

Newly designed taillights with plastic lenses for improved optics were located outside of the body to give the best appearance and maximum protection. Dual taillights available as extra equipment could be converted to combination taillights and turn signals. The license plate was moved to the cross sill under the tailgate and lighted on all pickups except the Power Wagon.

Engines and chassis

Dodge engineers incorporated many new mechanical features and engineering improvements into Functional Design pickups. These changes resulted in an improved line by providing greater durability, improved performance, lower operating cost and easier servicing.

The most notable change was the addition of V-8 power. On June 1, 1954, a V-8 became available in half-, three-quarter- and one-ton models. The 241 ci light-duty V-8 was an ohv engine with polyspherical heads. Also, at this time, the 218 L-6 was dropped from the line making the 230 L-6 the standard engine for all pickups. The power output of the 230 was increased by raising its compression ratio to 7.25:1 from 7.0:1, and by redesigning the manifold and through the use of a new camshaft.

This attractive 1954 woody wagon with Cantrell body was built on a half-ton chassis. Its DeLuxe equipment includes chrome wire wheels, whitewalls, radio, V-8 engine, chrome front bumper with chrome grille guards, chrome trim items on grille and under headlights, and chrome rearview mirror.

A new, three-speed transmission with higher ratios became standard for half-ton six-cylinder pickups. The heavy-duty three-speed transmission was continued for half-ton eight-cylinder Pickups and all three-quarter-ton and one-ton pickups. The Truck-O-Matic transmission continued for half- and three-quarter-ton six-cylinder models only.

All pickup frames were redesigned to permit the use of either six- or eight-cylinder engines. An extra cross-member was added at the rear of the engine, ahead of the transmission, to permit removal of the gearbox without disturbing the frame.

To eliminate engine movement and vibration, the clutch and brake pedals were mounted directly to the frame, independent of the engine. The clutch and brake pedals were also of a new two-piece design. This new pedal-mounting system, along with a new connecting linkage design, required less effort to operate the clutch. For the first time ever, rubber pedal pads became standard equipment.

In all, Dodge catalogued a total of eighty-seven improvements and changes for 1954. Together, these changes contributed to making Dodge one of the most stylish, practical and durable pickups anywhere.

Dependable Functional Design trucks went into production on July 1, 1953, and continued without change until March 1, 1955. An improved model followed in April 1955.

Standard and optional equipment

Standard equipment for the half-ton pickup included five disk wheels with 4.50 in. drop-center rims and 6.00x16 four-ply tires, double-acting hydraulic shocks front and rear, one-pint oil bath air cleaner, underslung tire carrier, long running boards with rear fenders, front bumper, 360 watt, 45 amp generator, 100 amp battery, short-arm left-side rear-view mirror, 2,200 lb. capacity front axle, 3,300 lb. capacity rear axle, 900 lb. capacity front springs, 1,200 lb. capacity rear springs, 10 in. clutch, three-speed transmission, dual vacuum wipers, ventilating wings in cab doors, left-side interior sun visor, and optional rear axle gear ratios 4.1:1 and 4.78:1.

Extra-cost optional equipment for the half-ton pickup included one-quart oil bath air cleaner, $1.45; armrest on left cab door, $3; four-pinion rear axle, $7; high-side pickup box, 6½ ft. long, $8.25, and 7½ ft. long, $9; rear bumper, $8.25; Deluxe Cab equipment, $23.50; Custom Cab equipment, $49; stainless-steel wheel covers, set of four, $13; turn signals, $16; domelight, $4.15; electric fuel pump, $4.15; generator for high charging at low speeds, $10; Dodge-Tint glass, $12.30; engine governor, $7.15; grille guards, two to set, $4.40; recirculating heater, $40; fresh-air heater, $60; dual electric horns, $12.40;

horn ring on steering wheel, $2.50; bright finish hubcaps, $1.50; long-arm, adjustable, left-side rearview mirror, $2.10, right-side, $3.20; interior rearview mirror, $2.75; bright metal radiator grille panel bar center caps and grille panel side moldings, $3; replaceable-element oil filter, $9.25; pickup box and rear fenders painted to match cab, any standard Dodge Truck color, $6.40; foam rubber seat back padding for Standard cab, $11.50, Deluxe cab, $7.50; foam rubber padding for seat cushion for Standard cab, $9; auxiliary taillamp, $2.55; hand throttle control, $2.50; three-speed heavy-duty transmission, $20; same with Fluid Drive, $63; four-speed transmission with 11 in. clutch, $71.90; Truck-O-Matic transmission, $110; rear-quarter windows, $12.30; dual electric wipers, $8.40.

Specifications and prices

B6–108 half-ton, 108 in. wheelbase and B6–116 half-ton, 116 in. wheelbase. Powered by an L-6 engine 3¼x4⅜ in. bore and stroke, 218 ci, advertised 100 hp, three-speed transmission, 6.00x16 four-ply tires.

C6–116 three-quarter-ton, 116 in. wheelbase, all specifications same as half-ton, except 7.00x15 six-ply tires.

D6–116 one-ton, 116 in. wheelbase, same as C6–116, except L-6 engine 3¼x4⅝ in. bore and stroke, 230 ci, advertised 110 hp, 6.00x16 six-ply front and 7.00x16 six-ply rear tires.

D6–126 one-ton, 126 in. wheelbase, same specifications as D6–116.

Late in the model year, an ohv V–8 engine of 3¹⁄₁₆x3¼ in. bore and stroke, 241 ci, advertised 145 hp, was released as an extra-cost option for all light-duty trucks.

B6–108 half-ton Series
Pickup, $1,331
Panel, $1,528
B6–116 half-ton Series
Pickup, $1,357
C6–116 three-quarter-ton Series
Pickup, $1,462
Stake, $1,518
Platform, $1,459
D6–116 one-ton Series
Pickup, $1,536
Stake, $1,586
Platform, $1,527
D6–126 one-ton Series
Pickup, $1,568
Stake, $1,638
Platform, $1,562

Production

The production skid which began in 1953 continued into this, the first year of the Functional Design Era. Total production of 104,966, while not a satisfactory number, was in line with the downturn suffered by the industry. Hardest hit was the light-duty category, or primarily, pickups.

The biggest losers (no one won) were Dodge, GMC and the independents, due to a fierce truck-sales-leadership battle being waged by Ford against Chevrolet. In those days, all truck producers belonged to one of two categories, the Big Four, consisting of Chevrolet, GMC, Ford and Dodge, or the Independents, made up of Divco, International Harvester, Studebaker and Willys. From 1952, the independent's market share fell from 30.1 to 21.8 percent. One other factor which contributed to a decline in Dodge truck sales was the fact that Dodge car sales dropped 48 percent from 1953, Dodge's poorest showing since 1938!

Dodge production in 1954 was divided between Canada, 9,124, San Leandro, California, 3,640 and Warren, Michigan, 92,232. Production by weight class, United States only, was 35,670 half-ton, 12,391 three-quarter-ton and 13,906 one-ton. Military production was 5,586 three-quarter-tonners. In spite of the low sales total, Dodge actually gained in market share, rising from 9.5 to 9.6 percent.

This was the last year for the 218 ci L-6 as the 230 became the standard six for the entire light-duty line, with a V–8 optional. Production ceased at the San Leandro plant in early 1955.

1955 C–1 and C–3 Series

The new 1955 trucks brought to market the finest combination of power, economy, load-carrying ability and driver comfort Dodge had offered to date. Cabs had been restyled with emphasis on driver comfort and visibility. Windshields now wrapped around the front of the cab and a wraparound rear window was optional, and cabs equipped with both appeared to be almost all glass. New windshield wipers with

---

Functional Design Radios

The radio for a Functional Design Dodge truck was a dash-mounted unit. The correct Mopar radio for C Series trucks is the Model 611–T. It is a three-piece radio consisting of control unit, power unit and speaker assembly.

Installation is similar to that of the Model 610–T radio as used from 1951 to 1953. The owner will have to cut out and drill his own mounting hole, slightly to the left and below the instrument cluster, as C Series trucks were not equipped with radio knockout plates.

It is rare to see the correct Mopar radio installed in a Functional Design truck, but they should be obtainable if you are patient and search diligently.

more powerful motors helped to clear the larger glass area. Dodge now offered four levels of cab trim: Standard, Deluxe, Custom and Custom Regal.

Standard cab seat upholstery was a combination of gray speckled vinyl and black vinyl, door panels

These front and rear three-quarter views of an April 5, 1955, clay model raised more questions than they answered. Up to the back of the doors, this clay was almost a stock Second-Series 1955 Functional Design cab. Dodge designers had given one style treatment to the right side and a second treatment to the left side. Both styles were more carlike than trucklike. One got the sense that Dodge's design group in 1955 was forward thinking in its approach to light-duty truck styling. Light-duty trucks in 1955 were still hard-working, no-nonsense trucks, not the mostly passenger-car trucks we have today. This truck may be the first proposal for a Club Cab pickup, which was eventually pioneered by Dodge in 1973. Or, it could be a six-passenger, two-door pickup. The closest vehicle I am aware of to compare it to was the 1957–1958 International Travelette, which was a passenger-carlike, six-passenger pickup. Even though this truck never went into production, it is historically significant because it demonstrates that Dodge designers were thinking and planning products 10 to 20 years into the future.

were edged in black with Chilean Beige binding and the roof headlining was also Chilean Beige. The Deluxe, Custom and Custom Regal cabs contained the following equipment, not found in the Standard Cab.

Equipment	Deluxe	Custom	Custom Regal
Dual electric wipers	X	X	X
Domelight and dual door switches	X	X	X
Air foam seat cushion	X	X	X
Air foam seat back cushion		X	X
Latex hairpad seat back	X		
Armrest, driver's side		X	
Armrest, both sides			X
Windshield visors, two sides		X	X
Ashtray		X	X
Wraparound rear window		X	X
Special trim		X	X
Glovebox door lock			X
Cigar lighter			X
Dash panel liner		X	X
Perforated headlining and insulation			X
Sound deadener on floor		X	X
Identification plate	X	X	X
Chrome windshield molding			X
Entire grille, Chilean Beige			X
Chrome hooded headlight doors			X
Ram's-head hubcaps one-half, three-quarter ton			X
Single air-note horn	X	X	
Dual air-note horn		X	X
Painted mirrors		X	X

New features of the instrument panel included a combination headlight and panel light switch that pulled out to turn on the headlights and rotated to turn the panel lights on and off as well as to control the intensity of the panel lights. All knobs were now black plastic. For maximum reliability and accuracy the temperature gauge was now electrically-operated. The speedometer registered up to 110 mph thanks to new V-8 power. The glovebox doorhandle was restyled and the choke control knob was moved to the left of the driver for better accessibility.

These two photos of a full-sized clay dated August 16, 1955, were puzzling. At first glance the cab appeared to be almost a production version of the 1957–1960 Power-Giant Era model, but on closer examination it was clearly different. Notice the short hood and how the front wheelwell opening extended back into the door. This may have been a styling exercise to develop a cab-over pickup. Its grille design was close to the 1958 production grille. The box was a new fender-side-type proposal. The rear fenders were grotesque—too big and too carlike. It would appear to be a real challenge to remove the side-mounted spare. We are lucky that nothing from this clay model ever reached production, except the general grille design.

This photo of an October 18, 1955, full-sized clay unveils an interesting truck. Its cab was the production 1955–56 Functional Design Era cab. The hood and front fenders were close to the 1957 production models. Evidently Dodge considered identifying light-duty models with a nominal rating designation as seen by the "H" on the right front fender. At this time Dodge did use a letter to identify mediums and heavies only; in fact, an H was a two-tonner. Light-duty models were B, C and D for half-, three-quarter- and one-ton respectively. The most interesting element of this clay is its cab-wide box. If the rocket and chevron trim pieces were eliminated, Dodge would have had the most attractive truck of its day. The box, tailgate and bumper were somewhat similar to the October 5, 1953, clay (see page 86). This was, unfortunately, the end of the line for these ideas as no part of this attractive box went into production. Dodge management may have made a mistake by not releasing this stylish truck for immediate production as it was certainly way ahead of the market.

The new front-end sheet metal remained unchanged from 1954, except for the painting on the grille. The grille bars were now painted Chilean Beige for Standard and Deluxe cabs; the entire grille opening and bars were painted Chilean Beige for the Custom Regal cabs.

The hood nameplate was larger and the V-8 medallion was a one-piece, stamped design. Deluxe, Custom and Custom Regal models had identification plates on the front fenders under the Job-Rated medallion.

New C-3 model

A new lightweight half-ton pickup model C-3-BL6 was introduced. Only available with a six-cylinder engine and with a maximum GVW of 4,250 lb., this was the same truck as the standard half-ton model B-3-B6.

The C-3-BL6 model differed from the standard half-ton B-3-B6 model in that its tire size was 6.70x15 four ply, its rear spring capacity was 750 lb., an oil-wetted-type air cleaner was used in place of the oil-bath type, a short tailpipe was used in place of the full length pipe, headlight rims were painted body color, only a side-mounted spare was offered without a hubcap, the seat was adjusted by relocating four bolts, the Dodge name embossed on the tailgate was not painted, the cab's interior back trim panel was omitted, and a lug wrench was the only tool provided.

The only extra equipment items were 1,200 lb. rear springs, turn signals, a second taillight, combination fuel and vacuum pump, oil filter, heater, heavy-duty cooling and rear bumper.

At $1,367 list, this special model sold for $40 less than the lowest-priced, standard half-ton pickup.

Dodge built thousands of these special half-ton right-hand-drive Panels for the Postal Service. Truck shown is a First-Series 1955.

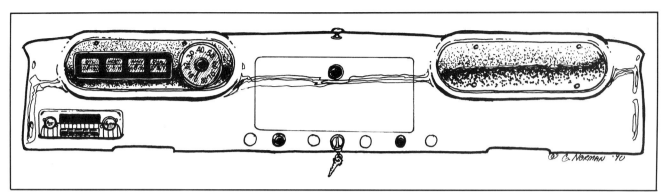

The correct original equipment Mopar radio for Functional Design Era trucks was Model 611-T. A radio was not a factory installed accessory, it was installed either by the dealer or by the owner himself. A dash knockout plate was not provided at the factory, therefore, the installer was required to cut out and drill the instrument panel according to instructions shown on a template supplied with the radio. The radio was located below and slightly to the left of the instrument cluster as seen in this drawing of a 1954 instrument panel. Greg Norman

Forty dollars in those days went a lot further than it does today.

Engine and chassis

A new 260 ci, single rocker, arm shaft, 169 hp, V-8 engine was available for all pickups. Dodge trucks shared this engine with the 1955 Plymouth cars. The 260 V-8 featured non-positive valve rotators for both intake and exhaust valves; valve guides integral with the head and vacuum spark advance. Compression ratio was 7.6:1.

The Whale Nose half-ton Post Office truck with walk-in body by Fageol was also built in large quantities in 1955 and 1956.

This truck's short 95½ in. wheelbase made it extremely maneuverable and easy to drive.

New transmission options included a Chrysler-built, PowerFlite automatic for half-, three-quarter-, and one-ton pickups, replacing the Truck-O-Matic. The standard three-speed with overdrive was available only for the half-ton model.

PowerFlite combined a high-performance torque converter and a simple, automatic, two-speed, planetary gearbox to provide exceptional acceleration with smooth operation. The clutch pedal was eliminated and a selector lever on the steering column allowed the driver to select Drive, Low, Reverse, or Neutral.

Standard and optional equipment

Standard equipment for the half-ton pickup included five disk wheels with 4.50 in. drop-center rims, 6.70x15 four-ply tubeless passenger-car-type tires, hydraulic shocks front and rear, one-pint oil bath air cleaner, underslung tire carrier, long running boards with rear fenders, front bumper, 360 watt 45 amp generator, 100 amp battery, short-arm stationary left-side rearview mirror, 2,500 lb. capacity front axle, 3,300 lb. capacity rear axle with two-pinion differential, 900 lb. capacity front springs, 1,200 lb. capacity rear springs, 10 in. clutch, three-speed transmission, dual vacuum wipers on Standard Cab, vent wings on cab doors, left-side interior visor, and optional rear axle ratios 3.73, 4.1:1 and 4.78:1.

Extra-cost optional equipment for the half-ton pickup included one-quart oil bath air cleaner, six-cylinder, $1.65, eight-cylinder, $3.95; armrest left door, $3.30; ashtray, $1.65; four-pinion differential, $6.60; rear bumper, $11.25; Deluxe Cab equipment, $26.50; Custom Cab equipment, $51; Custom Regal Cab equipment, $79; four chrome hubcaps, $1.65, set of five, $3; increased cooling, $10; four chrome wheel covers, 15 in. wheels, $16.50; directional signals, $23.50; domelight, $5.50; generator for high charging at low engine speed, $11.25; Dodge-Tint glass, $17.50; engine governor, $10; pair grille guards, $5.50; recirculating heater, $41.50; fresh-air heater, $62.50; dual electric horns, $14.50; horn ring on wheel, $3; left-side, long rearview mirror, $2.50, right side, $3.95; interior mirror, $3; replaceable-element oil filter, $12; electric fuel pump, $16; foam rubber padding for seat back, $11.25, for seat cushion, $11.25; 1,400 lb. capacity rear springs, $3.65; 1,750 lb. capacity rear springs, $6.60; right-side sun visor,

In 1954, Dodge restyled and renamed its half-ton panel as the Town Panel. With its sleek, new, gracefully rounded style and abundant chrome trim, it was at home on the boulevard functioning as a sedan delivery. Or, when it was in standard trim it was ideal for performing the hard work of a tradesman.

$3; hand throttle control, $3; side-mounted spare tire carrier, $10.25; three-speed transmission with overdrive, $100; three-speed, heavy-duty with 10 in. clutch, $40, with 11 in. clutch, $45; four-speed transmission with 11 in. clutch, $70; PowerFlite, $165; wraparound rear window, $29; and dual electric wipers, $11.25.

Specifications and prices

Half-ton models tires were changed to 6.70x15 four-ply tires. Base engine for all pickups was an L–6, 3¼x4⅝ in. bore and stroke, 230 ci, advertised 110 hp; optional engine ohv V–8, 3⁹⁄₁₆x3¼ in. bore and stroke, 260 ci, advertised 169 hp.

BL6–108 half-ton Series
Pickup, $1,367
B6–108 half-ton Series
Pickup, $1,407
Panel, $1,630
B6–116 half-ton Series
Pickup, $1,433
Stake, $1,512
Platform, $1,446
C6–116 three-quarter-ton Series
Pickup, $1,532
Stake, $1,598
Platform, $1,532
D6–116 one-ton Series

Pickup, $1,584
Stake, $1,650
Platform, $1,584
D6–126 one-ton Series
Pickup, $1,624
Stake, $1,690
Platform, $1,624

Dotty Dodge, with eye-catching custom paint and deluxe chrome trim, was a special show truck prepared for a May 1956 auto show in California.

This pilot-model 1955 half-ton Carryall became the production Town Wagon midway in the 1955 model year. Its unique experimental two-tone paint caused it to have somewhat of a military look.

Dotty Dodge's cab interior was typical of the high-line 1956 models. Dotty had everything, including V-8 engine and a PowerFlite automatic. Only in 1955 and 1956 was the automatic transmission's gear selector lever column-mounted. Beginning in 1957, it was moved to the dash and remained dash-mounted until 1969.

Production

Thanks to a healthy jump in production during the second quarter when new models went into production, the 1955 output of 107,405 exceeded 1954 by 2.3 percent. This total was not all that pleasing as total industry output climbed by 21.8 percent, which caused Dodge's market share to fall to 8.1 percent, a 15.6 percent dip. Canada built 11,054 trucks, California built none and the balance was accounted for by the Warren, Michigan, plant. This was the last year for Korean war military production and only seven of these units left the factory. Production by weight class, United States only, was 37,767 half-ton, 7,029 three-quarter-ton and 15,282 one-ton.

1956 C-3 Series

The pickups Dodge introduced in the spring of 1955 continued largely unchanged for the 1956 model year, but several engineering refinements would gradually be incorporated, which contributed to making them even better trucks and tougher competitors.

Second-Series 1955 and 1956 Dodge trucks are easy to spot due to their wraparound windshields and rear windows. Grille bars and grille openings were painted Chilean Beige, as seen on this 1955 top-of-the-line Custom Regal half-ton. The wrap-around rear window was standard equipment on Custom Regal models. A distinguishing feature between 1955 and 1956 Pickups was that in 1956, Pickup flareboards were made flat.

Due to a trend toward higher compression ratios and increased loads on the truck's electrical systems, Dodge went to 12 volt electrical systems on all models early in 1956. Also, all models, except the Power Wagon, now had ignition-switch starting.

Dodge adopted tubeless tires as standard equipment for all models except the Power Wagon. Tube-type tires became an extra-cost option.

The best way to determine if a Functional Design Era truck is a 1955 or a 1956 model comes from the year specified on the vehicle's title and registration. Some 1955 trucks that were not sold by the time the 1956 model year began in October 1955 were no doubt sold as new 1956s. Engine numbers for C-3 model trucks for 1955, and those 1956s built up to April 1956, began with a 300 series three-digit engineering code. For example, a six-cylinder, half-ton pickup's engine number might read T334-xxxx

(the last digits being a sequential number). A V-8 equipped truck's engine number would start with the prefix VT334. Power Wagons always used an engineering code of T137.

Dodge maintained its policy of incorporating new features into the trucks as they were ready, not just when a new model year arrived. The new low-slung, road-hugging, Forward Look styling of Chrysler Corporation's cars, brought out for 1955, really wouldn't be seen in Dodge trucks until the introduction of the 1957 model trucks with the Forward Look theme.

Starting in Spring 1956 (probably May or early June), Dodge introduced the C-3/T400 Series, which was like the T300 Series except for a few details. The engine size was increased from 260 to 270 ci, Job-Rated fender badges were replaced by new arrowhead-shaped Forward Look emblems, and a

This April 4, 1956, scale clay was a forward-thinking design exercise. It appeared to be a mid-engine layout. In many ways, it reminds one of the 1967 Dodge Deora. Or at least it was an interesting, early personal pickup design. However, its sides would have been much smoother and cleaner in style without the 1957 Plymouth tailfins, but then tailfins were mandatory on all vehicles of this era.

new lever-type parking brake control, which featured a knob used to adjust the tightness of the brake, was mounted on the driver's left side, under the dashboard. On pickups, the low-side box was discontinued and the flare rails on top of the side boards were flattened down to better mate with pickup covers.

Engine numbers for late–1956 models began with the 400 Series engineering code. A six-cylinder, half-ton pickup's engine number would be T434-xxxx. V–8 trucks would start with VT434.

The C–3/T400s continued until October 1956 when the 1957 K Series was unveiled. Grand totals of about 67,000 C–3T300 and 24,000 C–3/T400 Dodge light trucks were produced.

Standard and optional equipment

Standard equipment for the half-ton pickup included five disk wheels with 4.50 in. drop-center rims, 6.70x15 four-ply tubeless passenger-car-type tires, hydraulic shocks front and rear, one-pint oil bath air cleaner, underslung tire carrier, long running boards with rear fenders, front bumper, 360 watt 45 amp generator, 100 amp battery, short-arm stationary left-side rearview mirror, 2,500 lb. capacity front axle, 3,300 lb. capacity rear axle with two-pinion differential, 900 lb. capacity front springs, 1,200 lb. capacity rear springs, 10 in. clutch, three-speed transmission, dual vacuum wipers on Standard Cab, vent wings on cab doors, left-side interior visor, and optional rear axle ratios 3.73, 4.1:1 and 4.78:1.

Extra-cost optional equipment for the half-ton pickup included one-quart oil bath air cleaner, six-cylinder, $1.65, eight-cylinder, $3.95; armrest left door, $3.30; ashtray, $1.65; four-pinion differential, $6.60; rear bumper, $11.25; Deluxe Cab equipment, $26.50; Custom Cab equipment, $51; Custom Regal

A 1956 three-quarter-ton Stake with Standard cab, as seen by its small rear window and painted hubcaps. Note the flat flareboards on the half-ton Pickup parked with its box pointing toward the stake.

Cab equipment, $79; four chrome hubcaps, $1.65 set of five, $3; increased cooling, $10; four chrome wheel covers, 15 in. wheels, $16.50; directional signals, $23.50; domelight, $5.50; generator for high charging at low engine speed, $11.25; Dodge-Tint glass, $17.50; engine governor, $10; pair grille guards, $5.50; recirculating heater, $41.50; fresh-air heater, $62.50; dual electric horns, $14.50; horn ring on wheel, $3; left-side, long rearview mirror, $2.50, right side, $3.95; interior mirror, $3; replaceable-element oil filter, $12; electric fuel pump, $16; foam rubber padding for seat back, $11.25, for seat cushion, $11.25; 1,400 lb. capacity rear springs, $3.65; 1,750 lb. capacity rear springs, $6.60; right-side sun visor, $3; hand throttle control, $3; side-mounted spare tire carrier, $10.25; three-speed transmission with overdrive, $100; three-speed, heavy-duty with 10 in. clutch, $40, with 11 in. clutch,

1954-1966 Town Panel and Town Wagon

Two trucks which are rapidly becoming popular with light truck collectors are Dodge's Town Panel and Town Wagon Series of 1954-1966.

In 1954, Dodge management went all out to capture more of the closed delivery market. Dodge did not have the resources to develop both a Sedan Delivery and a Panel, so instead, designed one double-duty vehicle. The Town Panel, as it was renamed, with its "swept-back exterior" presented a more polished, modern, passenger-car-type appearance for those customers who needed a prestigious, boulevard-type, delivery vehicle.

The Town Panel was available in either of two trim levels to fit it to the job. In standard trim, the Town Panel appealed to the tradesman who needed a rugged, no-nonsense truck, and in Deluxe trim, it suited the needs of a merchant who delivered light packages door to door.

The 1954 Town Panel shared the same 108 in. wheelbase, half-ton truck chassis with the other half-ton models, and was powered by the dependable Dodge 218.

Late in the 1954 model year, when Dodge's first light-truck V-8 engine, the Power-Dome, became available (the most powerful engine in any light-duty truck, by the way), it too became available in the Town Panel. The V-8 engine delivered high road speeds, excellent fuel economy and exceptional acceleration.

In April 1955, the C-3 Series began and continued unchanged through the 1956 model year. The C-3 Series featured a new wraparound windshield for added visibility, the 218 engine was replaced with a 230 engine, and the Power-Dome V-8 was increased to 259. For the first time, a fully automatic transmission, the two-speed PowerFlite, was an extra-cost option.

Exterior improvements enhanced the C-3 Series Town Panel's modern shape, including chrome-plated windshield moldings coupled with chrome-plated hooded headlight and taillight rims and chrome-plated hubcaps with ram emblems. In addition, the grille panel reveal was painted Chilean Beige to add to its beauty and to emphasize streamlined, road-hugging lowness.

Introduction of the Town Wagon occurred late in the 1955 model year. The Town Wagon combined rugged truck construction with passenger-carlike styling, comfort and handling ease. The interior could be fitted for six passengers, leaving room for 90 cu. ft. of cargo or for eight passengers and minimum cargo. Both rear seats could be readily removed, thus converting the Town Wagon to a cargo hauler. This versatile cargo or people mover had a 1,575 lb. payload capacity. The addition of power brakes and power steering made these two beauties even more attractive.

In 1957, the Town Panel and Town Wagon were updated with the Corporate automobile-type Forward Look by the addition of an all-new grille, forward-thrusting fenders and hooded headlights. Dodge truck hoods had been the side-opening, butterfly type since the early 1930s, but finally changed to a one-piece, alligator type, which could be opened a full 90 degrees for easier servicing. The Power-Dome V-8 engine grew to 315 ci. A convenient dash-mounted, push-button-controlled, LoadFlite two-speed automatic transmission became an extra-cost option.

Also, for 1957 the first W100 "Go-anywhere," four-wheel-drive, Power Wagon, Town Wagon and Town Panel models became available for those customers who needed a high-ground-clearing and multiple-use workhorse to carry passengers, payloads or both. Both Power Wagon models could be powered with L-head six or V-8 engines, with three- or four-speed manual transmissions, or the optional, dash-mounted, push-button, LoadFlite automatic (only available with V-8 engine). An optional front-mounted, 8,000 lb. winch added even more off-road performance.

For 1958, Dodge designers face-lifted the front-end appearance with a new full-width hood and grille that made the frontal appearance much more massive and broader through the use of horizontal lines in the grille and wide-spaced dual headlights. Its new front bumper wrapped further around the fenders for added protection, and because it was more massive, it added to the truck's overall lower and wider appearance. This style, with only a few minor changes, remained basically the same through 1966, the last year these models were built. Wheelbase length was stretched to 114 in. in 1961 to make these older models consistent with the new half-ton pickup. Also in 1961, the L-6 engine was dropped in favor of the modern overhead-valve 225 slant six. This package remained basically unchanged through 1966.

This 1956 half-ton long-box Pickup belongs to Bob and Hazel Seymour of Anchorage, Alaska. The Seymours bought their Dodge new, and continue to use it for everyday transportation. Bob is retired so he has the time to maintain his Dodge in like-new condition.

This beautifully restored 1956 short-box six-cylinder half-ton Pickup belongs to Thomas Traynor of Yorktown Heights, New York.

$45; four-speed transmission with 11 in. clutch, $70; PowerFlite, $165; wraparound rear window, $29; dual electric wipers, 11.25.

Specifications and prices

All specifications remained the same as in 1955, except that advertised horsepower of the 230 six-cylinder increased to 115.

B6-108 half-ton Series
Pickup, $1,530
Town Panel, $1,760
Town Wagon, $2,057
B6-116 half-ton Series
Pickup, $1,556
Stake, $1,629
Platform, $1,563
C6-116 three-quarter-ton Series
Pickup, $1,653
Stake, $1,726
Platform, $1,660
D6-116 one-ton Series
Pickup, $1,711
Stake, $1,784
Platform, $1,718
D6-126 one-ton Series
Pickup, $1,750
Stake, $1,836
Platform, $1,770

Production

Is there any consolation in having a bad year, but a better year than the other guys? That's what happened in 1956 when total Dodge output was 104,028, or down 3.2 percent; the industry slipped by 9.5 percent. Dodge gained 6.2 percent in market share to 8.6 percent. Canada accounted for 12,768 trucks. Breakdown by weight class, United States only, was 32,844 half-ton, 9,552 three-quarter-ton and 14,294 one-ton.

Chapter 7

Power-Giant Era 1957–1960

Looking solely at sales and market share figures for the 1957–1960 period, this was a bad era for Dodge trucks. Dodge had enjoyed good sales from 1939 to 1947 with its Job-Rated trucks and again from 1948 to 1952 with the Pilot-House trucks. Then, sales began to slide in 1953 and continued to decline until hitting rock bottom in 1960 when market share fell all the way to 6 percent. Sales in 1961 fell again, but

The 1957 half-ton Pickup's cab and box were unchanged from 1956, but all sheet metal from the cowl forward was new to create the Forward Look. The Custom cab was equipped with a wraparound rear window as standard equipment.

because total industry sales also fell, market share remained at 6 percent. Fortunately, sales began to take off again with the 1962 model year, and have been strong ever since.

There is more, however, than just sales results. The pickups which rolled out of Dodge's Mound Road Truck Plant in the 1957–1960 years are much more interesting, innovative and exciting than bare sales figures would lead one to believe.

1957 K Series

Dodge adopted an all-new model numbering system in 1957. For example, in 1956 a half-ton pickup was designated a C-3-B6. The letter C indicated the Series (1954–1956), the number 3 indicated the sub-series (late 1955 or 1956), the letter B indicated half-ton and the 6 stood for six-cylinder engine. In 1957, the same truck was designated a K6-D100 with K meaning K Series of 1957, 6 a six-cylinder engine, D a conventional cab vehicle and 100 indicating half-ton.

Two new pickups in 1957 were the three-quarter-ton K6-D200 and K8-D200. GVW ratings on these three-quarter-ton pickups increased from 5,800 to 7,500 lb. In order to offer the best truck value in this class, Dodge redesigned the three-quarter-ton models using these new components: a 2,800 lb. capacity front axle, 6,500 lb. capacity full-floating rear axle with 8¾ in. diameter ring gear; new 12⅛x2 in. front brakes, 13x2½ in. rear brakes; a more powerful 315 ci V-8 engine; fin and tube radiator core; heavier frame; increased capacity propeller shaft; front springs of 1,000 lb. capacity and rear springs of 1,950 lb. were standard; a 3,000 lb. rear spring or 3,100 lb. rear spring with auxiliary leaf were extras.

Bodywork and interior

Dodge claimed its 1957 K Series pickups had an all-new Forward Look with new cabs and bodies. The truth is that the cab on a 1957 Dodge pickup originated in early 1955. Also, Dodge pickup boxes for 1957 carried over without change from the previous year. In 1956, Dodge trucks had featured Func-

Half- and three-quarter-ton 4x4 Pickups with conventional cabs were new for 1957. With the addition of these new models Dodge strengthened its leadership position in the 4x4 market. An engineering pre-production W100 half-ton is shown. Pro- *duction models displayed Power Wagon nameplates on each side of the hood. Also new in 1957 were model numberplates on each front fender, which served to identify light-duty model's nominal tonnage ratings.*

tional Designed cabs with "full-circle" visibility. In 1948, when the Pilot-House Era began, drivers enjoyed vastly improved all-around visibility due to a much larger windshield, side glass, rear glass and new rear-quarter windows. The term Pilot-House cab gradually fell out of use as time passed, but was revived again in April 1955 when a wraparound windshield and a wraparound rear window were added. Now Dodge drivers could look out through "full-circle" visibility.

Even though the cab was not really new, all sheet metal from the cowl forward was. K Series Dodge pickups took on an entirely new appearance due to a new grille, hooded headlights, parking lights, bumpers and ornamentation.

An alligator-type hood that opened a full 90 degrees was a Dodge first. The hood was so designed that it opened to either 48 degrees or to a full 90 degrees with practically no effort. The 90 degree opening presented a wide-open engine compartment, eliminating the necessity of removing the hood for engine repairs, while the 48 degree opening was adequate for routine servicing.

When viewed from the side, the front fender line extended over the hooded headlight and then angled back as it ran down to the bumper. This forward-thrusting look caused the truck to appear to be always in motion even while standing still, thus giving rise to the term Forward Look. The Forward Look was also an advertising slogan shared with Chrysler automobiles in 1957.

The attractive new grille was a one-piece design with headlight hoods and a top horizontal bar formed into a full-width grille panel. The chrome-plated lower grille bar and center strut were separate pieces bolted to the grille, and the top horizontal bar was

Six 1957 Power-Giants line up for a group photo. From left to right they are a D100 half-ton Pickup, D100 Town Panel, D300 one-ton pickup, D600 Stake, D900 dump and C700
COE tractor trailer. The forward-thrusting hooded headlights help create the Forward Look, a styling and marketing theme shared with corporate autos.

capped with a chrome molding. The grille was painted body color except for the lower reveal and the inside of the headlight hoods, which were painted Mojave Beige.

New ornamentation included the Dodge name in individual letters across the top of the grille and a large V ornament on the front of the hood for eight-cylinder models. Six-cylinder models did not have an ornament. The V–8 hood emblem on 1956 pickups was quite small, but for 1957, Dodge offered a V symbol which would have made Cadillac proud. All pickups displayed a Forward Look emblem and a model numberplate on each front fender.

Dodge marketed two cabs for 1957, the Standard and Custom. The Standard cab was standard for half-ton through two-ton conventional models. The

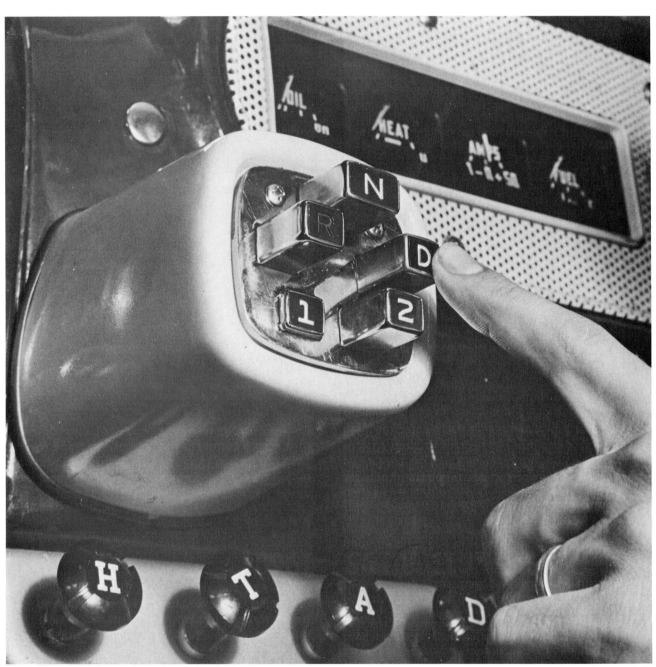

Dash-mounted, push-button-controlled LoadFlite three-speed automatic was new for 1957 and was a Dodge exclusive. Because of the absence of a Park position button, owners of trucks equipped with an automatic had to maintain their truck's emergency brake in good working order. The push-button automatic was also available on half- and three-quarter 4x4s, but only when equipped with a V–8.

106

Custom cab was standard equipment for two-and-a-half-, three- and four-ton conventional models, all COE models, and extra equipment for half-ton through two-ton conventional models.

The Standard cab was trimmed in a brown saran material with light, buff-colored facings. The Custom cab seat back cushion was upgraded with a glamor treatment in which the light, buff-colored facings of the seat extended into the back cushion, giving the appearance of a divided seat.

Seat and back cushions for the Standard cab were cotton sisal. The seat cushion for the Custom cab was foam rubber, and the back pad was latex-treated curled hair, with foam rubber available at extra cost.

Dodge designers painted the steering wheel and column black and provided a chrome horn button with a gold embossed Forward Look emblem.

Black with white lettering was used on all instrument panel control knobs, except for the wind-shield wiper knob which was chrome. The glovebox doorknob was black plastic with a chrome insert. The steering-column-mounted gearshift lever was also black, as was the handbrake lever, four-speed transmission shift lever and ashtray.

All door trim panels, sun visors, armrests and escutcheons were light buff. Headlining on standard cabs was light, buff-embossed cardboard with light buff binding; for the Custom cab the headlining was light, buff-perforated cardboard with Tufflex insulation between the headlining and roof panel.

Other new cab safety, comfort and, appearance details included chrome-plated window cranks with black knobs, a chrome-plated turn signal switch lever with black knob, glovebox door painted body color, black instrument bezels and an integral-switch dome-light on all models. Doors were equipped with safety-type rotary locks and pull-type handles, and both doors could now be locked from the outside. Single-speed electric wipers were used on Standard cab and

A Custom cab shows off the 1957 half-ton's luxurious and attractive interior. It was roomy and comfortable with its adjustable, chair height, foam rubber padded seat cushion.

Perforated headliner for sound deadening, armrests, sun visors, door and dash liners, and two-tone fabrics helped create its good-looking and cozy interior.

This 1957 W200 three-quarter-ton Power Wagon wrecker is still in daily use by Dan Welle Motors located on Sinclair Lewis' "Main Street" in Sauk Centre, Minnesota.

two-speed wipers on Custom cab. The extra-cost wraparound rear window provided excellent all-around vision. The outside mirror was painted body color while the inside mirror was painted light buff. Hubcaps on half-ton pickups were painted chrome metallic while chrome-plated hubcaps with rams head ornament were extra cost.

Engines and chassis

All 1956 transmissions carried over except that the Chrysler-built LoadFlite three-speed push-button automatic replaced the PowerFlite automatic for D100, D200, W100 and W200 pickups.

Greatly increased power due to a larger V-8 engine boosted performance dramatically for the new Dodge pickups. This V-8 had a polyspherical head and not the Hemi head. Displacement was 315 from 3.63x3.80 in. bore and stroke, compression 8.5:1, horsepower 204 at 4400 rpm and gross torque 290 at 2400 rpm. The standard engine continued to be the old standby 230 ci L-6 in D100, D200, D300, W100, W200 and W300.

Mojave Beige was the standard color for all light-duty model wheels as well as front bumpers. Two-tone color combinations consisted of Mojave Beige for the upper color and any standard color for the lower color. Cab color was also the standard color for all pickup boxes and rear fenders. Pickup box floors, however, were always painted black regardless of cab or box color. On all light-duty trucks, except the original Power Wagon, black was the standard color for running boards and Mojave Beige was the standard color for the grille panel lower opening, reveal and headlight door inserts.

In addition to the driving ease offered by the push-button LoadFlite automatic, light-duty Dodge trucks could be ordered, for the first time ever, with power steering and power brakes. At last pickups were becoming civilized.

All 1957 Dodge pickups came equipped with tubeless tires, except for the one-ton Power Wagon.

New 4x4 light-duties

A midyear introduction (January 1957) rounded out Dodge's 4x4 lineup and firmly established Dodge as the industry's 4x4 leader. Introduced were half-ton and three-quarter-ton 4x4s in conventional cab styling to complement the original military-styled one-ton Power Wagon and the two-ton conventional

This rear view clearly shows the station wagon rear fenders on Louis Wentworth's 1957 Sweptside. The Sweptside's fenders and rear bumper were borrowed from the 1957 Dodge two-door Suburban station wagon. Louie is from McCall Creek, Mississippi.

Floyd Minor of Council Bluffs, Iowa, owns this restored 1957 Sweptside.

cab Power Wagon introduced just the year before. Dodge, alone of the Big Three, built 4x4 trucks of half-, three-quarter-, one- and two-ton capacities.

Not only did the new half- and three-quarter-ton 4x4 models offer conventional cab styling with seating for three husky men, but also a powerful V–8 engine and Chrysler's own three-speed automatic. Automatic was only available with V–8 power, however.

Chevy also introduced twelve 4x4 models in April 1957. Other new 4x4 models included Willys in December 1956, IH in November 1956, and GMC in June 1957. Dodge booked an order for 2,900 military 4x4s in 1957 as well as several million dollars of spare parts for World War II vintage military trucks.

Basic Dodge factory-installed extra equipment to make 4x4s even more versatile and hard working

included a vacuum brake booster, Custom cab equipment, pintle hook, power takeoff assembly, radiator overflow tank, foam rubber padding on seat cushion and back cushion, extra-capacity front and rear springs, power steering, choice of three transmissions—heavy-duty three-speed, four-speed and automatic—wraparound rear window and 6,000 lb. capacity winch.

Make no mistake, these conventional cab 4x4s with new sheet metal were not the same trucks as the original Power Wagon. Their axles, transfer case and other mechanical components were of lighter-duty construction; the original Power Wagon is in a class by itself.

Standard and optional equipment

Standard equipment for the half-ton pickup included one-pint oil bath air cleaner, 2,500 lb. capac-

The Dodge Sweptside's companion was a DeSoto Sweptside, which featured 1956 Plymouth rear fenders. The DeSoto was given more detailed bodystyling elements than was the Dodge, as seen by the canted tailgate, special truck-type rear bumper, skirt located between the tailgate and bumper, special two- *tone paint scheme and chromed DeSoto full wheel covers. The DeSoto was an export truck. Judging by the palm trees in the background this truck appeared to be located on a tropical island.*

Sweptside D100

In 1957, Chevrolet's Camero Carrier was in its third year and Ford had just released its exciting new Ranchero car-pickup. Ford and Chevy were making Dodge look bad as Dodge didn't have a model to compete with either. Ford further contributed to Dodge's woes by announcing a new cab-wide Styleside pickup in 1957. As a result, Dodge dealers were putting a lot of heat on the factory to give them something to sell against Ford and Chevy's new products.

There was an almost unknown but important group at Dodge Truck called the Special Equipment Group. The SEG worked primarily with fleet users, but was also involved with individual sales. Throughout most of its history, Dodge Truck needed every sale possible, so was always anxious to accommodate a customer's special needs. The SEG could modify or change any standard Dodge truck in any way. Changes included such things as replacing standard tires with a special-size tire, modifying frame lengths, changing engines (substituting a diesel engine for a gas engine, for example) and so on. Because the SEG's work did not require a release from Central Engineering, they were able to quickly and efficiently solve individual customer problems. In later years, as government regulations covering safety and environmental issues became a larger factor in car and truck manufacturing, the SEG's ability to respond quickly and efficiently became restricted until the unit had to be dissolved.

Because the Sweptside was released late in the 1957 model year, little in the way of literature, sales material or photographs was produced. This photo was the only official black and white Chrysler Corporation photo of a 1957 Sweptside I know of (one of four of the same truck). For collectors looking for Sweptside material, the most commonly found Sweptside pieces are the several magazine ads that were produced.

The SEG helps explain why collectors occasionally find a Dodge truck that varies from standard in some way. If the change appears to have been done at the factory, chances are good that it was an SEG modification. The SEG is the reason a collector can't say, "That item is not correct or never offered."

Joe Berr, SEG manager, recognized that Dodge must do something and do it quickly. His challenge was in developing a new product without spending a lot of money, which wasn't available, on tooling and engineering.

Berr had an idea. He went over to the Dodge car assembly plant, appropriated a pair of rear fenders and a rear bumper from a 1957 Dodge two-door Suburban Station Wagon, and brought them back to the SEG shop where he had a D100 116 in. wheelbase Custom cab pickup. After removing the stock fenders, Burt Nagos welded the station wagon fenders to the pickup's box. The station wagon's rear bumper fit like a glove, but the tailgate had to be cut down to fit between the long fenders. Chrome trim pieces, custom-made to fit the cab, continued the lines running forward from the station wagon fenders. A two-tone paint job, full chrome wheel covers and wide white sidewalls were added and the Sweptside D100 was born. A few key Dodge truck dealers evaluated the new creation. "Build it," they said. "We can sell this beauty!"

The Sweptside D100 fit perfectly into Dodge Division's overall marketing strategy for 1957 as Dodge heavily promoted what they called Autodynamics, an attempt to tie car and truck lines together in order to convince a purchaser of a Dodge car or truck to go all the way with Dodge by buying both products. As the Sweptside D100 was part car, but more truck, it fit right in with Autodynamics.

In Dodge's car line, Autodynamics meant a low-slung beauty, which appeared to be in motion even while standing still. The Hemi V-8 saw to it that Dodge cars had plenty of go.

The 1957 truck line also featured Forward Look Styling with hooded headlights and forward-thrusting front fender lines. An optional Power-Dome V-8 engine, which could be coupled to the industry's first push-button automatic transmission, outperformed the old flathead six. The Sweptside, when equipped with power steering and power brakes, gave its owner the driving ease of a passenger car while retaining the toughness of a commercial vehicle.

Sweptside D100s were always built in the SEG Shop as a special product; they were never assembled on the production line with other pickups.

Today's truck collectors prize Dodge Sweptside D100s as one of the most desirable and collectible light trucks of the 1950s. They are appreciated for their beauty, as well as their scarcity. Introduced as a midyear 1957 model, they had only one full year of production in 1958. Production ceased in early 1959 because Dodge had announced its new cab-wide box Sweptline pickups at the start of the 1959 model year.

ity front axle, 3,600 lb. capacity rear axle with 3.73, 4.1:1 or 4.89:1 ratios, front bumper, 11 in. clutch, 17.4 gallon fuel tank mounted under cab, 450 watt 30 amp generator, short-arm left-side mirror, long running boards and rear fenders, front and rear shocks, underslung tire carrier, three-speed transmission, single taillight and five steel stud disk wheels with 6.70x15 four-ply tires.

Extra cost optional equipment for half-ton pickup included one-quart oil bath air cleaner, right-side armrest, 60 amp battery, chrome-plated front bumper, chrome-plated or painted rear bumper, Custom cab equipment, side-mounted spare tire, increased cooling, brightmetal wheel covers for 15 in. wheels, turn signals, V-8 engine, electric fuel pump, generator for high charging at low engine speed, tinted glass, engine governor, chrome or painted grille guards, chrome headlight door inserts, perforated headliner for Standard cab, recirculating heater, fresh-air heater, dual horns, horn ring, chrome hubcaps, hydraulic jack, cigar lighter, glovebox door lock, longarm exterior left- or right-side mirror, interior mirror, windshield bright outer molding, replaceable-element oil filter, two-tone paint, foam rubber padded seat back, foam rubber padded seat cushion, 1,200 lb. front springs, 1,750 lb. rear springs, 750 lb. Easy-Ride rear springs, power steering, right-side interior sun visor, hand throttle, three-speed transmission with overdrive, three-speed heavy-duty transmission, four-speed transmission, three-speed LoadFlite automatic with push-buttons, wraparound rear window, windshield washers and dual electric windshield wipers.

Specifications and prices
D100–108 half-ton, 108 in. wheelbase, and D100–116 half-ton, 116 in. wheelbase; three-speed transmission, 6.70x15 four-ply tires.

D200–116 three-quarter-ton, 116 in. wheelbase, three-speed transmission, 7x17.5 six-ply tires.

D300–126 one-ton, 126 in. wheelbase, three-speed transmission, 7x17.5 six-ply tires.

Standard engine for all light-duty trucks was an L–6, 3¼x4⅝ in. bore and stroke, 230 ci, advertised 120 hp. Optional engine was an ohv V-8, 3.63x3.80 in. bore and stroke, 315 ci, advertised 204 hp.

D100–108 half-ton Series
Pickup, $1,653
Town Panel, $1,906
Town Wagon, $2,197
D100–116 half-ton Series
Pickup, $1,679
Stake, $1,764
Platform, $1,698
Sweptside, NA
D200–116 three-quarter-ton Series

Pickup, $1,833
Stake, $1,918
Platform, $1,852
D300–126 one-ton Series
Pickup, $1,885
Stake, $1,979
Platform, $1,914

Production
Production of 1957 models began on September 12, 1956, and new models were introduced to the public on October 30, 1956, the same day as all Chrysler Corporation car lines. Production for 1957 was dismal, dropping 19.3 percent to 83,977 in a year that industry production declined only 3.8 percent. Due to this big drop, market share declined 15.1 percent to 7.3 percent, its lowest point since 1932! Canadian production sank to 7,378, its lowest total since 1939.

1958 L Series
L Series Dodge trucks had an all-new appearance due to the new sheet metal from the cowl forward and, even though the cab itself carried over without change. The primary reason for redesigning the front end was to provide a wider engine compartment to facilitate engine servicing. This was accomplished by redesigning front fender housings and engine compartment splash shields. New cab door hinges permitted doors to swing outside of the front fender housings, which increased door openings by 15 percent for greater ease of entry and exit.

Since 1948, Dodge truck grilles had been made from a one-piece, full-width and full-height panel. This design was dropped in favor of a narrower grille panel which fit snugly between the front fenders. The new grille was made of three horizontal bars mounted in the large opening between the headlights, with a fourth bar in a separate smaller opening just above the front bumper. Damaged grille bars could be quickly and easily replaced by simply unbolting them.

Ornamentation for conventional models included the Dodge name in individual letters across the front of the hood. A model numberplate on both sides of the hood was integrated into an attractive grille, which covered openings in the hood-side panels. These openings permitted engine heat to escape. The word Dodge and the numeral 6 or 8 was attached to each front fender.

Interiors
Upholstery for the Standard cab was a brown saran enriched with gold threads and facings of colored sandalwood. Custom cab upholstery was a breathable vinyl, with a topaz pattern on either black or brown background, depending on body color. The

Custom cab seat back cushion had a deluxe or glamor treatment in which the topaz-colored facings extended a short distance into the back cushion panel in a long V shape. The seat cushion had topaz-colored bolsters at each end where wear was most pronounced.

The Standard cab seat cushion and back pad were made of cotton sisal. The seat cushion pad for the Custom cab was foam rubber, and the back pad was a latex-treated, curled hair. A foam rubber back pad was available as extra-cost equipment.

Other cab interior features that contributed to driver comfort, convenience and appearance included a chrome turn signal switch with knob, case and cover painted sandlewood, glovebox door painted body color and the knob sandlewood plastic with chrome insert; glovebox door lock was standard equipment for Custom cab and extra for Standard cab; silver-colored instrument bezels, instrument panel trim plate embossed anodized aluminum; new domelight with integral switch located at the rear of the cab above the rear window; new two-piece headlinings, designed to mount close to the roof panel for maximum headroom, became standard for both cabs; Standard cab rooflining was sandlewood-colored embossed cardboard; Custom cab rooflining was topaz-colored, perforated embossed cardboard with topaz binding; Tufflex insulation between the headlining and roof on the Custom cab for reduced heat and noise; Standard cab equipped with single-speed electric wipers; Custom cab with variable-speed wipers; Standard cabs could be equipped with variable speed wipers at extra cost; outside mirror painted body color, inside mirror painted sandlewood available at extra cost; new, deep-center steering wheel was painted sandlewood in Standard cab and topaz in

A top-of-the-line Sweptside sits proudly in front of five other 1958 models. Left to right, a D100 half-ton Pickup, D100 Town Wagon, D300 one-ton dual-wheel Stake, D100 Town Panel and D800 tractor trailer.

Custom cab; in both cabs, the steering column jacket was painted sandlewood; horn button was plastic, with a chrome shield design on a red background having two chrome and black borders; sandlewood-colored plastic was used for all instrument panel control knobs and lettering was storm charcoal; steering-column-mounted shift lever was painted sandlewood with a bright metal knob.

For safety reasons, the Orscheln handbrake lever handle was painted Dodge Truck Red as it was quite easy to accidentally release it when exiting the truck. With the quality Orscheln parking brake, the parking brake could be adjusted by the driver by simply turning the end of the handle. This fast, easy method took up cable slack without the use of tools.

Two-tone embossed cardboard was used for the Standard cab door trim panels; the background color was sandlewood with a storm charcoal painted design and sandlewood color used on bindings and fasteners. The soft, padded door trim panel used for the Custom cab assisted in deadening noise inside the cab. The panel covering was a two-tone vinyl with

A 1958 W200 three-quarter-ton Power Wagon shows off its restyled grille and front fenders, which were common to all 1958 trucks. Dual headlights were an option early in the year, but later in the year became standard equipment. Power Wagon models were equipped with medium-duty truck-type bumpers. From 1957 up to 1968 the term Power Wagon became somewhat confusing in that the original, 1946 military-styled 4x4 and the 4x4s with conventional cabs were both called Power Wagons. The original Power Wagon did not change in style from year to year, but the conventional cab Power Wagon's style changed along with all other trucks.

topaz background. Storm charcoal was used for Standard cab armrests and topaz for Custom cab armrests. Window crank handles were chrome with sandlewood plastic knobs. The roof-mounted radio was painted sandlewood with chrome knobs, the gun-metal-colored dial had eggshell lettering. A black rubber floor mat was standard for all cabs.

Features of the new six- and eight-cylinder-powered one-ton 4x4 pickups, rated at 10,000 lb. maximum GVW, included: Spicer Model 70 front and rear axles with interchangeable complete differential assembly, ring gear, pinion and wheel bearings. The front axle was rated for 4,500 lb. and the rear for 7,500 lb. with ratios of 4.88 and 5.87:1. The transfer case and power takeoff were the same as on half- and three-quarter-ton models for maximum interchangeability. Bendix 13 x 2½ in. front and rear brakes were used for maximum interchangeability and the Duo-

Servo design provided equal braking in either direction. An extra-heavy-duty frame was well-suited for off-road operation; the frame size was 8.09, flange width 2.78, thickness .210 and section modulus 6.44 in. A 25 gallon fuel tank was mounted outside the frame on the right side as standard equipment. A second 25 gallon tank was mounted on the left side, available as extra equipment. Four-speed syncro-mesh transmission was standard equipment, with LoadFlite three-speed automatic as extra equipment.

Features of the six- and eight-cylinder-powered half and three-quarter-ton 4x4 pickups included a Spicer Model 44F front axle rated at 3,000 lb. with ratios of 4.09 and 4.89:1. A Chrysler-built rear axle rated at 3,600 lb., with ratios of 4.11 and 4.89:1 on half-ton models, a Chrysler-built rear axle rated at 6,500 lb., with ratios 4.11 or 4.89:1 was used on three-quarter-ton models. Service brake size on half-

The DeSoto half-ton Pickup was a badge-engineered truck and differed from a Dodge only in name. The DeSoto, however, was an export-only vehicle. This DeSoto was somewhat *similar to the 1957 DeSoto Sweptside in that it was also an upscale truck as seen by its chrome front bumper, DeLuxe cab, whitewall tires and two-tone paint.*

ton models was 12⅛x2 in. front and rear, and on three-quarter-ton models 12⅛x2 in. front and 13x2½ in. rear. The standard fuel tank was 18 gallons mounted at the rear of the frame; a 37.5 gallon rear-mounted tank was available at extra cost. Power steering was available at extra cost, and a three-speed, heavy-duty transmission was standard with a four-speed transmission or LoadFlite three-speed automatic with pushbutton control as an extra-cost item with the V–8 engine only. A single lever controlled the transfer case for convenience and ease of operation of front axle engagement and high-low shift.

The extensive improvements for the L Series Dodge Trucks were not limited to styling features alone. Many engineering and mechanical innovations contributed to greater vehicle durability, payload capacity, and serviceability. These improvements included: replaceable cartridge-type oil filters supplanting the sealed-type for all except fleet orders (this change occurred late in K Series production);

new, improved Cleveland S–55 propeller shafts became standard for conventional models D100, D200, D300, Forward Control Models P300 and 4x4 Models W100 and W200; maximum GVW rating for D300 increased from 8,800 to 9,000 lb; front axle ground clearance increased by 1¹¹⁄₃₂ in. for Models D100, D200, D300, and P300 by redesigning the front axle and suspension; horns relocated as far forward as possible to improve audibility; polarized, multiple connectors of molded plastic and completely sealed replacing the exposed type; Oriflow shock absorbers for more control over spring oscillations. The ride was greatly improved for Model D100 with a new, low-rate, 900 lb. capacity front spring, and new progressive-type rear springs. Standard springs were rated at 1,050 lb.; extra equipment springs were available at 1,350 lb. capacity.

Shift patterns for four- and five-speed transmissions were embossed and painted on top of the gearshift knobs. New, larger-diameter steering columns

This 1958 Dodge half-ton was identical to the DeSoto half-ton except for its grille guards and Dodge nameplates.

designed to accommodate built-in turn signals and drop center steering wheels—a decided safety improvement—became standard for all models except Power Wagon. For easier servicing, the battery location was changed to under the hood. Red warning lights for generator and oil pressure replaced ammeter and oil pressure gauge, except for on the Power Wagon. The light switch was relocated to the left of the driver for better accessibility and the windshield wiper switch was relocated from the top of the instrument panel to the face of the panel at the right of the driver for easy reach. An electric tachometer became available as an extra-cost option. Limited-slip differential became available for the Model D100 rear axle and for front and rear axles of the W100.

Standard and optional equipment

Standard equipment for the half-ton pickup included one-pint oil bath air cleaner, 2,500 lb. capacity front axle, 3,600 lb. capacity rear axle with 3.73:1, 4.1:1 or 4.89:1 ratios, 50 amp battery, painted front bumper, 11 in. clutch, Standard cab equipment, standard six-cylinder engine, 17.4 gallon fuel tank mounted inside frame, 450 watt generator, Sahara Beige-painted hubcaps, short rearview mirror, 4.50x15 in. rims, front and rear shocks, 900 lb. capacity front springs, 1,050 lb. capacity rear springs, underslung tire carrier, tubeless tires 6.70x15 four-ply three-speed transmission, single taillight, five-stud wheels, and dual electric single-speed wipers.

Extra-cost optional equipment for the half-ton pickup included one-quart oil bath air cleaner, right-side armrest, 60 amp battery, chrome front bumper, chrome or painted rear bumper, Custom cab equipment, side-mounted spare tire carrier, chrome trim package of hood ornament, hood, fender and door moldings, chrome grille bars, headlight trim plate, increased cooling, set of four or five chrome wheel covers, Full-Traction differential, turn signals, V–8 engine, electric fuel pump, generator for high charging at low speeds, tinted glass, engine governor, chrome-plated or painted grille guards, dual headlights, perforated headliner with insulation, recirculating heater, fresh-air heater, dual horns, chrome hub caps, hydraulic jack, cigar lighter, cab corner lights, glovebox door lock, long-arm adjustable rearview mirrors, interior mirror, outer bright windshield moldings, replaceable-element oil filter, two-tone paint, roof-mounted radio, foam rubber seat cushion and seat back, 1,200 lb. front springs, 1,350 lb. rear springs, power steering, interior right-side sun visor, electric tachometer, hand throttle, three-speed transmission with overdrive, four-speed transmission, LoadFlite push-button transmission, wraparound rear window, windshield washers and dual variable-speed electric wipers.

Specifications and prices

All same as 1957
D100–108 half-ton Series
Pickup, $1,714
Town Panel, $1,985
Town Wagon, 6 pass., $2,262
Town Wagon, 8 pass., $2,308
D100–116 half-ton Series
Pickup, $1,752
Stake, $1,837
Platform, $1,782
Sweptside, $2,124
W100–108 half-ton 4x4 Series
Pickup, $2,594
Town Panel, $2,865
Town Wagon, 6 pass., $3,143
Town Wagon, 8 pass., $3,189
W100–116 half-ton 4x4 Series
Pickup, $2,629
Stake, $2,715
Platform, $2,660
D200–116 three-quarter-ton Series
Pickup, $1,945
Stake, $2,031
Platform, $1,975
W200–116 three-quarter-ton 4x4 Series
Pickup, $2,747

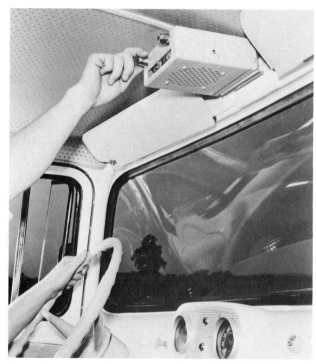

The ceiling-mounted transistor radio in this 1958 pickup was typical for the years 1957–1960. An aerial extended from the top of the radio through the cab's roof.

Stake, $2,832
Platform, $2,777
D300–126 one-ton Series
Pickup, $2,000
Stake, $2,106
Platform, $2,041
W300–129 one-ton 4x4 Series
Pickup, $3,173
Stake, $3,278
Platform, $3,214

Production

Introduction date for 1958 models was October 31, 1957. Unfortunately, 1958 was a year of general economic recession causing total industry production to fall by 20.1 percent to a twenty-year low. Production at Dodge was about in line with the industry, that is, off by 22.7 percent, for a total of 64,948, Dodge's lowest total since 1938. Market share of 7 percent was off by 4.1 percent from 1957. Canadian production amounted to 6,280.

In 1958, imported light-duty trucks began to take a big enough market share (4 percent) to be visible. Volkswagen, who sold the industry's only van and a pickup, was the chief culprit.

1959 M Series

Dodge's evolutionary product improvement policy continued for 1959, highlighted by a new pickup, the Sweptline. The new Sweptline, with its smooth-sided cab and wide box, was available in half-, three-quarter- and one-ton models with box lengths of 6½, 7½ and 9 ft.

The handsome Sweptline box gave Dodge pickups a whole new beauty. However, this first Sweptline bodystyle only lasted two years as the all-new Dart pickup replaced it in 1961. The Sweptline pickup has been part of the Dodge truck line since. As a matter-of-fact, since 1986, Sweptline is the only pickup model Dodge builds.

While definitely a step ahead in beauty, the wide-box, high-styled Sweptline also offered more utility. The Sweptline's box measured 16¾ in. wider and ¾ in. longer on the 108 in. wheelbase half-ton model and 126 in. wheelbase one-ton model, but on the 116 in. wheelbase three-quarter-ton model, a full 9 in. longer. These added inches in width and length added to a 30 percent increase in load-carrying space. In addition, the Sweptline's 9 in. wider tailgate and all-steel floor made loading and unloading easier.

The 1959 Sweptside was the rarest Sweptside of all because of its short production run. It was dropped in January 1959. It makes one cringe to see these cement contractors use a Sweptside for rough, heavy-duty work.

Twin taillights were standard equipment and added a new dimension in safety.

The addition of the Sweptline pickup caused Dodge to rename its narrow-box pickup model to prevent confusion. The name Utility Line was first proposed, but this was later shortened to Utiline—a name which continued until 1985 when the narrow box was dropped. A dual-rear-wheel, one-ton pickup was available only in the Utiline Series. The fenders used on the "dually" one-ton are not the same fender

A 1959 Sweptline pickup with cab-wide box. This glamorous new top-of-the-line offering was the reason Dodge discontinued the Sweptside in January 1959. This Sweptline pickup box saw service only on 1959 and 1960 Dodge pickups. Dodge later sold the tooling for this box to Studebaker. Note the roof-mounted radio aerial at the front and center of the cab.

118

as used on the smaller Utiline pickups; instead it is a wider version of the rear fender style as used from 1948 to 1952.

Although offered at new model introduction time, the top-of-the-line Sweptside D100 pickup came to the end of its run in mid-January 1959, when it became obvious that the Sweptline pickup filled that market niche well. Due to its short production year, the 1959 Sweptside D100 pickup is now a rare model.

Bodywork and interior

Styling changes for the rest of the lineup included a new grille that was simpler and more attractive. Also, above the grille, a nameplate with the word Dodge embossed on it in red letters replaced the nameplate made up of individual letters. A single chrome spear on both sides of the hood followed by a model numberplate replaced more elaborate ornamentation from 1958.

New concealed running boards added to the smooth, sleek look of the Sweptline pickup. Concealed running boards also served to strengthen cab construction.

Conventional cab Power Wagons used all the above ornamentation and also displayed a Power Wagon nameplate on each front fender. Dodge did not make conventional cab Power Wagon pickups in the Sweptline Series this year.

Plain gray-painted hubcaps were standard equipment for half-ton models and extra equipment for three-quarter-ton models. Chrome hubcaps or wheel covers could be ordered for half-ton models only. One-ton models were not equipped with hubcaps.

A standard Dodge pickup carried little chrome trim as chrome was used only on the hood front nameplate, hood-side spear and model numberplate, and the trim ring around the parking lights. Buyers could select either of two extra-cost trim and molding packages. One package included chrome grille bars and headlight trim plates. The other package included all of the above plus chrome moldings on the hood, fenders and cab doors. A molding package for Sweptline pickups consisted of chrome moldings on pickup box side panels.

Standard cab interiors featured seats upholstered with Saran cloth, and long-wearing vinyl facings and bolsters in two color combinations. The headlining was of two-piece construction of embossed fiberboard in Sand Dune White. Embossed fiberboard was also used for door trim panels in two color combinations. A black, deep-dish steering wheel with black and gold trim or a silver wheel with black and silver trim completed the handsome interior package.

For the first time in several years, Dodge designers created an instrument panel of conventional arrangement. That is, all instruments were grouped together in a hooded cluster directly in front of the driver, the glovebox returned to the right side, and an integral ashtray became a standard item. All other control knobs were positioned in a horizontal line below and at the center of the instrument panel.

A typical Dodge touch was to mount the radio to the ceiling as it had been since 1957. The radio was attached to the cab roof in an easy-to-reach location between the sun visors. The correct Mopar radio for 1957–1960 Dodge trucks is Model 700, a small, compact, but powerful transistor radio.

Quality features of the Custom cab not found in the Standard cab included a left-side armrest; treated black fiberboard dash liner with ¾ in. fiberglass insulation; soft, sound-absorbent, door trim panels upholstered in gold or silver vinyl; ¾ in. jute pad under rubber floor mat; embossed and perforated fiberboard headlining with insulation cemented to headlining panel. Two seat trim combinations harmonized with outside paint colors, one with a brown background and white designs, gold facings and bolsters, the other with a black background and white designs silver facings, and bolsters.

Two-tone color combinations could be ordered on any pickup. Two-tone cabs featured a chrome molding to separate the Sand Dune White area above the molding from the choice of color for areas below the molding.

Engines and chassis

Chassis and mechanical improvements included suspended brake and clutch pedals; hydraulically-actuated clutch; new, improved Warner three-speed transmission, four-speed transmission standard for the D300 Model; larger and improved hydraulic brakes and improved master cylinders; new 3.54:1 rear-axle ratio for D100; new Spicer rear axle for D200 and W100; oil filter integral with the new 318 ci V–8; oil filters standard equipment on all V–8s; new, improved engine mountings; improved frames and improved ride and handling; new Spicer 60 rear axles rated at 4,500 lb. for D100 increased GVW from 5,100 to 6,000 lb.

The major mechanical advancement for 1959 was the use of new suspended clutch and brake pedal mountings. Suspending the pedals from brackets mounted to the cowl eliminated the necessity for pedal shaft holes through the floorboards and resulted in improved cab sealing. This also allowed the clutch and brake master cylinders to be mounted on the firewall for easier servicing.

In order to provide the best possible ride, the quietest operation and to help minimize maintenance, the Pickup's suspension systems were completely redesigned. For starters, the springs were straddle-mounted in tension-type shackles on the rear only, which used rubber bushings. A new one-piece design was also used for both shackles and brackets. This new-type shackle and bushing provided the following advantages: it eliminated the need for lubrication and insured a more constant friction level as the friction in grease-type bearing surfaces varies greatly depending on the amount of grease used; contributed to a lower noise level; eliminated sound transfers from unsprung components; increased roll stability; and simplified replacement of rubber bushings.

Increasing front spring width from 1¾ to 2 in. and rear spring width from 1¾ to 2½ in. added considerably to a better ride and easier handling.

Standard and optional equipment

Standard equipment for the half-ton pickup included one-pint oil bath air cleaner, 2,500 lb. capac-

ity front axle, 3,600 lb. capacity rear axle with 3.54:1, 4.1:1, 4.89:1 for the V–8 and 4.1:1 or 4.89:1 six-cylinder rear axle ratios, three-speed transmission, 50 amp battery, Sand Dune White painted front bumper and hubcaps, Standard cab equipment, 11 in. clutch, 230 ci six-cylinder standard engine, 17.4 gallon fuel tank mounted inside frame, 525 watt generator, short-arm rearview mirror, 15x5 in. rims, front and rear shocks, 900 lb. capacity front springs six-cylinder, 1,000 lb. V–8, 1,050 lb. capacity rear springs, underslung tire carrier, 6.70x15 four-ply tires, single taillight, five five-stud wheels, and dual electric, single-speed wipers.

Extra-cost optional equipment for the half-ton pickup included one-quart oil bath air cleaner; left-side armrest; 60 amp battery; chrome-plated front bumper; chrome or painted Sand Dune White rear bumper; spare tire carrier inside-mounted on Swept-line pickups and side-mounted for Utiline pickups; chrome trim package 1 included grille bars, headlight

The Tradesman was new for 1958 and could be outfitted to suit the requirements of any various businesses. The term

Tradesman was later applied to Dodge vans. This three-quarter-ton model is a 1959.

panel; chrome trim package 2 included grille bars, headlight panel, moldings on hood, fender housings and cab doors; increased cooling; chrome wheel covers set of four or five; Custom cab equipment; full-traction differential; signal lights; V–8 engine; electric fuel pump; generator for high charging at low engine speeds; tinted glass; engine governor; chrome or Sand Dune White grille guards; recirculating heater; fresh-air heater; hood ornament; dual electric horns; chrome hubcaps, set of four or five; heavy-duty instrument cluster included electric tachometer, oil pressure gauge and ammeter; hydraulic jack; cab marker lights; glovebox door lock; long-arm adjustable mirrors left and right; interior mirror; brightmetal moldings on Sweptline pickup; replaceable-element oil filter; two-tone paint, upper portion Sand Dune White, lower any standard color;

roof-mounted radio; foam rubber seatback and seat cushion; 1,000 lb. capacity front springs six-cylinder, 1,200 lb. eight-cylinder; 1,350 or 1,750 lb. capacity rear springs; power steering; 20 in. diameter steering wheel; auxiliary taillamp; hand throttle; three-speed transmission with overdrive; four-speed transmission; LoadFlite automatic; wraparound rear window; windshield washers; variable-speed dual electric windshield wipers.

Specifications and prices

Same as 1957 and 1958 except that optional V–8 was changed to 3.91x3.31 in. bore and stroke, 318 ci, and advertised 205 hp. Engine for W300 4x4, L–6, 3.43x4.5 in. bore and stroke, 251 ci, and advertised 125 hp.

D100–108 half-ton Series
Utiline Pickup, $1,781

Because 1960 was the last year of the Power-Giant Era, changes were limited. This half-ton 1960 Sweptline Pickup shows off its new grille panel and minor ornamentation changes, which were its only appearance changes.

Sweptline Pickup, $1,797
Town Panel, $2,062
Town Wagon, six pass., $2,336
Town Wagon, eight pass., $2,382
D100-116 half-ton Series
Utiline Pickup, $1,816
Sweptline Pickup, $1,832
Sweptside Pickup, $2,189
Stake, $1,902
Platform, $1,852
W100-108 half-ton 4x4 Series
Utiline Pickup, $2,589

Town Panel, $2,870
Town Wagon, six pass., $3,144
Town Wagon, eight pass., $3,190
W100-116 half-ton 4x4 Series
Utiline Pickup, $2,624
Stake, $2,710
Platform, $2,660
D200-116 three-quarter-ton Series
Utiline Pickup, $1,899
Sweptline Pickup, $1,915
Stake, $1,985
Platform, $1,935
W200-116 three-quarter-ton 4x4 Series
Utiline Pickup, $2,729
Stake, $2,815
Platform, $2,765
D300-126 one-ton Series
Utiline Pickup, $2,062
Sweptline Pickup, $2,078
Stake, $2,168
Platform, $2,108
W300-126 one-ton 4x4 Series
Utiline Pickup, $3,202
Stake, $3,407
Platform, $3,348

Elliott Kahn of Clearwater Beach, Florida, photographed this not-quite-stock condition 1960 Power Wagon Town Panel at a Florida car show. All Town Panel and Town Wagon Power Wagons are highly prized and sought after by collectors for their uniqueness, practicality and toughness.

Paul McLaughlin of Albuquerque, New Mexico, spotted this original-condition, 1960 half-ton pickup quietly parked and waiting for a new owner. This pickup is a "plain vanilla" model as seen by its small back window and absence of chrome trim, but it does have the high-line Sweptline box. Its black bumper, headlight trim and wheels are not correct; they should be Mojave Beige.

Production

Dodge introduced its new models on October 24, 1958. The downward trend in production continued in 1959, falling 19.7 percent to 77,767 in a year when industry production rose 27.8 percent. Naturally, market share fell again, to 6.5 percent. Canadian production was 6,087.

1960 P Series

In 1960, Dodge Truck management decided to move into the rapidly expanding medium- and heavy-duty market with new, cab forward C models powered by both gas and diesel engines. Dodge light-duty models improved in a number of minor ways, but were essentially carried over from 1959 without major change as Dodge was busy preparing a whole new generation of light-duty models for 1961, one of those rare years when everything from the wheels up changed.

Engine and chassis

On V-8 engines only, the oil-bath-type air cleaner, standard with Dodge since 1941, was dropped in favor of a replaceable-paper-element filter. V-8 engine buyers could still order the oil-bath type at extra cost if so desired. Dodge continued to make the oil-bath air cleaner standard equipment on six-cylinder engines.

In the interest of quieter operation, the fan on the 230 ci six was slowed by reducing fan speed to an engine speed ratio from 1.23:1 to 0.95:1 Cooling efficiency was maintained by using an 18 in. diameter fan.

Bodywork and interior

A one-piece Dodge nameplate on the front of the hood was new. The plate had a painted background with embossed letters and border. In addition, a diecast Dodge name and model series plate was attached to both sides of the hood. All 4x4 models used the name Power Wagon in place of Dodge. An attractive new grille, constructed of a single piece of aluminum with attached center medallion, added to the truck's appearance. The lower grille bar did not change. Chrome windshield moldings and chrome headlight trim rings continued as extra equipment.

Seat upholstery in the Standard cab was trimmed with a random stripe, black and beige saran without a bolster. The Custom cab upholstery used a black and gold woven checked saran with chain-pattern gold mylar, black saddle grain facings and bolsters. Welts were chain-pattern gold mylar.

The roof headlining was two pieces of embossed meadboard in Sand Dune White. This meadboard was a high-quality, moisture-proof material made by laminating films of plastic on both sides of fiberboard.

Door trim panels on Standard cabs were printed cardboard with the upper section matching the color and pattern of the seat trim material and the lower section matching the black saddle-grain facings. On Custom cabs, the door trim panels were saddle-grain background painted black with painted gold pattern. Bindings and fasteners for either scheme were black.

The steering wheel, steering column, handbrake lever and gearshift linkage were painted black, while clutch and brake pedal shafts were painted body color.

Two-tone paint schemes on P Series trucks were an exact duplicate of the M Series: Sand Dune White above the chrome moldings and any standard paint color below.

Standard and optional equipment

Standard equipment for the half-ton pickup was the same as 1959 except that the hubcaps were painted metallic gray.

Extra-cost optional equipment for the half-ton pickup was the same as 1959.

A rear view of Rod's 1960 Fargo reveals big, bold block letters spelling Fargo pressed into and painted on its tailgate.

This is a truck which doesn't exist! That is, Dodge did not build Sweptsides in 1960. Sweptside production terminated in January 1959. Rodney Harlan of Anaheim, California, purchased it several years ago with the understanding that it was in fact a 1960 Sweptside. Its serial number and engine number are correct for a 1960 half-ton, but we are at a loss to explain how it came to have a Sweptside body. It could be a fake; that is, a former owner could have mounted the body from an earlier Sweptside on the 1960 chassis or it could possibly be a special-order built by Dodge.

Rod Lindsey of Victoria, British Columbia, Canada, spent 2½ years restoring this 1960 Fargo half-ton to original specifications doing all the work himself. It has been a consistent trophy winner ever since. Rod's Fargo is powered by the correct Chrysler big-block L-6.

Specifications and prices

Same as 1959.

D100–108 half-ton Series
Utiline Pickup, $1,812
Sweptline Pickup, $1,826
Town Panel, $2,119
Town Wagon, six pass., $2,384
Town Wagon, eight pass., $2,431

D100–116 half-ton Series
Utiline Pickup, $1,847
Sweptline Pickup, $1,860
Stake, $1,931
Platform, $1,883

W100–108 half-ton 4x4 Series
Utiline Pickup, $2,578
Sweptline Pickup, $2,591
Town Panel, $2,884
Town Wagon, six pass., $3,150
Town Wagon, eight pass., $3,196

W100–116 half-ton 4x4 Series
Utiline Pickup, $2,612
Sweptline Pickup, $2,626
Stake, $2,696
Platform, $2,648

D200–116 three-quarter-ton Series
Utiline Pickup, $1,952
Sweptline Pickup, $1,966

Stake, $2,036
Platform $1,988

W200–116 three-quarter-ton 4x4 Series
Utiline Pickup, $2,719
Sweptline Pickup, $2,732
Stake, $2,803
Platform, $2,755

D300–126 one-ton Series
Utiline Pickup, $2,096
Sweptline Pickup, $2,110
Stake, $2,202
Platform, $2,143

W300–129 one-ton 4x4 Series
Utiline Pickup, $3,299
Stake, $3,406
Platform, $3,346

Production

New 1960 models went on display at Dodge dealers across the country on October 9, 1959. Sales this year weren't as bad as some because total production declined only 1.9 percent versus 19.7 percent the year before. Industry production was up by 6.7 percent, however, causing Dodge's market share to fall to 6 percent. Dodge management didn't know this at the time, but this is the lowest Dodge's market share would ever drop. After 1960, Dodge production and sales set off on a steady upward climb.

Chapter 8

Sweptline Era 1961–1971

1961 R Series

In 1960, Dodge Truck's market share was stuck at 6 percent, the lowest market penetration by Dodge since 1932. In fact, Dodge's sales had been falling at a sickening rate since 1953. To breathe life back into the truck division, Dodge used the same tactic it had used in 1933 to break out of that sales slump: an all-new truck with styling based on the passenger-car line was introduced, and truck sales immediately shot up and remained strong until 1952. For 1961, Dodge traded on its hot Dart passenger car, which had been new for 1960, and the Dart pickup was born.

These clays dated August 20, 1956, were two early proposals for the next-generation R truck, which was launched in 1961 (the Sweptline Era). Little of what we see here became reality. However, we do see the beginnings of some design elements that did reach production. For example, the basic cab roofline and windows were similar to the 1961 truck. And the 1961 grille is somewhat of a combination of the egg-crate type shown on the clay with the side-mounted spare, and the dual headlights from the other clay were somewhat akin to the 1961 style.

One of the first loads of 1961 Sweptline Era pickups pulls out of the Mound Road plant aboard a Dallas & Mavis rig. The C800 diesel-powered tractor was a new series with the 1960 model year. The C-series of gas and diesel medium- and heavy-duty trucks were Dodge's main offering through 1975.

Dodge's marketing strategy was for a reengineered pickup that was new from the ground up and featured "passenger car styling and handling characteristics with exceptionally high fuel economy de-

This scale clay of December 11, 1957, was another proposal for the 1961 Sweptline Era or R pickup. This truck's front-end treatment had grown closer in shape to the truck that was built. This truck had taken a step backward, however, in terms of its roof and windshield designs. The windshield was too tall and made the roof appear ready to blow off. An interesting trim idea shown on this clay was the plate designating its nominal size located immediately below the vent window. The smooth flow of its side was due to the fact the box was integral with the cab.

rived from the new inclined engines," in the words of Dodge General Manager M. C. Patterson. Don't be confused here; Patterson said the new Dart pickup featured "passenger car styling" but not that it shared sheet metal with Dodge cars. Patterson continued: "Our Dart pickup has a low wide silhouette with clean lines that flow smoothly from front to rear; a new drop-center frame, coupled with balanced design suspension and wide treads, gives the Dart exceptional road stability. Our two inclined overhead valve engines, designed for fuel economy, will interest every truck owner who wishes to reduce his fuel costs. We believe these engines will enable our new light-tonnage models to operate more economically than any comparable trucks on the road." In other words, Dodge management's strategy was to design and engineer a lower, wider, sleeker, more stylish and more fuel efficient truck to attract potential pickup buyers back to Dodge.

The drop-center frame siderails slanted downward at the cowl and slanted up again just aft of the cab, thus allowing the cab to sit 3 in. lower for easy entry and exit. Without a doubt, the Dart pickup was technologically far superior to any previous Dodge pickup, evidenced by its new ohv slant six, car-like styling, new frame, roomy, luxurious and comfortable cabs, alternator (an industry first), longer and wider springs, longer wheelbases and new easier steering due to relocating the steering gear, which now also had higher ratios for "passenger car handling ease."

These April 29, 1958, photos of a full-sized clay show the 1961 Sweptline Pickup approaching its final form. Here again Dodge designers used one design treatment on the right side and a second on the left side. The right side's shape was close to the final design that went into production. The grille was also close to production, as was the hood with its louvers, but the rear end and tailgate had not been finalized. The roofline windshield, rear and side window styles were all close to the production model. The nominal size (100) plate was not yet right and the parking lights were missing.

The first double-level Dodge panel since 1938? This August 21, 1958, photo of a full-sized clay pictured the 1961 Sweptline Pickup almost as introduced. This particular model, of course, was never released for production, but certainly it was an interesting design exercise as it made use of existing components. That is, a panel-type upper body was married to a Sweptline pickup box. Or, could we consider it a factory built pickup topper without windows?

An interesting fact is that half- and three-quarter-ton pickups shared the same frame, while one-ton pickups used a frame with straight siderails. One-ton pickup cabs sat higher, so Dodge engineers inserted a filler panel between the front bumper and the bottom of the grille panel to fill in the gap caused by the cab being perched higher on the frame. One-ton pickups offered the option of applied running boards that were identical to the standard running boards as used on medium-duty trucks.

The Sweptline pickup box was completely redesigned to complement the new styling theme. The box width was increased four inches, boosting cubic volume by thirteen percent. The increased width permitted a styled appearance of an integral cab and body by extending the side panel forward, close to the cab door trailing edge.

Engines and chassis

No changes were made in V–8 engines for 1961, but the six-cylinder engine lineup changed dramatically. This was the first year for the new, and now world famous, slant six. Two versions were introduced in 225 ci and 170 ci displacements. The 230 ci L–6, whose roots went all the way back to 1933, was now history. The only L–6 left was the 251 which became standard equipment this year for Power Wagon.

The 170 slant six was restricted to two trucks, the D100 pickup and P200, the smallest forward-control model; Dodge called it a "high economy" engine. This was the first year Ford offered its Econoline pickup and Chevrolet its Corvan pickup, both of which had smaller six-cylinder engines than Dodge's 170 slant six. Volkswagen, the pioneer in small, economical deliveries, had an even smaller four-cylinder

This 1961 Dart half-ton pickup's chrome bumper, full wheel covers, chrome side trim and two-tone paint identify it as a top-of-the-line model. The Dart nameplate lasted only one year. Dart pickups did not return in 1962.

engine. Without a compact truck line of its own to compete in this newest market segment, the 170 slant six allowed Dodge light-trucks to be almost as economical to operate as compacts. Fleet buyers were another reason the 170 was used. For light loads they wanted all the fuel economy possible, and some fleet buyers also preferred under-powered trucks which couldn't be hot-rodded.

Dodge set the pickup industry on its heels with the introduction of the alternator. Developed and built by Chrysler, the alternator charged even at idling speeds and reached its peak charge rate quickly. The charging system consisted of an alternator, rectifier assembly and voltage regulator. The alternator produced alternating current which the rectifier converted to direct current, while the regulator controlled the voltage. An alternator weighed 43 percent less than a comparable generator.

A new heavy-duty three-speed transmission, New Process Model A745, replaced the former three-speed transmission as standard equipment for D100, W100, D200 and W200 pickups. The three-speed transmission with overdrive was dropped.

In the final analysis, except for the wheels, the 1961 pickups were new from the ground up.

Standard and optional equipment

Standard equipment for the half-ton pickup included 35 amp alternator, 2,500 lb. capacity front axle, 3,600 lb. capacity rear axle with 3.58:1, 3.91:1, 4.56:1 ratios, 50-amp battery, external contracting parking brake on transmission, 10 in. hydraulic clutch, 225 slant six engine, one-pint oil bath air cleaner, 18 gallon inside, fuel tank behind seat, front and rear shocks, 1,025 lb. capacity front springs, 1,100 lb. capacity rear springs, 17 in. steering wheel, 6.70x15 four-ply tires, three-speed Chrysler A745 transmission, five five-stud disk wheels, dual single-speed wipers, metallic gray hubcaps, exterior mirror, wheel wrench and jack, left-hand sun visor, underslung spare tire carrier, electric horn, domelight and single taillight.

Extra-cost optional equipment for the half-ton pickup included one-quart oil bath air cleaner (six and V–8 engines); 40 amp alternator; driver's side armrest; chrome front bumper; painted rear bumper; chrome rear bumper; bright finish hubcaps, set of five; inside box tire carrier for Sweptline and side-mounted for Utiline pickup; cigar lighter, increased cooling; anti-spin differential; directional signals; 170 ci slant six (no extra charge); 318 ci V–8; oil pressure gauge; tinted glass; engine governor; fresh-air heater; recirculating heater; dual electric horns; heavy-duty instrument cluster; hydraulic jack; cab marker lights; auxiliary taillight; interior rearview mirror; long-arm adjustable rearview mirror, 5 in.

round or 5x7 in. head, right and left sides, replaceable-element oil filter; two-tone paint, radio; foam rubber seat cushion; 1,250 lb. capacity front springs; 1,400 or 1,750 lb. capacity rear springs; power steering; interior right-side sun visor; hand throttle control; four-speed transmission; three-speed automatic transmission; dual electric variable-speed wipers; full-width rear window; windshield washers.

Specifications and prices

D100 114 in. and D100 122 in. wheelbase half-ton, three-speed transmission, 6.70x15 four-ply tires.

D200 122 in. wheelbase three-quarter-ton, three-speed transmission, 6.50x16 six-ply tires.

D300 133 in. wheelbase one-ton, four-speed transmission, 8x17.5 six-ply tires.

Standard engine for all D100, D200 and D300 pickups was the 225 ci ohv six. The 170 ci ohv six was a no-cost option for the D100 only. A 318 ci ohv V–8 was an option for all pickups.

W100 114 in. wheelbase half-ton, three-speed transmission, 6.50x16 six-ply tires.

W200 122 in. wheelbase three-quarter-ton, three-speed transmission, 7x17.5 six-ply tires.

W300 133 in. wheelbase one-ton, four-speed transmission, 8x19.5 eight-ply tires. WM300 126 in. wheelbase one-ton, four-speed transmission, 9.00x16 eight-ply tires.

Standard engine for W100 and W200 was the 225 ci ohv six. Standard engine for W300 and

This 1961 225 slant six engine's appearance was typical of all slant sixes. From the left side, all routine servicing could be performed, including oil level, oil filter, water filter, air cleaner and battery. Also, Dodge scooped the industry in 1961 with its exclusive alternator.

WM300 was the 251 ci L-6. Optional engine for W100, W200 and W300 was the 318 ci ohv V-8. No other engine was available for the WM300.

D100-114 half-ton Series
Dart Utiline Pickup, $1,812
Dart Sweptline Pickup, $1,826
Town Panel, $2,119
Town Wagon, $2,384
Town Wagon, eight pass., $2,431
D-100 122 half-ton Series
Dart Utiline Pickup, $1,847
Dart Sweptline Pickup, $1,860
Stake, $1,931
Platform, $1,883
W100-114 half-ton 4x4 Series
Dart Utiline Pickup, $2,534
Dart Sweptline Pickup, $2,547
Town Panel, $2,840

Town Wagon, $3,106
Town Wagon, eight pass., $3,152
D200-122 three-quarter-ton Series
Utiline Pickup, $1,952
Sweptline Pickup, $1,966
Stake, $2,036
Platform, $1,988
W200-122 three-quarter-ton 4x4 Series
Utiline Pickup, $2,586
Sweptline Pickup, $2,599
Stake, $2,670
Platform, $2,622
W300 one-ton 4x4 Series
Utiline Pickup, $3,304
Stake, $3,411
Platform, $3,351
D300-133 one-ton Series
Utiline Pickup, $2,130

This photo dated August 16, 1960, showed the first slant six engine installation in a Dodge pickup.

A husky, medium-duty D700 chassis cab leaves the plant on its way to a new owner with a Town Wagon on its back and a Town Panel in tow.

A 1961 Town Wagon built for the US Navy. The Town Wagon and Town Panel were marketed through 1966 without change in both 4x2 and 4x4 versions.

Stake, $2,235
Platform, $2,176

Production

Finally, in 1961, Dodge hit the bottom of the long downhill production slide which began in 1953. As a matter-of-fact, total production in 1971, the last year of the Sweptline Era, was over three times greater than the 1961 output. Total production for calendar-year 1961, including Canada, was 64,886, or a decline of 6.4 percent over 1960. Market share held steady at 6 percent because total industry output dropped by 6.2 percent.

A strike at Dodge's Warren, Michigan, plant in December proved costly, because 4,300 less units were built in December than in November.

In August, the Government awarded contracts to Dodge for production of 10,254 trucks, 8,503 military 4x4s and 1,751 Forward Control delivery trucks for the Post Office.

Production by weight classes for the model year was as follows: D100 28,143, W100 615, D200 3,831, P200 1,191 (P models are Forward Control delivery trucks), W200 532, D300 4,908, P300 275 and W300

387. Military production was 3,190, and Canada built 6,496 trucks. Six-cylinder engines dominated in 1961 taking 67.6 percent of the total to 32.4 percent for V–8 engines.

1962 S Series

In the spring of 1961, Dodge management appointed Phil Buckminster to head Dodge Truck. Bucky, as he was called, was given the job of making Dodge Truck successful or Chrysler would get out of the truck business. It was too late in the model year to make a difference in 1961, but in 1962, Bucky began to show results as both sales and market share increased substantially. Bucky had set the wheels in motion in 1961, and began engineering and design work for the Compact Van, which was launched in midyear 1964. Dodge's Compact Van would later prove to be the most important new product Dodge Truck ever developed. It quickly proved to be a winner—a bases loaded home run—and established Dodge as the van leader, a position held to this day.

The formal introduction date for 1962 models was September 28, 1961. In mid 1962, however, Dodge renewed its former policy of dropping the annual introduction of new models in favor of introducing improvements as soon as they were perfected. Dropping the annual changeover also eliminated styling changes made merely for sake of change.

The Dart pickup disappeared after 1961. The pickup didn't change, only the name. In fact, no name was associated with 1962 pickups except Sweptline or Utiline. The Dart name had to be dropped because the Dodge car division would reveal a new compact car called Dart in 1963. It wouldn't be good to associate a full-sized, brawny truck with a compact car. Dodge's compact cars in 1961 and 1962 were called Lancers, a name which didn't interfere with the truck side of the business.

Because 1962 was only the second year for the new pickups, few appearance or mechanical changes were made. However, a redesigned grille greatly improved the 1962 truck's appearance. Gone was the light egg-crate-type grille of 1961, replaced by a restyled grille insert that contributed to a heavier, more massive look. A model numberplate was inserted in the center of the grille and Dodge nameplates replaced the model numberplates that had previously been attached to the front fenders.

Wider use was made of Chrysler-built electrical components in 1962 Dodge pickups as now all alternators, voltage regulators, distributors, solenoid shift starters and ballast resistors were sourced from Chrysler.

Additional engineering improvements included a new 18 in. steering wheel for D300 pickups. The

W100 and W200 Power Wagons for 1962 were powered by either a 225 slant six or a 318 V–8. One-ton W300 Power Wagons along with the military-style Power Wagon were powered by a 251 ci L-6. Transmission choices were three- or four-speed manuals. An automatic was not offered.

W300 steering gear changed to Gemmer Y–4D–335 from Gemmer Y–5D–375 to reduce steering effort and increase steering gear life. Outside running boards on D300 pickups became a mandatory, extra-cost item. All pickups were equipped with a mechanically-actuated stoplight switch, rather than a hydraulically-actuated switch. Inside-of-box spare tire carrier on Utiline pickups was replaced by a new, underslung carrier as standard equipment. A new, heavy-duty front axle was available as extra equipment for W200 pickups.

Dodge installed a turbine engine in a medium-duty truck, ran it 290 miles to Chicago as a test, and placed it on display at the Chicago Automobile show. A Chrysler spokesman said, "The Dodge Turbo Truck has been created as a research vehicle to explore the many facets of gas turbine engine application in the trucking industry." The CR2A gas turbine engine installed in the truck was the same type as used by Chrysler in various experimental gas turbine automobiles at that time.

Standard and optional equipment

Standard equipment for the half-ton pickup remained the same as in 1961.

Extra-cost optional equipment for the half-ton pickup remained the same as in 1961.

Specifications and prices

No specification changes from 1961.
D100–114 half-ton Series
Utiline Pickup, $1,800
Sweptline Pickup, $1,814
Town Panel, $1,998
Town Wagon, $2,263
Town Wagon, eight pass., $2,310
D100–122 half-ton Series
Utiline Pickup, $1,835

Does something look odd here? This Dodge nameplate was proposed for 1962 but was not approved. Production truck nameplates were made up of individual letters bolted to the hood. Dodge pickup's front-end styling, including grille, which began in 1962, continued without change up to midyear 1965.

Sweptline Pickup, $1,848
Stake, $1,919
Platform, $1,871
W100–114 half-ton 4x4 Series
Utiline Pickup, $2,474
Sweptline Pickup, $2,487
Town Panel, $2,780
Town Wagon, $3,046
Town Wagon, eight pass., $3,092
D200–122 three-quarter-ton Series
Utiline Pickup, $1,940
Sweptline Pickup, $1,954
Stake, $2,024
Platform, $1,976
W200–122 three-quarter-ton 4x4 Series
Utiline Pickup, $2,525
Sweptline Pickup, $2,538
Stake, $2,609
Platform, $2,561
W300–133 one-ton 4x4 Series
Utiline Pickup, $3,304
Stake, $3,411
Platform, $3,351
D300–133 one-ton Series
Utiline Pickup, $2,118
Stake, $2,233
Platform, $2,164

Production

Dodge truck production hit the bottom of its long slide and in 1962 headed up with a vengeance, shooting all the way up to 102,484 units—an impressive 43.6 percent gain! Market share also recovered rather well, up to 7.7 percent, which was a 28.3 percent improvement over 1961.

Production by weight classes for the model year were as follows: D100 30,144, W100 677, D200 5,969, P200 1,887, W200 1,083, D300 5,656, P300 651 and W300 418. Military trucks totalled 14,322, and Canadian production was 6,382.

1963 T Series

No changes were made whatsoever in styling or ornamentation on 1963 Dodge trucks no doubt due to the new policy of "no annual model changes" that Dodge instituted in 1962.

Engines and chassis

A new version of the 225 slant six was introduced this year. The 225–2 Premium replaced the 251 L–6 in various medium models including the W300 pickup. Only the Power Wagon continued to use the 251 L–6. Premium components that enabled the 225–2 to power medium-ton trucks included roller timing chain, bi-metal connecting rod bearings, stellite-faced exhaust valves, roto caps on exhaust valves and polyacrylic valve stem seals.

Miscellaneous other changes in the pickups included replacing 1,100 lb. front springs with 1,350 lb. springs on W100 and W200 pickups; Model W300 pickup 2,450 lb. rear springs replaced by 3,250 lb. springs; pickup cab seat was given improved coil springs and seatback was made adjustable for angle; full-depth, foam seats were made standard on Custom cabs and extra on Standard cabs; the attached running boards, which were made mandatory, extra-cost equipment in 1962, were now made standard equipment for D300 pickups.

This was the year for the first-ever Dodge-built crew cab pickups. Prior to 1963 Dodge crew cabs were built by outside converters. Only D200 and W200 three-quarter-ton pickups on 146 in. wheelbase were available, but with either Utiline or Sweptline bodies.

Standard and optional equipment

Standard equipment for the half-ton pickup remained the same as in 1962. Extra-cost optional equipment remained the same as in 1962 but added traffic-hazard warning switch; undercoating; trim package 1, consisting of bright finish moldings on hood, cowl, door and cab back; trim package 2, consisting of bright finish front bumper and moldings on hood, cowl, doors, cab back and body sides; three trailer towing packages.

Specifications and prices

All specifications remained the same except the standard engine in the W300 was changed to the 225–2, which was the 225 six equipped with premium features for service in medium-duty models. Optional engine for W300 was changed to the 318–2, which was the 318 V–8 equipped with premium features for service in medium-duty models.

D100–122 half-ton Series
Utiline Pickup, $1,844
Sweptline Pickup, $1,857
Stake, $1,928
Platform, $1,880
D100–114 half-ton Series
Utiline Pickup, $1,809
Sweptline Pickup, $1,823
Town Panel, $2,007
Town Wagon, $2,272
Town Wagon, eight pass., $2,319
W100–114 half-ton 4x4 Series
Utiline Pickup, $2,486
Sweptline Pickup, $2,499
Town Panel, $2,792
Town Wagon, $3,058
Town Wagon, eight pass., $3,104
D200–122 three-quarter-ton Series
Utiline Pickup, $1,949
Sweptline Pickup, $1,963

Stake, $2,033
Platform, $1,985
D200–146 three-quarter-ton Series
Crew cab Utiline Pickup, $2,557
Crew cab Sweptline Pickup, $2,571
W200–122 three-quarter-ton 4x4 Series
Utiline Pickup, $2,537
Sweptline Pickup, $2,550
Stake, $2,621
Platform, $2,573
W200–146 three-quarter-ton 4x4 Series
Crew cab Utiline Pickup, $3,256
Crew cab Sweptline Pickup, $3,269
D300–133 one-ton Series
Utiline Pickup, $2,147
Stake, $2,252
Platform, $2,193
W300–133 one-ton 4x4
Utiline Pickup, $3,313
Stake, $3,420
Platform, $3,360

Production

Following the lead set in model-year 1962, 1963 kept pace with a respectable 17.8 percent increase or 120,678 total trucks built. The industry's total increased 17.2 percent, meaning that Dodge's market share stayed constant at 7.7 percent.

Production by weight classes for the model year was as follows: D100 41,018, W100 1,283, D200 11,657, P200 3,117, D300 6,674, P300 646 and W300 515. Production in Canada capped off at 9,691, and 13,500 military trucks were built. Dodge gasoline-powered trucks in 1963 were led by sixes at 65.2 percent of total; V–8s took 34.8 percent.

This was the best year for Dodge truck production since the slump that began in the 1953 model year. Thankfully the downturn was now history.

1964 V Series

In 1964, Dodge's most exciting and interesting collector pickups of the decade were introduced, the Custom Sports Special and the compact A100.

The Custom Sports Special went into production in 1964 after consumer testing by motor-minded Californians in 1963. A Custom Sports Special was an extra-cost option package available on D100, D200, W100 and W200 122 in. wheelbase Sweptline pickups only.

135

Dodge tested the waters before going into production with the Custom Sports Special by placing a preproduction model in the hands of the motoring press in California for testing and evaluation, and to get a reading on consumer reaction. The auto writers loved it, and it was their enthusiasm for this wild sports pickup that convinced Dodge management to produce it.

In reality, the Custom Sports Special was an option package added to the buyer's choice of D100, D200, W100 or W200 pickups in either Utiline or Sweptline models. The Custom Sports Special was a pickup with sporty looks inside and out. The option package of standard items included luxurious black vinyl bucket seats with a console between them (these items came from a Dodge passenger car); plush carpeting from the firewall to the top of the gas tank behind the seats; dual armrests and sun visors; an easy-to-read instrument cluster; chrome grille, bumper and roof moldings; and four 1 in. wide sports car racing stripes extending over the roof and hood; the racing stripes were white when the body color was dark, and black when the body color was light.

Bucket seats, with a console in pickups, are old hat today, but in 1964 this cab interior package was revolutionary. Nevertheless, it received immediate acceptance from normally conservative truck buyers. Dodge offered an optional Bucket Seat Package for all cab models shortly after introducing the Custom Sports Special because bucket seats proved to be so popular.

Dave Mayer of Lynnwood, Washington, is the owner of this outstanding 1964 D100 Utiline. Dave consistently wins the best truck award at Slant 6 Club of America meets.

This 1964 Custom Sports Special is owned by Marlan Ramsey of Edina, Minnesota. It is the only Custom Sports Special I know of. This truck is in original condition and is used by his son as a daily driver. Marlan intends to restore it in the near future.

Dave's slant six engine is as clean and nice as the rest of his truck.

Under the hood, Dodge offered everything from economical to wild. Base engine was the 140 hp slant six 225. Options were the 318 with 200 hp and the 426 Wedge V–8, rated at a whopping 365 hp. The 426 Wedge featured 10.2:1 compression ratio, a four-barrel carburetor, high-lift, long-duration camshaft, hydraulic lifters and required premium fuel. Neither Chevrolet nor Ford at the time could offer anything approaching the 426 in size or performance. With the high-performance 426 engine, the following equipment was mandatory: power steering, heavy-duty instrument cluster and tachometer, Loadflite automatic, rear-axle struts and dual exhaust.

Putting the power to use, the buyer could choose from a three-on-the-tree; a four-speed with synchros in third and fourth mounted on the floor; or a three-speed, push-button automatic.

Because the Custom Sports Special was not a model as such, there are no separate production figures. It is suspected that few were sold because virtu-

ally none exist today. Or, it could be that they were driven into the ground. If you stumble on one, especially a 426 powered Custom Sports Special, buy it. It's a rare and valuable truck, which will not only appreciate, but be a lot of fun to own and drive.

Dodge's first compact pickup, the A100, was announced to the public early in January 1964 for production in February. Dodge was the last to enter the compact market, a market pioneered by Volkswagen back in the 1950s. Being the last one in has certain advantages because it allows one to study thoroughly the competition and play a little game of one-upmanship. This is exactly what Dodge did, and immediately established itself as the compact truck leader, as the van business was called in those days. This is a leadership position Dodge has never relinquished.

Dodge's A100 pickup scooped the competition in that it could haul 2,130 lb. of payload versus 2,050 lb. for its closest competitor, provided the largest

By 1964, light-duty trucks were playing a major role in recreational use, including pickup slide-on campers, toppers, *trailer towing and, in this case, a 1964 three-quarter-ton cab chassis fitted with a Roll-A-Long Sportster housecar.*

137

1964–1970 A 100 and A108 Compact Trucks

Dodge fumbled its Route-Van program, but a decade later Dodge hits a bases-loaded home run with its compact truck line. Since 1953, Dodge's sales performance had been shaky due in large measure to the intense sales rivalry between Ford and Chevrolet. In 1961, Ford and Chevrolet inserted their import fighters into the light-duty truck wars; these were Ford's Econoline van and pickup, and Chevrolet's Corvair van and pickup. The marketplace decided early on that Ford's entry was on target but that Chevrolet missed the mark (Chevrolet debuted its conventionally styled Chevy Van in 1964). Econoline's immediate sales success was very much noticed by Dodge.

In 1962, Dodge launched a compact truck program of its own. Dodge Truck at this time had its back up against the wall. Its fortunes had to improve and improve fast if it was going to remain in the truck business, so the pressure was on. The first thing they did was to go out and buy ten Econoline vans to study. One of these they literally cut in half to better examine its construction. Dodge engineering had learned some hard lessons from the Route-Van's lack of body structural integrity; there was no way they were going to repeat that mistake. After thoroughly studying the Econoline, it became apparent to Dodge engineers what they needed to do. Their conclusion was that Ford's Econoline was basically good, but Dodge engineering believed they could build a superior van by designing in more structural quality. This was done by beefing up the body with more and heavier gussets, more welds, more metal bends and supports, and the use of heavy-duty hinges on all passenger and cargo compartment doors.

Product development is naturally easier, faster and less expensive when one can draw "inspiration" from someone else's efforts. All of the Big Three owed a tip of their hats to Volkswagen for pioneering the van business; the van's basic size, shape, small engine size and even the name "compact" were borrowed from Volkswagen's Micro Bus and Combi. The streets of America would look far different today if Volkswagen had not shown the way. Fortunately, Dodge engineering did its work well. By creating a van which became an immediate sales success, Dodge took over as the van leader, a position they have maintained a hammerlock on to this day.

Dodge engineering developed their compact truck with the express goal of maintaining Dodge's reputation for dependability and toughness. In addition to greater body structural integrity, Dodge compacts were powered by a larger standard engine and its optional engine was also larger. Plus, Dodge offered the only heavy-duty three-speed, steering-column-mounted manual transmission. Greater strength and power allowed Dodge to handle bigger payloads, and Dodge again led the field with the largest payload rating of any compact. Going hand-in-hand with its larger payloads and toughness were heavier front and rear axles, and larger brakes. Finally, Dodge was the only one in the compact truck field to offer, as extra equipment, both 14 in. and 15 in. wheels and tires.

Dodge was not content to sit idly by and continue its exceptional compact line as it was. Instead, for its second year, a V-8 engine became an option, the only V-8 engine in any compact truck. The 273 ci V-8 produced 174 gross hp. Both slant sixes—the 101 hp 170 and the 140 hp 225—were retained. The V-8 added a new dimension to the compact's performance. Now, due to greater power, an owner could make deliveries much faster, and when not on the job, he could make better time carrying a pickup camper and pulling a boat trailer keeping up with traffic on the freeways.

Nothing changed for 1966, but 1967 was a most important year for Dodge's compact line. New was the A108 Extended Van built on a 108 in. wheelbase, versus the A100's 90 in. wheelbase. An A108 is easy to distinguish from an A100 because the additional body length was added between the front passenger door and side cargo doors, not tacked on to the body's rear as was done with second-generation vans.

In 1967, along with a bigger body, Dodge also provided a larger engine, the 210 hp 318 V-8. The 273 V-8 was dropped, but the two slant sixes carried on as before. The A100 pickup did not change, and it was also available with the 318 V-8.

After the 1967 major new product introductions, no changes were made at all in 1968. The 1969 introduction was almost as quiet, the only new item of note being an optional, roof-mounted factory air conditioner. Sadly, however, 1969 would be the last year for the A100 pickup. One peculiar event of note for 1970 is that the Sportmans Wagons (passenger vans) only, which were merchandised as cars (station wagons), not trucks, and officially tabulated by the industry as cars, were now powered by a new 198 ci 120 hp slant six as its base engine with the 225 as an option.

Early in the spring, Dodge released its second-generation van. This was basically the large Dodge van still in production. The new van meant the end of the A100 and A108 vehicles. A pickup was not included in the new lineup. Dodge had been building the industry's only compact pickup since 1967, the last year Ford built its Econoline pickup.

All 1964–1970 Compact Van and Pickup models are sought after by collectors, especially the unique A100 Pickup as it was the lowest production item and is therefore more desirable. Seek out compacts powered by the 225 six or the V-8 for superior performance. Also, look for a pickup equipped with cab corner windows, which not only enhances its appearance, but improves drivers' vision as well.

A D100 half-ton Pickup was cut open and specially prepared for the car show circuit. This show truck was equipped with a slant six, and its style was typical of 1962 to Second-Series 1965 pickups.

standard and optional engines, largest optional wheels at 15 in., largest fuel tank at 21 gallons, largest brakes, more comfortable bucket seats, and a long list of optional and custom equipment items including rear-quarter windows.

A100 pickups are still readily available, but one seldom sees a well maintained or even a fully restored one. These economical and fun pickups could grow in demand and value in the coming years.

Standard and optional equipment

Standard equipment for the half-ton pickup remained the same as in 1963.

Extra-cost optional equipment for the half-ton pickup remained the same as in 1963, but added seatbelts, Camper Package and Custom Sport Special Package.

Specifications and prices

A100 90 in. wheelbase compact, three-speed transmission, 6.50x13 four-ply tires. Standard engine was the 170 six, optional engine was the 225 six.

D100 114 in. and 122 in. wheelbase half-ton, three-speed transmission, 6.70x15 four-ply tires.

D200 122 in. wheelbase three-quarter-ton, three-speed transmission, 6.50x16 six-ply tires.

D300 133 in. wheelbase one-ton, four-speed transmission, 8x17.5 six-ply tires.

Standard engine for all D100, D200 and D300 pickups was the 225 six. The 170 six was a no-cost

This photo dated July 30, 1959, was the earliest design proposal I know of for the Compact pickup. The general concept was close to the A100 Pickup of 1964, even though no details were similar to the finished design.

Less than three years earlier, April 16, 1962, this ⅛ in. scale clay of a Compact pickup was closer in shape to the final Compact A100 pickup.

option for D100 only. A 318 V–8 was an option for all pickups.

W100 114 in. wheelbse half-ton, three-speed transmission, 6.50x16 six-ply tires.

W200 122 in. wheelbase three-quarter-ton, three-speed transmission, 7x17.5 six-ply tires.

W300 133 in. wheelbase one-ton, four-speed transmission, 8x19.5 eight-ply tires. WM300 126 in.

Less than two years before its mid 1964 model year introduction, this September 1962, A100 Pickup proposal appeared to be the final model. If you have exceptional vision you will be able to read the nameplate on its door—Saratoga. Saratoga was a nameplate used on Chrysler cars for many years, but was not used for the A100 pickup or any Dodge truck.

wheelbase one-ton, four-speed transmission, 9.00x16 eight-ply tires.

Standard engine for W100 and W200 was the 225 six. Standard engine for W300 was the 225–2 and for the WM300 the 251 L–6. Optional engine for W100 and W200 was the 318 V–8, for the W300 it was the 318–2 V–8. No other engine was available for WM300.

D100–114 half-ton Series
Utiline Pickup, $1,809
Sweptline Pickup, $1,823
Town Panel, $2,007
Town Wagon, $2,272
Town Wagon, eight pass., $2,319
D100–122 half-ton Series
Utiline Pickup, $1,844
Sweptline Pickup, $1,857
Stake, $1,928
Platform, $1,880
A100–90 half-ton Series
Pickup, $1,752
Panel Van, rear doors only, $1,893
Van, $1,943
W100–114 half-ton 4x4 Series
Utiline Pickup, $2,486
Sweptline Pickup, $2,499
Town Panel, $2,792
Town Wagon, $3,058
Town Wagon, eight pass., $3,104
D200–122 three-quarter-ton Series

Dodge designed, engineered and equipped its Compact A100 pickup with a larger engine, heavier axles, heavier springs, *and bigger wheels to enable it to outwork its two major competitors. The pickup had a load capacity of 2,130 lb.*

Utiline Pickup, $1,949
Sweptline Pickup, $1,963
Stake, $2,033
Platform, $1,985
D200–146 three-quarter-ton Series
Crew cab Utiline Pickup, $2,557
Crew cab Sweptline Pickup, $2,571
W200–122 three-quarter-ton 4x4 Series

Utiline Pickup, $2,537
Sweptline Pickup, $2,550
Stake, $2,621
Platform, $2,573
W200–146 three-quarter-ton 4x4 Series
Crew cab Utiline Pickup, $3,256
Crew cab Sweptline Pickup, $3,269
D300–133 one-ton Series

The Dodge A100 Compact Van, when introduced in 1964, was the last van of its type to come to market. Therefore, Dodge's Compact Van was styled better, built better and *equipped with more power to give it the ability to work harder. In 1964, with the van shown, Dodge established itself as the industry's van leader.*

Utiline Pickup, $2,147
Stake, $2,252
Platform, $2,193
W300–133 one-ton 4x4 Series
Utiline Pickup, $3,313
Stake, $3,420
Platform, $3,360

Production

Due to the excitement created by introducing the Custom Sports Special pickups and the A100 line of compact trucks, Dodge production continued on its uphill climb to 148,692, gaining 23.2 percent on the way. Market share bounced up to 8.9 percent, a healthy 15.6 percent gain, making the 1964 market share Dodge's best showing since 1954. Dodge truck total production more than doubled the total posted in 1961.

Production by weight classes for the model year was as follows: D100 53,912, W100 1,285, D200 13,030, P200 2,473, W200 3,044, D300 6,451, P300 873, W300 518 and compacts 10,252. Canadian production was 13,062, and military trucks totalled 8,081.

1965 A Series

Second-series 1965 Dodge pickups were reengineered, revised and redesigned to make them better able to handle slide-in pickup campers. In keeping with its policy of no annual model changes, the new models went on sale in the spring of 1965 without a great deal of fuss, in spite of the fact that second-series 1965 trucks were extensively and dramatically changed.

Bodywork and interior

First of all, the wheelbase on D100, D200 and W200 models was stretched to 128 in. to provide better weight distribution for hauling big loads, in particular, campers. Going hand-in-hand with the longer wheelbase was a new 8 ft. pickup box. The 8 ft. length provided tremendous utility for those who hauled standard 8 ft. long construction items such as plywood panels, wallboard and studs.

Along with the longer box, Dodge engineers provided a full-width tailgate, a full 65 in. wide and operable with a single-handle, double-latch mechanism opened easily with one hand. Hinged steel straps replaced chains to hold the tailgate in a horizontal position. A wider tailgate was another concession to pickup camper buyers.

One last concession for pickup camper owners was to redesign the rear of the Sweptline box to make it perfectly vertical, not "tumblehome," or slightly off vertical.

Another important improvement in Sweptline body construction was the new full-depth, double-wall sides. Dodge's double wall was full height, not

Delivering light loads as seen here was a typical application for an A100 Van. Its larger standard slant six engine and, beginning in 1965, its powerful V–8 (the only V–8 in its class) enabled it to more quickly deliver its assigned route.

This husky A100 Pickup is taking on a man-sized load of fertilizer. Cab corner windows (not shown here) were an optional item that improved the appearance of the A100 Pickup, but more importantly added to driving safety.

In 1965, Dodge Truck operated under a policy of no annual model changes for change sake. The 1965 model half-ton shown here was discontinued about midyear and replaced without fanfare by a restyled and reengineered Second Series model.

ordinary double wall as used by both Ford and Chevrolet, which extended up only two-thirds of the box's height.

Dodge designers gave 1965 models an even better outward appearance with a new full-width grille. The new grille lent a wider, lower and more massive look to the front end. It no longer had a model numberplate, which instead was placed on each front fender below the Dodge nameplate. Single headlamps replaced the old duals to reduce replacement costs. In the rear, new slim-line taillights added to the all-new appearance. Now taillight, brake light and directional signal were all housed in a single unit. For the first time ever, all Dodge pickups were factory equipped with turn signals as standard equipment.

In keeping with the trend to upgrade pickup cab interiors, Dodge greatly improved both the Standard cab and Custom cab interiors. Upholstery trim, door trim panels, sun visors and roof trim panels were now

a bright and attractive white, a big improvement over the gray trim used in prior years.

Cab interiors were also upgraded in that separate interior comfort and appearance packages were made available. The comfort package included a left-hand armrest, right-hand sun visor, cigar lighter, cab insulation, full foam rubber seat cushion, three new upholstery colors and a breathable, vinyl seat upholstery.

The appearance package consisted of a white steering wheel with full chrome horn ring, textured-metal door trim panels, bright instrument panel trim, chrome grille, mylar windshield and rear window moldings, Delta emblems on lower rear front fenders, Custom nameplate below the vent window and bright drip moldings.

Engines and chassis

Dodge further strengthened its hold on the compact pickup market by making big news by adding a hard-working, 174 hp, 273 ci V-8 engine to its compact truck line. Now anyone with a heavy load to haul, such as a camper, could now do so. The hefty V-8 provided the extra power needed for hauling

This Dodge ad promoting the wide variety of available campers was typical for 1965. Clockwise from upper left was a D200 Crew Cab with slide-on camper, A100 Sportsman Wagon, Dodge Motor Home, D200 Camper Special pickup with slide-on camper, D200 chassis cab with camper body, A100 Pickup with fiberglass special slide-on camper and a W200 4x4 Pickup with slide-on camper.

A Second-Series 1965 Dodge ad touted its reengineered Pickup with a new, double-wall box, new longer 128 in. wheelbase, new cab-interior styling and a tailgate that could be operated with one hand.

heavy loads around town and on the highway. Dodge teamed the V-8 with its heavy-duty, A745 three-speed transmission or with the optional three-speed LoadFlite automatic. The same two transmissions were used on half- and three-quarter-ton pickups with new dash-mounted, automatic transmission gearshift levers; push-button transmission controls were dropped.

In 1965, Dodge first announced, along with all Chrysler car lines, a five year or 50,000 mile engine and drivetrain warranty. This was something the other major manufacturers didn't adopt until late in the 1980s.

Standard and optional equipment

Standard equipment for the half-ton pickup remained the same as in 1964.

Extra-cost optional equipment for the half-ton pickup remained the same as in 1964.

The Custom Sports Package consisted of bucket seats, custom carpeting, 1 in. stripes, bright mylar molding around windshield and rear window, Dodge Delta emblems on B posts, bright molding on instrument panel, textured-metal door trim panels, bright horn ring, armrests, sun visors, additional insulation, console with lighter and map light, black carpet over gas tank cover, chrome grille, chrome drip moldings, Custom nameplates, chrome trim on instrument cluster, hood around dials and knobs, white steering wheel and chrome front bumper, $255.30

The High Performance Package for the D100 consisted of engine Model 426 Wedge, rear axle struts, rear axle ratios of 3.23:1, 3.55:1 or 3.91;1, 1,750 lb. capacity rear springs, A727 Loadflite auto-

The cutest camper of all was the A100 Pickup equipped with the fiberglass Cam-Pact slide-on unit that was sized and styled to fit the 90 in. wheelbase A100 Pickup. The available V-8 engine provided ample power to speed vacationers along at freeway speeds without slowing for hills.

The front grille on Dodge pickups changed from 1961 to 1962, and then kept with the new design until mid 1965. The front-end shape was much the same, but the new grille radically altered the look. Greg Norman

1965 - 66   1967 - 68

Midway through 1965, the front end was revamped and the modification lasted through 1966. For 1967-1968, the front was completely redesigned yet again. Greg Norman

matic, vacuum brake booster, heavy-duty instrument cluster, power steering and 6,300 rpm tachometer, $1,235.60. The High Performance Package was available with or without the Custom Sports Package. It could be ordered on D100 or D200 128 in. wheelbase Utiline or Sweptline pickups.

Dodge management was serious about capturing as much of the pickup camper market as possible.

In addition to the lengthened wheelbase, longer body and wider tailgate, Dodge marketed eight pickup camper packages. Based on 128 in. wheelbase D100, D200, D200 crew cab (160 in. wheelbase) and W200, the Camper Packages featured special base equipment of a heavy-duty nature, plus either Deluxe or Custom Camper Packages for the above four models. These packages added comfort and appearance items

`69          `70 - `71

Changes to the front end were minor after 1969, with a redesign of the grille being the focus for 1970-1971. Greg Norman

146

'61 - EARLY '65

MID '65 - '71

The rear-end appearance changed more slowly on Dodge pickups. Here are the two designs for 1961 through early 1965 and from mid 1965 through to 1971. Greg Norman

to the basic Camper packages. An attractive and functional fiberglass slide-on camper unit was available for the A100 pickup too, now that the 273 V-8 was available.

Specifications and prices

All specifications remained the same except at midyear wheelbase lengths on the long wheelbase half-ton D200 and W200 models changed from 122

The major front-end style change in midyear 1965 was the elimination of dual headlights and the broadening of the grille, *which caused Dodge trucks to look wider and heavier. This truck was an early 1966 Standard cab Utiline half-ton.*

in. to 128 in. The 273 ci ohv V–8 also became an optional engine for A100 compacts.

D100–114 half-ton Series
Utiline Pickup, $1,833

Tadd Faubion of Portland, Oregon, is a Slant 6 Club of America member who proudly displays his Second-Series 1965 D100 Sweptline pickup at Club events.

Sweptline Pickup, $1,847
Town Panel, $2,088
Town Wagon, $2,378
Town Wagon, eight pass., $2,424
D100–128 half-ton Series
Utiline Pickup, $1,868
Sweptline Pickup, $1,881
Stake, $1,952
Platform, $1,904
A100–90 half-ton Series
Pickup, $1,752
Panel Van, $1,893
Van, $1,943
W100–114 half-ton 4x4 Series
Utiline Pickup, $2,510
Sweptline Pickup, $2,523
Town Panel, $2,813
Town Wagon, $3,079
Town Wagon, eight pass., $3,125
D200–128 three-quarter-ton Series
Utiline Pickup, $1,973
Sweptline Pickup, $1,987

The Second-Series 1965 Pickup featured more than a new front appearance. The wheelbase on long-box half-ton and three-quarter-ton Pickups was stretched from 122 to 128 in., rear styling was updated and the Sweptline box, as seen here, was made of full double-wall construction. The box was given a new full-width tailgate, which could be operated by a one-hand tailgate latch. The new tailgate also eliminated the old-fashioned chains.

Stake, $2,057
Platform, $2,009
D200–146 three-quarter-ton Series
Crew cab Utiline Pickup, $2,581
Crew cab Sweptline Pickup, $2,595
W200–128 three-quarter-ton 4x4 Series
Utiline Pickup, $2,561
Sweptline Pickup, $2,574
Stake, $2,645
Platform, $2,597
W200–146 three-quarter-ton 4x4 Series
Crew cab Utiline Pickup, $3,280
Crew cab Sweptline Pickup, $3,293
D300–133 one-ton Series
Utiline Pickup, $2,171
Stake, $2,276
Platform, $2,217
W300–133 one-ton 4x4 Series
Utiline Pickup, $3,337
Stake, $3,344
Platform, $3,384

Production

Although posting a lower percentage gain than in the past three years, production was still on the upswing, topping off at 160,792 or a gain of 8.1 percent. Market share actually dropped a bit to 8.3 percent because total industry production was up by 16.4 percent over 1964.

Production by weight classes for the model year was as follows: D100 55,465, W100 1,145, D200 15,697, P200 1,002, W200 2,532, D300 7,952, P300 1,159, W300 675 and compacts 38,883.

Canadian production was 17,340, and military was 8,475. Six-cylinder engines were installed in 58.8 percent of total gas-powered trucks and V–8s took a 41.2 percent share.

1966 B Series

Due to the extensive changes made in the 1965 pickup line, changes for 1966 were minimal.

While still in the line, the Custom Sports Special had its fangs pulled: the 426 was no longer an option. Base engine was the 225 and the 318 V–8 optional. In the end, the engine lineup remained the same with the other full-sized pickups. The 426 had only been used in the Custom Sports Special, never in any other Dodge truck model, in any year. At least one special-order Custom Sports Special left the factory with a Hemi 426.

A major new offering, standard on D300 and W300, and optional on D100, D200, W100 and W200, was a new close-ratio, four-speed manual transmission, the NP 435, which permitted higher speeds in lower gears. A driver could now shift into third at a high speed to either pass or climb a grade,

yet another example of Dodge catering to the camper market.

All Camper Special models now carried a Camper Special nameplate on each front fender, the only visual appearance change for 1966.

Standard and optional equipment

Standard equipment for the half-ton pickup included six-cylinder 225 engine, 6.70x15 four-ply tubeless passenger-car-type tires, five 5 in. disk wheels, 2,500 lb. capacity front axle, 3,600 lb. capacity rear axle with 3.23:1, 3.55:1 or 3.91:1 ratio, 1,025 lb. capacity front springs, 1,100 lb. capacity rear springs, hydraulic shock absorbers front and rear, three-speed transmission, one-pint oil bath air cleaner, 35 amp alternator, 53 amp battery, 10 in. clutch, directional signals, metallic gray painted hubcaps, interior and exterior mirror, front bumper, electric horn, domelight, wheel wrench and jack, left-hand sun visor, underslung spare tire carrier and seatbelts.

Extra-cost optional equipment for the half-ton pickup included full-width rear window; one-quart oil bath air cleaner; 46 or 59 amp alternator; right-side armrest; 70 amp battery; chrome-plated front bumper; painted or chrome-plated rear bumper; inside box spare tire for Sweptline and outside-left-mounted for Utiline; 11 in. clutch for 225 engine; increased cooling; anti-spin rear axle; 318 ci V–8 engine; oil pressure gauge; tinted glass; engine governor; fresh-air heater; custom fresh-air heater; dual electric horns; chrome-plated hubcaps; heavy-duty instrument cluster; hydraulic jack; cigar lighter; cab marker lights, exterior rearview mirror; trim molding package for Sweptline pickups; two-tone paint; radio; foam-padded seat and seatback; front springs 1,250 lb. capacity front springs; 1,400 or 1,750 lb. capacity rear springs; power steering; four-speed transmission; three-speed automatic transmission; right-side sun visor; traffic hazard warning switch; hand-throttle; undercoating.

Specifications and prices

A100 90 in. wheelbase compact, three-speed transmission, 6.50x13 four-ply tires. Standard engine was the 225 six, optional engine was the 273 V–8.

D100 114 in. and 128 in. wheelbase half-ton, three-speed transmission, 6.70x15 four-ply tires.

D200 128 in. wheelbase three-quarter-ton, three-speed transmission, 6.50x16 six-ply tires.

D300 133 in. wheelbase one-ton, four-speed transmission, 8x17.5 six-ply tires.

Standard engine for D100 and D200 was the 225 six, standard engine for D300 was the 225-2 six. Optional engine for D100 and D200 was the 318 V–8 and for the D300 the 318-2 V–8.

W100 114 in. wheelbase half-ton, three-speed transmission, 6.50x16 six-ply tires.

W200 128 in. wheelbase three-quarter-ton, three-speed transmission, 7x17.5 six-ply tires.

W300 133 in. wheelbase one-ton, four-speed transmission, 8x19.5 eight-ply tires. WM300 126 in. wheelbase one-ton, four-speed transmission, 9.00x16 eight-ply tires.

Standard engine for W100 and W200 was the 225 six. Standard engine for W300 was the 225–2 six and for the WM300 it was the 251 L–6. Optional engine for W100 and W200 was the 318 V–8, for the W300 it was the 318–2 V–8. No other engine was available for WM300.

D100–114 half-ton Series
Utiline Pickup, $1,868
Sweptline Pickup, $1,882
Town Panel, $2,110
Town Wagon, $2,426
Town Wagon, eight pass., $2,490
D100–128 half-ton Series
Utiline Pickup, $1,905
Sweptline Pickup, $1,918
Stake, $1,990
Platform, $1,942
A100–90 half-ton Series
Pickup, $1,972
Panel Van, $2,020
Van, $2,133
W100–114 half-ton 4x4 Series
Utiline Pickup, $2,547
Sweptline Pickup, $2,560

This cab interior is typical of Second-Series 1965 and 1966 Pickups equipped with the optional Comfort Package. The Comfort Package added to a Standard cab full-depth foam rubber seat and seatback, combination fabric and vinyl uphol- stery, driver's armrest, right sun visor, cigar lighter and extra cab insulation. Plus, the luxury touches of ceiling lining, two-tone interior, chrome trim, radio and dash-mounted automatic shift lever.

Town Panel, $2,835
Town Wagon, $3,127
Town Wagon, eight pass., $3,191
D200–128 three-quarter-ton Series
Utiline Pickup, $2,015
Sweptline Pickup, $2,031
Stake, $2,103
Platform, $2,054
D200–146 three-quarter-ton Series
Crew cab Utiline Pickup, $2,661
Crew cab Sweptline Pickup, $2,675
W200–128 three-quarter-ton 4x4 Series
Utiline Pickup, $2,598
Sweptline Pickup, $2,611
Stake, $2,683
Platform, $2,635
W200–146 three-quarter-ton 4x4 Series
Crew cab Utiline Pickup, $3,403
Crew cab Sweptline Pickup, $3,416
D300–133 one-ton Series
Utiline Pickup, $2,193
Stake, $2,301
Platform, $2,242
W300–133 one-ton 4x4 Series
Utiline Pickup, $3,374
Stake, $3,482
Platform, $3,422

Production

Dodge posted a double win in 1966 as both total production and market share climbed. Production was 169,830 and market share was 8.5 percent, a 2.4 percent gain for each category.

Production by weight classes for the model year was as follows: D100 52,140, W100 1,964, D200 24,334, P200 1,757, W200 2,948, D300 7,667, P300 1,132, W300 651 and compacts 40,442.

Canadian production was 16,691, and military 3,171. V–8 engine installations continued to gain on the sixes by capturing 47.5 percent of production in 1966, versus 52.5 percent for sixes.

1967 C Series

Again in 1967, Dodge pickup styling carried over without change, but this year significant changes were made in the engine lineup.

The power output of the 318 was increased from 200 to 210 hp by increasing its compression ratio from 8.25:1 to 8.5:1. This higher-output 318 also became the V–8 option for A100 pickups as the 273 V–8 was dropped. Dodge's compact pickup continued to be the industry leader in power and performance.

With the addition of an optional 383 ci, 258 hp V–8, Dodge owned the distinction of offering the most powerful engine in the full-size pickup field.

The 383 was optional for D100, D200, D300, W100 and W200. It was ideal for heavily loaded campers or for use wherever top performance was desired on or off the road.

Cab interiors took on a whole new appearance for the 1967 in that the dash was now padded and finished in a non-reflective black paint. Also, dual padded sun visors became standard equipment on all pickups. In the interest of additional safety, backup lights and emergency flashers became standard equipment.

The Custom Sports Special was continued, but this would be its last year. As with all other pickups, the 383 V–8 was an option which provided the Custom Sports Special with gut-wrenching performance.

Standard and optional equipment

Standard equipment for the half-ton pickup remained the same as in 1966.

Extra-cost optional equipment for the half-ton pickup remained the same as in 1966.

A100 Compact Vans were built on this line at the Missouri Truck Plant beginning in 1967.

An early, extended A100 Van proposal that did not go into production. Additional body length on this prototype was added onto the cargo area behind the rear axle. Production

A108 Van's added the 18 in. of space to the body between the stretched wheelbase.

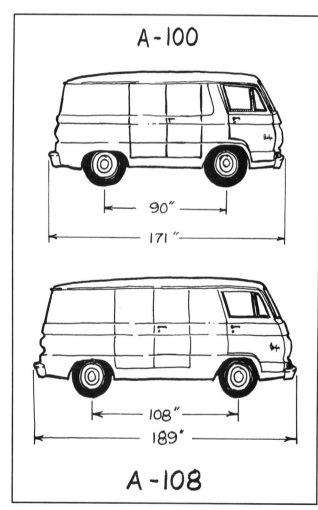

A-100

90"

171"

108"

189"

A-108

Wheelbase and overall length comparison between the A100 and A108 Vans. Greg Norman

Specifications and prices

No change from 1966 except the optional engine for A100 compacts was changed to the 318 V-8 from the 273 V-8.

D100-114 half-ton Series
Utiline Pickup, $2,019
Sweptline Pickup, $2,045
D100-128 half-ton Series
Utiline Pickup, $2,055
Sweptline Pickup, $2,080
Stake, $2,153
Platform, $2,105
A100-90 half-ton Series
Pickup, $1,989
Panel Van, rear doors only, $2,076
Van, $2,126
A108-108 half-ton Series
Panel Van, rear doors only, $2,232
Van, $2,282
W100-114 half-ton 4x4 Series
Utiline Pickup, $2,678
Sweptline Pickup, $2,691
D200-128 three-quarter-ton Series
Utiline Pickup, $2,158
Sweptline Pickup, $2,186
Stake, $2,257
Platform, $2,209
D200-146 three-quarter-ton Series
Crew cab Utiline Pickup, $2,841
Crew cab Sweptline Pickup, $2,855
W200-128 three-quarter-ton 4x4 Series
Utiline Pickup, $2,778
Sweptline Pickup, $2,791

Stake, $2,865
Platform, $2,815
W200–146 three-quarter-ton 4x4 Series
Crew cab Utiline Pickup, $3,534
Crew cab Sweptline Pickup, $3,547
D300–133 one-ton Series
Utiline Pickup, $2,324
Stake, $2,432

Platform, $2,373
W300–133 one-ton 4x4 Series
Utiline Pickup, $3,534
Stake, $3,644
Platform, $3,584

Production

After five straight years of production gains, the 1967 production turned down slightly, by 7 percent,

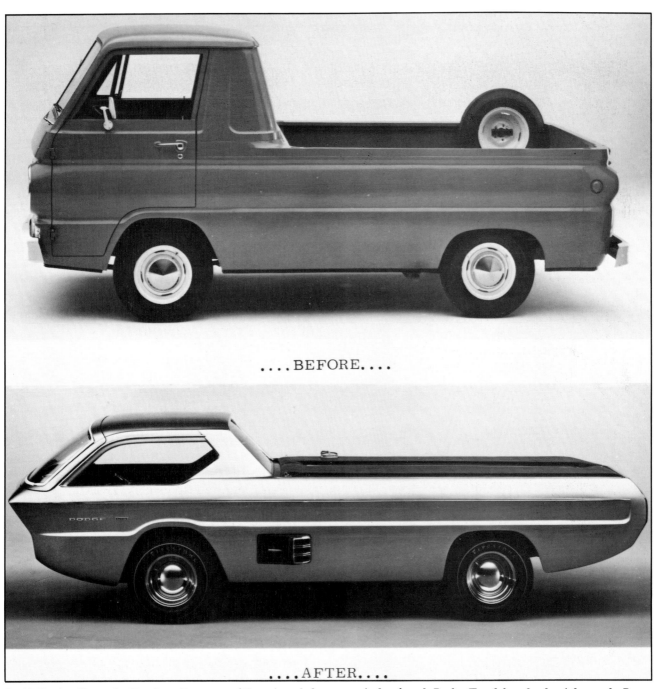

.... BEFORE ....

.... AFTER ....

In 1967, the Alexander Brothers Company of Detroit styled and built this futuristic Dodge Deora from a stock production A100 pickup. The Deora was fully functional and built entirely of steel. Dodge Truck bought the rights to the Deora and sent it out on the car show circuit for promotion.

or a total of 158,002. The industry total dropped by 7.8 percent, increasing Dodge's market share total by 1.2 percent to 8.6. In light of this, Dodge's performance was quite satisfactory.

Production totals by weight classes for the model year were as follows: D100 35,586, W100 1,006, D200 18,089, P200 936, W200 3,734, D300 6,890, P300 3,379, W300 667 and compacts 40,112.

Canadian production was 16,137, military 4,503 and 30,667 trucks were built in the new Missouri plant, which went into production this year. For the first time ever, for the industry as a whole, V–8 engines outsold sixes 50.7 to 49.3 percent. For Dodge, the numbers were reversed, 50.2 percent for sixes and 49.8 percent for V–8s.

Dodge celebrated its Golden Anniversary as a truck builder this year, 1917 to 1967.

1968 D Series

Exterior appearance changed for the better in 1968 due to a new, more attractive, massive-looking grille as well as redesigned headlight rims and parking lights.

Cab interiors received a facelift too with the addition of color-keyed upholstery fabrics. Interiors of A100 pickups were available in four vinyls only—blue, tan, green or black—colors that were also available in full-size pickups, but full-sized pickups offered an optional fabric in a combination of the same four colors.

Larry Gerber of Walnut Creek, California, is another Slant 6 Club of America member with a trophy-winning truck. His 1967 A100 Pickup is complete with the rare and highly desirable cab corner windows.

Sad to say the Custom Sports Special did not return for 1968. However, Dodge did plug a new model into its slot, the glamorous Adventurer. The Adventurer was basically the same concept as the Custom Sports Special, a pickup designed to be used for personal transportaton as well as a work truck, but with minor differences. The standard Adventurer's interior was equipped with a bench seat, but bucket seats with center console were an option. Adventurer was only available on half- and three-quarter-ton pickups and with Sweptline bodies only. An Adventurer nameplate attached on each side at the rear of the Sweptline body identified this top-of-the-line truck. Two-tone paint schemes were available as well as a vinyllike top on the D100 Adventurer only. The vinyl top was unusual in that it was actually a specially applied, stippled paint which looked like vinyl. Engine and transmission choices were the same as any full-size pickup.

Standard and optional equipment

Standard equipment for the half-ton pickup included 37 amp alternator, 2,500 lb. capacity front axle, 3,600 lb. capacity rear axle with 3.23:1, 3.55:1 or 3.91:1 ratios, 53 amp battery, 225 six-cylinder engine with 10 in. clutch, 18 gallon fuel tank inside behind seat, oil filter, front and rear shock absorbers, 1,025 lb. capacity front springs, 1,100 lb. capacity rear springs, 8.15x15 four-ply tires, three-speed transmission, five five-stud 15x5.5 in. wheels, windshield washer, dual electric variable-speed windshield wipers, metallic gray painted hubcaps, two exterior mirrors, front bumper, horn, wheel wrench and jack, padded instrument panel and sun visors, underslung spare tire carrier, domelight, turn signals, seatbelts, four-way emergency flashers, custom fresh-air heater with defrosters, dual armrests, full-width rear window, side marker reflectors and backup lights.

Extra-cost optional equipment for the half-ton pickup included one-quart oil bath air cleaner, 46 or 60 amp alternator, chrome front bumper, painted or chrome rear bumper, 11 in. clutch with 225 ci six-cylinder engine, anti-spin rear axle, 318 ci V-8 engine, 383 ci V-8 engine, oil-pressure gauge, tinted glass, engine governor, auxiliary heater under seat, dual horns, chrome hubcaps, heavy-duty instrument cluster consists of tachometer and oil pressure gauge, hydraulic jack, cigar lighter, cab-corner marker lights, interior rearview mirror, long-arm adjustable rearview mirrors, bucket seat package including center console and carpeting on floor and over gas tank, bucket seat package including all above plus cigar lighter, dash liner, roof headlining panel and additional insulation, textured vinyl roof in black or white, two-tone paint, radio, extra foam padding for seat cushion and back, third seatbelt, two belts with shoulder belts, 1,250 lb. capacity front springs, 1,400 or 1,750 lb capacity rear springs, power steering, hand-throttle, four-speed transmission, three-speed automatic transmission, undercoating and chrome wheel covers.

Specifications and prices

A100 90 in. and A108 108 in. wheelbase compact trucks, three-speed transmission, 6.95x14 four-ply tires. Standard engine for compacts was the 170 six; the 225 six and 318 V–8 were optional.

D100 114 in. and 128 in. wheelbase half-ton, three-speed transmission, 8.15x15 four-ply tires.

D200 128 in. three-quarter-ton, three-speed transmission, 6.50x16 six-ply tires.

D300 133 in. wheelbase one-ton, four-speed transmission, 8x17.5 six-ply tires.

A lineup of a few of the campers available from Dodge in 1968. A motor home was at the top of the hill, a three-quarter-ton pickup with slide-on camper unit below was followed by two Compact Wagons and Compact Van camper conversions.

155

1968–1971 Adventurer

There is a 1950 Dodge promotional movie in which the Power Wagon is touted as a family vehicle. One scene attempts to develop the duality of the Power Wagon by showing a grandmother, mother and young daughter driving the truck to town from the family ranch to spend a leisurely day shopping. It's a little hard to buy the idea that a Power Wagon would be acceptable for this function, but at the least, it was an interesting idea for the time.

The first time Dodge became interested in luxury, fashion, comfort and convenience was in 1953 when an effort was made to appeal to women drivers by promoting its half-ton pickup to serve as a dual-purpose vehicle for work and as the family's sole source of transportation. In 1953, Dodge offered a semi-automatic transmission, tinted windows and an upgraded interior. The results were crude compared to today, but nevertheless the movement toward a more civilized truck had begun.

Dodge's Custom Sports Special, which immediately preceded the Adventurer, was the first serious step toward marketing the pickup as an upgraded dual-purpose vehicle. The Custom Sports Special emphasized sports more than duality and, therefore, fell short in terms of creating a true dual-purpose truck.

The Custom Sports Special served its purpose, however, in that it put in place much of what has later become the norm for a high-styled, luxury truck: a significantly upgraded truck interior complete with bucket seats, console, carpeting and the like along with an upgraded exterior appearance using additional chrome trim and ornamentation.

On several occasions, Dodge crossed over names from the car side of the business to the truck side. The Adventurer is one of them. From the mid 1950s to its demise in 1961, Adventurer was the nameplate used by DeSoto for its top-of-the-line models. Adventurer is a good choice for the fanciest of all Dodge pickups as it conjures up visions of freedom and the open road and also maintains the exclusiveness once associated with the nameplate at DeSoto. About the last thing one would associate with the name was work.

The Adventurer was not a specific model, but rather two packages, interior and exterior packages which came only as a set. For example, the Adventurer Package for the first-ever Adventurer in 1968 sold at retail for $139.50 and consisted of Adventurer nameplates on pickup box and interior of doors, chrome front bumper, chrome grille, bright mylar moldings around windshield and rear window, Dodge Delta emblem on B posts, chrome drip moldings, 15 in. chrome wheel covers, exterior trim molding package with black or white filler in the side trim molding, carpeting including insulation, headlining including insulation, dash panel insulation, white steering wheel, chrome horn ring, chrome hood around instruments, chrome instrument face plate, complete body undercoating, cigar lighter and full foam bench seat with custom trim.

In addition to the base package, a buyer could also select a chrome rear bumper for $33.60, and a bucket seat package consisting of driver and passenger Bostrom bucket seats, console and additional carpet over the fuel tank for $117.90.

Adventurer Packages were offered only on D100 Sweptline 114 and 128 in. wheelbase pickups and D200 Sweptline 128 in. wheelbase pickups. It was not available on crew cab models. For aesthetic reasons, it is easy to understand why the Adventurer was only offered on Sweptline pickups and not Utiline pickups. But there is another reason as well. Dodge, as well as Ford and Chevrolet, did not want to build a narrow fender-side-type pickup box because its wooden floor and bolt-together-type construction were too labor intensive and costly to build. The all-steel Sweptline box was automatically welded into a single unit at less cost. It was in the best interest of all pickup manufacturers to woo customers away from the old-fashioned narrow box. Dodge was the first builder to discontinue its narrow box, in 1985, and the others have since followed suit.

A Dodge Truck document dated June 1967, indicated that the Adventurer Packages would be available for the A100 pickup, but this never happened. Dodge Truck marketing knew the days of the A100 were numbered and decided against it.

Because an Adventurer was a package, Dodge marketing found it easy to add, subtract from or modify to suit market conditions for promotions and the like. For example, in 1969, the Adventurer Package was expanded, both interior and exterior, to create an even more high-fashion and elegant statement. Power steering, power brakes, engines, transmissions, spring capacities, air conditioning and other mechanical components were always outside the scope of the Adventurer Package. A buyer could order his Adventurer with the mechanical options of his choice.

Truck development was an evolutionary process, not revolutionary, and so it was with the Adventurer. By 1970, Dodge designers put it all together. The new grille design created a fresh, new, clean overall style. With the addition of the Adventurer Package, the results were stunning. Dodge achieved a remarkably elegant passenger-car-styled pickup which delivered luxury, comfort and prestige. A pickup fully capable of living a double life of work and play.

For 1971, the last year of the Sweptline Era, the Adventurer was expanded to three offerings: the base Adventurer, mid-level Adventurer Sport and top-of-the-line Adventurer S.E. The main difference between the Sport and S.E. was that the S.E. had a wood-grain applique on its tailgate and lower body sides. In some opinions, the S.E. was overdone because of the wood-grain; wood-grain may be acceptable on a station wagon, but not on a truck.

Collectors are now becoming seriously interested in 1968–1971 Adventurers. They are prized because of what they are: beautiful, well-built trucks, equipped with all the goodies. When equipped with V-8s, automatics and full-power assists they are easy to drive and responsive.

Standard engine for D100, D200 and D300 pickups was the 225 six. The 318 V-8 and 383 V-8 were optional engines.

W100 114 in. wheelbase half-ton, three-speed transmission, 6.50x16 six-ply tires.

W200 128 in. wheelbase three-quarter-ton, three-speed transmission, 7x17.5 six-ply tires.

W300 133 in. wheelbase one-ton, four-speed transmission, 8x19.5 eight-ply tires. WM300 126 in. wheelbase one-ton, four-speed transmission, 9.00x16 eight-ply tires.

Standard engine for W100 and W200 was the 225 six. Standard engine for W300 was the 225-2 six and for WM300 it was the 251 L-6. Optional engine for W100 and W200 was the 318 V-8, for W300 it was the 318-2 and no optional engine was available for the WM300.

D100-114 half-ton Series
Utiline Pickup, $2,163
Sweptline Pickup, $2,189
D100-128 half-ton Series
Utiline Pickup, $2,200
Sweptline Pickup, $2,225
Stake, $2,300
Platform, $2,251
A100-90 half-ton Series
Pickup, $2,047
Panel Van, rear doors only, $2,132
Van, $2,183
A108-108 half-ton Series
Panel Van, rear doors only, $2,291
Van, $2,342
W100-114 half-ton 4x4 Series
Utiline Pickup, $2,818
Sweptline Pickup, $2,831
D200-128 three-quarter-ton Series
Utiline Pickup, $2,273
Sweptline Pickup, $2,301
Stake, $2,374
Platform, $2,325
D200-146 three-quarter-ton Series
Crew cab Utiline Pickup, $2,979
Crew cab Sweptline pickup, $2,993
W200-128 three-quarter-ton Series
Utiline Pickup, $2,922
Sweptline Pickup, $2,935
Stake, $3,011
Platform, $2,960
W200-146 three-quarter-ton 4x4 Series
Crew cab Utiline Pickup, $3,703
Crew cab Sweptline Pickup, $3,716
D300-133 one-ton Series
Utiline Pickup, $2,446
Stake, $2,556
Platform, $2,496

W300-133 one-ton Series
Utiline Pickup, $3,649
Stake, $3,762
Platform, $3,700

Production

Dodge production bounded back in 1968 from the slight downturn experienced in 1967, gaining 20.5 percent up to 190,341 total trucks. Market share didn't fare as well, dropping 1.2 percent to 8.5 percent due to the fact that industry total production increased 22.5 percent.

Production totals by weight classes for the model year were as follows: D100 49,770, D200 25,502, D300 6,287, W100 1,198, W200 5,308, W300 674, P200 7,612, P300 1,993, M300 4,869 (M models were motor homes) and compacts 52,790.

Canadian production was 16,572, military 5,046 and production in Missouri totalled 65,060. V-8 engine installations raced past sixes in 1968 by 56.6 to 43.5 percent.

Pickup cab interiors for 1968 were even more colorful and attractive due to a new color-keying program that gave the customer a choice of black, tan, blue or green heavy-grain vinyl upholstery. The headliner fabric complemented the seat colors. Two armrests were standard and door handles were recessed safely into the fiberglass door trim panels. This interior was the optional Comfort Package, which was even more plush with its vinyl bolster-type seat cushions in two-tone colors and a combination of vinyl and fabric upholstery.

In July 1967, 140,000 sq. ft. were added to the Warren, Michigan, truck plant.

1969 E Series

At this point in truck history, Dodge was striving to make pickups have the "appearance and environment of a passenger car," as the market for dual-purpose pickups was rapidly increasing. It was becoming commonplace for an entire family to take long trips in pickup campers. Dodge management hoped to increase the demand for its trucks by offering a higher level of comfort and attractiveness. Great strides were made along those lines in 1968 with the addition of color-keyed interiors and the introduc-

tion of the full-dress Adventurer models. An Adventurer could now be dressed up more than ever with several optional exterior and interior trim and equipment packages.

The trend toward more attractive pickups continued for 1969 with a restyled hood (at last the hood louvers which dated back to 1961 were dropped) and a new Dodge nameplate replaced the dated one on the front of the hood. A Dodge Delta insignia now appeared on the hood just above the Dodge nameplate on Adventurer models only.

Plush dual-purpose pickups were becoming so popular that in the February 1969 issue of *Motor Trend* magazine, writer V. Lee Oertle tested a full-

A glamorous 1969 D100 Adventurer Pickup interior with redesigned instrument panel. For the first time, air-conditioner outlets were dash-integral, and the automatic shift lever was moved from the dash to the steering column. Full-length upper instrument panel padding and a flip-up glovebox door were also new.

dress 1969 Dodge three-quarter-ton Adventurer pickup equipped with a 383 V–8 and a three-speed automatic transmission. His comments and observations bear repeating.

Concerning handling Oertle wrote, "Absolutely top-notch. The Dodge really hangs on." And, also, "In city traffic and during normal high-speed freeway driving, the Adventurer is a slick handler. Steering effort is almost non-existent. The power steering option is extremely quick, as well as effortless. It's a real pleasure to handle in any kind of situation."

Concerning performance he said, "Responsiveness of the 383 cubic inch V–8 could be described as *pleasantly alarming*. There seems to be no wind-up delay whatever in the automatic transmission. The split-second your foot touches that gas pedal the pickup literally hurls itself into the traffic stream. I'm not talking about beating the light, speeding, or anything that silly. Just healthy muscular acceleration. The big V–8 picks up the load and runs with it, as lightly as Tiny Tim through the tulips."

On cab comfort he wrote, "The interior of the Adventurer will shock someone fresh out of the bare-bones farm truck. Instead of bare-metal doors there are fiber glass trim panels. Carpets replace the usual rubber floor mats. Bright trim and tasteful use of every available cubic inch of space in that cab make it seem larger. It resembles a station wagon more than a pickup, particularly the thin-silhouette air conditioner under the dash. Naturally, the Adventurer's cab is heavily insulated against both heat and engine-room noise. Glare reducing instruments are clustered and very easy to read. The total impression of the Adventurer cab is one of spacious comfort, stylish awareness plus pride. You feel like it belongs in any neighborhood, with no excuses made because 'it's a truck.' From the vinyl covered cab roof to the careful use of extra nameplate moldings and sports hubcaps, the Adventurer is a real stand-out."

Other observations of outstanding features from the report, "1. The driving position could hardly be better. You sit up high, with the top of the steering wheel well below eye-level of even the shortest driver. 2. The side door window ledges have a unique step-down design, so that the forward ledge under the side-vent windows is high, and the rear portion where you rest your elbow is low. If you have ever tried to drive a deep-seated pickup model where your *elbow* is almost as high as your *ears* when resting on the sill, you'll like the Adventurer 'feel.' 3. Optional bucket seats in any other type of vehicle are pretty much a nuisance for a family man or a guy on a date. But in a pickup truck, they're as handy as a crescent wrench. Take three average-sized men, and one will have long legs. Put all three onto a pickup bench-seat

on a long haul and when drivers rotate, the long-legged passenger gets accordianed up against the dashboard. He can't rest and he can't stretch out. Bucket seats allow individual adjustments for leg room. The Adventurer goes a step further. A center-mounted bucket seat offers the same overall seat

Everyone's favorite was the 1969 D100 Adventurer Sweptline pickup. The dual-purpose Adventurer was at home putting in a hard day's work and out on the town in the evening.

Power Wagons in 1969 featured a single-lever transfer case control. A driver could slip into or out of four-wheel-drive with a simple flick of the wrist. Shown is a 1969 W100 half-ton Sweptline Pickup.

159

If we kept telling you all about the good things that come in the new Adventurer, there'd hardly be room left to show you the truck. But one more thing you should know is this. Just to make leading a double life easy for you, Adventurer has a standard 25-gallon gas tank so you don't have to head for the gas pump first thing every morning . . . or last thing at night. Go see Adventurer at your nearby Dodge Dealer's. One look will tell you everything else.

DODGE ADVENTURER
The **SPORTRUCK**
that leads a
double life

Dodge Trucks   CHRYSLER MOTORS CORPORATION

width as an ordinary bench seat. That third passenger can ride up front."

A major interior upgrade was a restyled instrument panel with the first-ever, dash-integral air conditioner in a Dodge pickup for both D and W models. A protective padding ran the full width of the instrument panel. A new instrument cluster faceplate with edge lighting, safety controls and knobs, passenger-car slide-type heater controls and a flip-up glovebox door added to the tailored look.

A step toward conventionality was moving the automatic gearshift lever and indicator to the steering column. After all, between the pushbutton selector and later lever selector, Dodge's automatic transmission selector had been on the dash since 1957! The dash-mounted shift lever continued for A100 pickups only. In 1969, Power Wagons dropped the two-lever system in favor of a single-lever transfer case that allowed the driver to quickly and easily shift into four-wheel-drive with just a flick of the wrist. It also was quieter running, lighter in weight and more durable than the old two-lever system.

Dodge engineers reengineered the ride qualities on half- and three-quarter-ton work-and-play pickups with what they called "Cushioned Beam Suspension." This was really a quick fix to enable Dodge to continue selling the only pickup built by the Big Three with a solid I-beam front axle. Independent front suspension would not be available until 1972. Cushioned beam consisted of modifying the existing suspension system with several new features: a sway bar, a new front leaf spring design with lower rates and plastic liners to reduce harshness, new tie rod ends, and shorter pitman arms to reduce friction, and increased steering ratio for easier handling.

Standard and optional equipment

Standard equipment for the half-ton pickup remained the same as 1968 except the dry-type air cleaner and 318 ci V-8 in addition to 225 ci six-cylinder engine became standard equipment.

Extra-cost optional equipment for the half-ton pickup remained the same as 1968 except for addition of instrument-panel-mounted air conditioner, 8.8 in. vacuum brake booster, power steering now available with six-cylinder engine, and four-speed NP435 available with close-spaced or wide-spaced ratios.

Specifications and prices

D100–114 half-ton Series
Utiline Pickup, $2,431
Sweptline Pickup, $2,470
D100–128 half-ton Series
Utiline Pickup, $2,470
Sweptline Pickup, $2,507
Stake, NA
Platform, NA

A100–90 half-ton Series
Pickup, $2,338
Panel Van, rear doors only, $2,415
A108–108 half-ton Series
Panel Van, $2,589
W100–114 half-ton 4x4 Series
Utiline Pickup, $2,982
Sweptline Pickup, $3,018
W100–128 half-ton 4x4 Series
Utiline Pickup, $3,018
Sweptline Pickup, $3,057
D200–128 three-quarter-ton Series
Utiline Pickup, $2,259
Sweptline Pickup, $2,596
Stake, NA
Platform, NA
D200–146 three-quarter-ton Series
Crew cab Utiline Pickup, $3,300
Crew cab Sweptline Pickup, $3,312
W200–128 three-quarter-ton 4x4 Series
Utiline Pickup, $3,271
Sweptline Pickup, $3,310
W200–146 three-quarter-ton 4x4 Series
Crew cab Utiline Pickup, $4,112
Crew cab Sweptline Pickup, $4,130
D300–133 one-ton Series
Utiline Pickup, $2,731
Stake, NA
Platform, NA
D300–159 one-ton Series
Crew cab Utiline Pickup, $3,517
W300–133 one-ton 4x4 Series
Utiline Pickup, $3,925
Stake, NA
Platform, NA

Production

Production dipped 5.1 percent in 1969, down some 10,000 trucks to 180,642. Market share also retreated to 7.9 percent, a 7.1 percent loss. Total industry production increased by 2.1 percent.

Dodge truck production by weight classes for the model year was as follows: D100 46,943, D200 21,839, D300 6,955, W100 2,405, W200 5,185, W300 1,553, P200 815, P300 468, M300 9,903, M400 1,834 and compacts 47,660.

Canadian production was 15,505, military 1,872; the St. Louis plant built 48,192 trucks.

Dodge was the first in the industry to make available power steering on compact vans and wagons with automatic transmissions.

Since the early 1960s, industry production of recreational vehicles increased nearly 25 percent annually. Truck-mounted campers increased 12.6 percent in 1969 over 1968, truck caps increased 44.5 percent.

The industry sold 69.7 percent of all gasoline-powered trucks with V–8 engines. The high demand for V–8 power was due to the fact that the interstate freeway system was nearing completion, and also that more and more trucks were being used to carry or pull recreational vehicles over the new freeway system. In 1969, Dodge sold 62.1 percent V–8 engines.

1970 F Series

Because 1971 would be the last year for this pickup series, little changed in 1970. The most important change in the pickup lineup was dropping the A100.

In March 1970, as a 1971 model, Dodge announced a second-generation van, basically the same full-size van as currently manufactured, and a pickup was not to be part of this new product offering. With the demise of the A100 pickup the 170 slant six was also dropped. Actually, Dodge dropped the 170 slant six in favor of the 198 slant six which was developed for the new, larger van series.

Exterior appearance changes were limited to a new grille of anodized aluminum with a deep textured insert and side marker lights were now rectangular, as opposed to round as in 1969. Inside appearance changes only dealt with instrument panel faceplate covers: silver and black plastic for standard interiors, bright chrome trim for custom interiors and wood-grained faceplates for the Adventurer.

Continuing to cater to the camper customer, Dodge engineers designed the industry's first easy-off tailgate which was standard on all D200 and W200 Sweptline pickups with Camper Special or Camper Custom packages. Without using tools, the tailgate could be quickly and easily removed and replaced by one person. Also, Camper Special models came equipped with a new wiring harness for rapid and reliable hookup of the camper's electrical system. Standard equipment on Camper Special models was a 25 gallon fuel tank, as well as an optional 23 gallon auxiliary tank.

Engineering improvements were limited to changes in transmissions. First of all, a three-speed automatic became an option for W100 and W200 pickups. Second, a new three-speed, fully synchronized manual transmission was made standard on all half- and three-quarter-ton pickups with the 383 V–8. It was also made standard on D200 and W200 crew cabs with six-cylinder engines. A fully synchronized four-speed for all pickups provided more versatility for rugged terrain or heavy loads.

Standard and optional equipment

Standard equipment for the half-ton pickup remained the same as in 1969.

If you are looking for a collector truck which will return a high rate of appreciation in the next decade, find a well-preserved and well-maintained 1970 or 1971 Adventurer. Buy one equipped with either a 318 or 383 V–8, automatic, air conditioning, power steering, bucket seats with center console, vinyl roof and as many other luxury options as possible, and you'll have a truck which you will be proud to own, drive and show as it appreciates.

Extra-cost optional equipment for the half-ton pickup remained the same as in 1969 except for the addition of wheel-lip and sill moldings.

Specifications and prices

Two changes were made in the compact truck line. The first was a new standard tire size of E78x14–B. The second was a new 198 ci six-cylinder engine, which became the standard offering; the 225 and the 318 were optional.

The only changes made in the D and W Series were in standard tire size offerings. They now were G78x15–B for D100 and W100, 8.00x16.5–D for D200 and W200, 8.00x16.5–D for D300, and 8.75x16.5–E for W300.

D100–114 half-ton Series
Utiline Pickup, $2,625
Sweptline Pickup, $2,667
D100–128 half-ton Series
Utiline Pickup, $2,668
Sweptline Pickup, $2,703
Stake, NA
Platform, NA
A100–90 half-ton Series
Panel Van, rear doors only, $2,608
Van, NA
A108–108 half-ton Series
Panel Van, $2,790
Van, NA
W100–114 half-ton 4x4 Series
Utiline Pickup, $3,210
Sweptline Pickup, $3,250
D200–128 three-quarter-ton Series
Utiline Pickup, $2,435
Sweptline Pickup, $2,703
Stake, NA
Platform, NA
D200–146 three-quarter-ton Series
Crew cab Utiline Pickup, $3,800
Crew cab Sweptline Pickup, $3,825
W200–128 three-quarter-ton 4x4 Series
Utiline Pickup, $3,535
Sweptline Pickup, $3,575
Stake, NA
Platform, NA
D300–133 one-ton Series
Utiline Pickup, $2,995
Stake, NA
Platform, NA
D300–159 one-ton Series
Crew cab Utiline Pickup, $3,820
Crew cab Sweptline Pickup, $3,770
W300–133 one-ton 4x4 Series
Utiline Pickup, $4,239
Stake, NA
Platform, NA

Production

After a slight downturn in 1969, production bounced right back in 1970 gaining 4.4 percent and topping off at 188,637 trucks. Market share at 9.6 percent was up a whopping 21.5 percent because the industry as a whole dropped 14.4 percent.

Dodge truck production by weight classes for the model year was as follows: D100 51,625, D200 21,816, D300 7,057, W100 3,441, W200 6,168, W300 1,029, P200 1,188, P300 521, M300 11,573, M400 1,687 and compacts 46,242.

Canadian production was 1,048, military 2,703, Missouri 54,784. A general economic recession in 1970 caused total car and truck sales to fall in 1970 over 1969, but Dodge, on the other hand, increased 4.4 percent. Ford and Chevrolet suffered from strikes in 1970, causing them to lose production. Only Dodge recorded a production gain in calendar 1970.

1971 G Series

As so often in the past when Dodge was in the last year of a dated truck platform, changes for the last year were minimal. And true to form, 1971 was no exception. The biggest change concerned a new model, the Sweptline Special D100 pickup.

The Sweptline Special D100 was a special, low-priced, light-duty half-ton which sold for almost $300 less than the cheapest Chevrolet half-ton, or $2,481.50. Built on a 114 in. wheelbase with a 6½ ft. box, its rear axle was rated at 3,600 lb. and the front axle at 2,500 lb. Dodge marketing ordered it designed specifically for the budget-minded buyer who had need for a light-duty truck. Power was by the 198 ci slant six, with the 225 slant six optional.

The Sweptline Special featured a white-painted grille, a special nameplate, and black and clear silver instrument cluster. Standard transmission was a three-speed manual, but an automatic transmission was also an available option. Other economy features included black wheels, 8.25x15–B tires, round, painted, 5 in. outside mirrors, 9¼ in. clutch, 3.91:1 rear axle ratio, black interior trim only, black and aluminum paint on dash cluster faceplate, and an inside mirror.

Above the Sweptline Special came the standard models, now called Custom. They featured an aluminum-painted grille insert, fender-side name-plates—Custom 100 or Custom 200—Dodge decal in the right corner of the tailgate, bright and black instrument cluster faceplate, standard painted mirror and standard automatic choke. Above the Custom were three trim levels of the Adventurer: Adventurer, Adventurer Sport and Adventurer S.E. The S.E. version was loaded with all available option packages, including lower body-side wood-grain applique.

Standard and optional equipment

Standard equipment for the half-ton pickup included 37 amp alternator, two armrests, 2,800 lb. capacity front axle, 3,600 lb. capacity rear axle, 46 amp battery, front bumper, 10 in. clutch six-cylinder and 11 in. clutch eight-cylinder engine, 225 ci six-cylinder engine, 318 ci V-8 engine, rubber floormat, 23 gallon fuel tank, bright finish grille, fresh air

The Dude Package on this 1971 D100 consisted of a Dude name decal in white or black applied to each side of the box, C stripe body decals, tailgate decal with Dodge identification, *chrome taillight bezels, body-color gas cap, body-color outside mirror and chrome hubcaps. The Dude Package was available only on Sweptline D100 and D200 Pickups.*

heater and defroster, single horn, padded instrument panel, instruments included fuel, ammeter, temperature gauge, oil pressure light and speedometer, turn signals, domelight, side markers, backup lights, four-way flashers, interior and exterior mirrors, seatbelts, shock absorbers front and rear, padded sun visors, 1,025 or 1,200 lb. capacity front springs for six-cylinder and 1,250 or 1,450 lb. front springs for eight-cylinder engine, 1,100, 1,300, 1,650 or 1,900 lb. capacity rear springs, G78x15–B(4PR) tires, three-speed transmission, five 5.5 inch five-stud wheels, wheel wrench, windshield washers, two-speed electric windshield wipers and full-width rear window.

Extra-cost optional equipment for the half-ton pickup included one-quart oil bath air cleaner, instrument-panel-mounted air conditioner, 50 or 60 amp alternator, anti-spin rear axle, 59 or 70 amp Mopar battery, bright finish front bumper, painted or bright finish rear bumper, step-type rear bumper for Sweptline pickups only, inside box spare tire carrier for Sweptline or outside box on left side for Utiline pickups, cigar lighter, 11 in. clutch for 225 six engine, increased cooling, 383 ci V–8 engine, 23 gallon auxiliary fuel tank, tinted glass, dual electric horns, bright finish hubcaps, heavy-duty instrument cluster, hydraulic jack, cab marker lights, interior and exterior mirrors, replaceable-element oil filter, oil pressure gauge, textured-vinyl roof painted black or white, two-tone paint, radio, third seatbelt, shoulder belts, 1,250 or 1,450 lb. capacity front springs for six-cylinder and 1,500 or 1,750 lb. capacity front springs for eight-cyliner, 1,400, 1,650, 1,750, 2,000, 1,950, 2,200, 2,600 or 2,900 lb. capacity rear springs, rear auxiliary springs, power steering, hand throttle control, four-speed transmission with either close ratio or wide ratios, three-speed automatic transmission, undercoating, and set of four wheel covers for 15 in. wheels.

Specifications and prices

B100 109 in. and 127 in. wheelbase half-ton vans, three-speed transmission, E78x14–B tires.

B200 109 in. and 127 in. wheelbase three-quarter-ton vans, three-speed transmission, G78x15–B tires.

B300 109 in. and 127 in. wheelbase one-ton vans, three-speed transmission, 8.00x16.5–C tires.

Standard engine for B100 and B200 was the 198, and the 225 and 318 were options. Standard engine for B300 was the 225, and the 318 was optional.

No changes to D and W Series pickups.
D100–114 half-ton Series
Custom Pickup, $2,790
Adventurer Pickup, $2,941
D100–128 half-ton Series
Custom Pickup, $2,826

This beautiful, original-condition 1971 Adventurer Sport is owned by Paul Peltier of Berlin, Wisconsin. Paul bought it as is and has only detailed it to restore its original beauty. In 1971, three Adventurers were offered: the base Adventurer, the middle-level Aventurer Sport and the top-of-the-line Adventurer S.E.

Adventurer Pickup, $2,977
Adventurer Sport, $3,089
Adventurer S.E., $3,191
W100–128 half-ton 4x4 Series
Utiline Pickup, NA
Sweptline Pickup, NA
Stake, NA
Platform, NA
D200–128 three-quarter-ton Series
Custom Pickup, $3,023
Adventurer Pickup, $3,174
Adventurer Sport, $3,287
Adventurer S. E., $3,388
D200–146 three-quarter-ton Series
Crew cab Utiline Pickup, $3,837
Crew cab Sweptline Pickup, $3,387

The instrument panel of Peltier's 1971 Adventurer Sport is as clean and uncluttered as its exterior.

D200–160 three-quarter-ton Series
Crew cab Utiline Pickup, NA
Crew cab Sweptline Pickup, NA
W200–128 three-quarter ton 4x4 Series
Utiline Pickup, $3,777
Sweptline Pickup, $3,770
Stake, NA
Platform, NA
W200–146 three-quarter-ton 4x4 Series
Crew cab Utiline Pickup, $4,664
Crew cab Sweptline Pickup, $4,664
D300–133 one-ton Series
Utiline Pickup, NA
Stake, NA
Platform, NA
D300–159 one-ton Series
Crew cab Utiline Pickup, NA
W100–114 one-ton 4x4 Series

Utiline Pickup, $3,275
Sweptline Pickup, $3,275
W300–133 one-ton 4x4 Series
Utiline Pickup, $4,185
Stake, $4,450
Platform, $4,395
Vans
B100–109 Van, $2,890
B200–109 Van, $3,116
B300–109 Van, $3,116
B100–127 Van, $3,027
B200–127 Van, $3,451
B300–127 Van, $3,523

Production

For the first time, Dodge production topped 200,000 trucks. Final total was 221,776, a large 17.6 percent increase over 1970. However, market share fell slightly to 9.4 percent because the rest of the

Was this the last 1971 pickup built? It could well be as it leaves the plant along with a 1972 half-ton Pickup and a 1972 one-ton Stake.

166

industry recovered from their slow year in 1970 and posted a healthy 20.2 percent increase in production.

Dodge truck production by weight classes for the model year was as follows: D100 47,323, D200 15,875, D300 5,881, W100 3,651, W200 5,112, W300 782, P200 929, P300 269, G400 3,636 (Postal Service trucks), M300 16,261, M400 3,025 and compacts 66,308.

Canadian production was 17,010, military none and Missouri 72,273.

Dodge installed V–8 engines in 70.6 percent of trucks equipped with gasoline engines.

1978–1979 Li'l Red Express
by D. J. Smith

Dodge built the Li'l Red Express truck as a limited-production, high-performance D–150 pickup truck in the years 1978 and 1979. Powered by a Police Pursuit 360 V–8, this muscle truck delivered its power through a modified transmission and heavy-duty suspension. All Li'l Reds were red in color and had a Li'l Red Express decal on both doors. The truck's working end used the familiar Dodge high-sided box, dressed up with wooden inserts on the sides and tailgate. The interior featured full instrumentation including a tachometer. The gauges could be seen easily through the Tuff-type steering wheel. Prices new, topped the $7,000 mark.

The radical idea for a high-performance truck originated with a prototype put together at the Chrysler's Truck Product Planning Division (TPPD). With the help of Dick Maxwell, Chrysler Performance Planning Group, and Tom Hover of the TPPD, the muscle truck moved from prototype to actual production. However, the Li'l Red was never more than a limited-production model and in 1978, its introductory year, only 2,000 were built.

The heart of the small-block limited-production E58 360 ci was the camshaft. The thumpy Chrysler 340 profile camshaft gave 252 degrees of intake and exhaust valve duration and a short 33 degrees of overlap. Aiding the engine's breathing, an induction package pulled fresh air from gravel pan orifices located between the bumper and grille. These fed to a large, dual-snorkel air cleaner that wore a dress-up chrome lid. The fresh-air induction system fed a big four-barrel ThermoQuad carburetor. At the output end, dual exhausts fed through a set of 2½ in. pipes to a set of A134-440 wedge mufflers. A set of vertically positioned, straight-through, chrome-plated, big-truck-type stacks completed the exhaust system. With a compression ratio of 8.2:1 this engine netted 225 hp at 3800 rpm.

A modified transmission governor from a 440 Wedge transmission in the heavy-duty Torqueflite gearbox kept power transfer at a maximum, while the rear differential, with a 3.55:1 gear ratio and a Sure-Grip anti-slip package, assured optimum acceleration and traction. The large-footprint Goodyear GT radials were sized at HR60x15 front and LR60x15 rear. They were mounted on slotted, chrome-plated rims sized at 15x7 inch front and 15x8 inch rear. To handle the power, and quite possibly to circumvent emission standards, the Li'l Red sat on a stiff 6,100 GVW suspension.

Performance was impressive on both the prototype and actual production models. In November 1977, *Hot Rod* ran a prototype to a quarter-mile time of 14.7 seconds at 93.0 mph. In June 1978, *Hot Rod* tested a production model which covered the quarter-mile in 15.77 seconds at 88.06 mph. *Car and Driver* claimed the Li'l Red could reach 100 mph in 19.9 seconds and had a top speed of 119 mph.

The Li'l Red Express was the first pickup truck developed for high-performance applications. It was produced in limited quantities for two years only. The truck's unique looks are stylish and make a definite power statement. Recently recognized for investment potential, the Li'l Red Express is affordable and has excellent resale. The latest price guides give the Li'l Red a 40 percent markup over the standard D–150 heavy-duty Dodge pickup trucks.

The July 1991 issue of Sport Truck *magazine featured an article based on selections from its readers, editors and outside truck experts to find the Ten Top Pickups of all time. The winner was the 1978–79 Dodge Li'l Red Express. Sport Truck said, "It is the last true American hot rod that was available from the factory." They say the 1978 model is more desirable because only 2,200 were built in the first year while 5,000 rolled off the line in 1979. In addition, the 1979 models were not as spirited due to detuning because of the introduction of smog equipment.*

Chapter 9

Power Wagon 1946–1968

According to the *History of the Dodge Division,* published by the Dodge Truck Division on March 30, 1951, "The basic design of this four wheel drive vehicle, was created to fulfill military needs, for a small, fast, powerful and rugged vehicle, capable of traveling equally as well on the road, or off the road. The civilian version of this newly, and well named "Power-Wagon" has been styled with a pleasing appearance, but the rugged driving units such as: Engine, Clutch, Transmission, Transfer Case, Front and Rear Driving Axles remain the same as used on the military models." The source of this statement was a description of the original Power Wagon dated March 11, 1946.

There's not much doubt as to the heritage of one of the world's most popular 4x4 trucks. The Power

This photo of the 170 in. wheelbase T234 dated October 17, 1945, showed without any doubt the genesis of the Power Wagon's styling. The T234 was the three-ton heavy-duty truck specially designed and built for the Chinese Army, better known by its nickname, The Burma Road truck. Dodge built 15,000 of them between October 1944 and March 1946.

Wagon's mechanical features, originally developed for use in the military three-quarter-ton T214, were ideally suited for a heavy-duty, general-purpose 4x4 designed for off-highway use and for service on unimproved roads. The mechanicals had been battle-tested in the 255,196 military trucks built for World War II. The three-quarter-ton T214 won the hearts of thousands of soldiers whose lives depended on them under the worst conditions.

Mounting the standard civilian cab on the military chassis was easy enough to do. To the civilian cab, Dodge engineers added a military-type hood and radiator shell, which by all appearances was taken from the famous T234 Burma Road truck, a military three-ton 4x2 which Dodge built 15,000 of for the Chinese Army late in World War II. The grille con-

sisted of thirteen heavy, vertical rods welded to a rectangular frame under the radiator shell. Simple, military-style flat front fenders, built heavy enough to double as body armor, completed the front-end appearance.

Long running boards ran from the back of the front fenders to the front of the rear fenders. The rear fenders were also simple in style—the non-skirted, cycle-type and very heavy-duty.

A new steel box had to be specifically designed to hold the loads this brute was capable of hauling. Early prototypes show a box borrowed from a conventional one-ton pickup, but this low-sided narrow box seemed like a miniature and looked out of place. Instead, Dodge engineers developed a super-sized, 8 ft. long by 4½ ft. wide and 22¼ in. high box, which

Dated July 3, 1945, this was the earliest Power Wagon photo known. At this time the Power-Wagon was officially designated a Farm Utility Truck. This prototype lacked name- *plates, but was equipped with combat wheels and a winch without cable.*

proved capable of hauling huge loads. A spare tire was mounted on the right side of the box between the rear fender and the cab.

To the military mechanicals, Dodge engineers added such features as a two-way power takeoff. The front shaft operated the winch mounted on the frame up front and the rear shaft powered auxiliary equipment or a pulley for belt operations. A mechanical governor was available which provided a wide range of constant speed settings to make it adjustable for belt pulley drive and any other type of auxiliary equipment driven by the power takeoff. Speed changes could be conveniently made by a control located in the cab. These items provided the civilian version with versatility for application in many kinds of industrial, agricultural, public utility, state highway and a multitude of other uses.

The naming of Dodge's new sturdy, go-anywhere truck is in itself an interesting story. Dodge marketing people used a unique, effective, and creative strategy to announce the name. How logical: announce it in a widely read publication which shared the name—*Power Wagon. Power Wagon* was a national magazine of the motor truck industry which began publication on March 15, 1906, and continued until March 1963. The March 1946 issue announced the new truck in an article entitled, "New Dodge Truck to be named 'Power-Wagon'." Quoting from the article, "Forest H. Akers, vice-president and director of sales of the Dodge Division of Chrysler Corporation, said the name Power-Wagon was chosen because it so aptly describes the functions of the new 94–horsepower truck; a self-propelled power plant capable of a wide range of industrial and agricultural power needs." Mr. Akers continued, "It was the avowed purpose of the engineers and designers of the Power-Wagon to create the most useful and versatile truck ever manufactured. How well they have succeeded is shown by the great variety of mobile and stationary power jobs it performs, in addition to serving as a haulage unit of unusual performance ability."

An earlier article in the January 2, 1946, issue of *Automotive and Aviation Industries* announced it as the Model WDX General Purpose truck. One month

This rear three-quarter view of the Farm Utility Truck showed the slightly modified 9 ft. box borrowed from a Job-Rated Era one-ton pickup. It is understandable why Dodge design engineers changed to the large box for production Power Wagons.

later, and a month before *Power Wagon* officially announced the new truck's name, it too called the Power Wagon simply a general-purpose, one-ton truck. Official Chrysler Corporation papers published in 1945 labeled early prototypes simply Farm Utility Truck. Interestingly, the October 16, 1943, issue of *Colliers* magazine ran a Dodge Truck Division ad which pictured the one-and-a-half-ton 6x6 version of the three-quarter-ton T214, over the caption, "Battle-Wagon by Dodge."

Power Wagons became available starting about March 1946. Still, it was considered a 1946 model.

To be sure, a number of engineering and mechanical refinements and improvements were made over the years, all of which improved the Power Wagon's load hauling or job performance ability, but basically, it ran as a continuous model from 1946 to 1968 (through 1978 for export only) without major mechanical or appearance changes. Why change a truck which was so inherently good, just for change's sake?

Model year improvements

1949   Changed to a heavy-duty, four-speed, spur-gear transmission as used on one-and-a-half-ton F Models.

1950   Four-blade radiator fan replaced six-blade fan.

1951   Mounting angle of transfer case revised to improve propeller shaft angle.

Addition of rubber engine mountings, front and rear.

Addition of rubber insulators for cab and box mountings.

1,600 lb. capacity front springs available as extra equipment.

3,000 lb. capacity rear springs available as extra equipment.

Pickup box side panels and fenders made

Two early production Power Wagons (photo dated May 6, 1946) outside the plant waiting to be delivered. The pickup was equipped with a high-side production box, which looked more in keeping with the rest of the truck. Both trucks, *however, were equipped with combat wheels. The frame of the Power Wagon on the left had been shortened and a fifth wheel installed. This truck was possibly the work of the Special Equipment Group.*

similar to the one-ton pickup's box.
Rear axle capacity increased from 5,500 to
6,500 lb.
Front axle capacity increased from 3,500 to
3,750 lb.

Instruments changed to style of B2 conventional trucks.
New spark plug covers.
Higher capacity fuel pump.
More powerful starter.

Fargo Power Wagons were an important export item for Chrysler Corporation. Power Wagons with DeSoto nameplates were also exported, and Fargo Power Wagons were sold in Canada. This photo, dated May 3, 1946, tells us that export sales began early. Domestic Power Wagons sales ceased in 1968, but export-only sales continued for another ten years.

Brakes changed to Cyclebond molded, tapered linings, and anodized brake cylinders.

1952   Standard B-3-D carburetor and sandwich-type governor became standard equipment, superseding the integral-type carburetor and governor.

1953   Compression ratio increased from 6.7:1 to 7.0:1.

1954   230 ci engine power output boosted by increasing the compression ratio from 7.0:1 to 7.25:1, by redesigning the manifold and by use of a new camshaft for longer-duration valve openings.

1956   Changed to 12 volt electrical system.

1957   Vacuum brake booster became available.

1961   The 251 ci L-6 engine replaced the 230 ci L-6 engine.
        Alternator became standard equipment.

1962   Lockout front wheel hubs became available as extra equipment.

1963   1,600 lb. front springs replaced 1,150 lb. springs.
        3,000 lb. rear springs replaced 2,500 lb. springs.

1948–1949 Standard and optional equipment

Standard equipment for the pickup model included five disk wheels with 5.50 in. rims. 7.50x16 eight-ply all-service tread tires, heavy-duty hydraulic shocks front only, one-quart oil bath air cleaner, side-mounted spare tire carrier, long running boards and rear fenders, two-speed transfer case, front bumper, channel-type reinforcements inside frame siderail, velocity-type engine governor, sealed-type oil filter, 3,500 lb. capacity front axle, 5,500 lb. capacity rear axle, 1,110 lb. capacity per spring front springs, 2,500 lb. capacity per springs rear springs, 10 in. clutch, four-speed transmission with power takeoff openings, dual vacuum windshield wipers, sun visor on left side, Deluxe seat cushion and back, and rear axle ratios of 4.89:1 with 7.50x16 eight-ply tires and 5.83:1 with 9.00x16 eight-ply tires.

Extra-cost optional equipment for the pickup model included Deluxe cab equipment consisting of vent wings in doors, domelight, armrest on left door, dual sun visors, dual electric windshield wipers, $40; draw bar, $20; generator for high charging at low engine speeds, $18.50; mechanical governor, $63; long-arm adjustable rearview mirror on left side, $2, right side, $3; replaceable-element oil filter, $7; pin-

This Cantrell-bodied four-door woody station wagon was a rare Power Wagon. It was set up for heavy-duty service as evidenced by its front-mounted winch.

tle hook, $10; power takeoff assembly, $65; pulley drive (pulley unit only), $73; rear driveshaft assembly (shaft assembly only), $72; rear shock absorbers, $31; auxiliary taillamp, $6; pair tow hooks, $5; winch and winch driveshaft, $200.

1958 Standard and optional equipment

Standard equipment for the pickup model included five disk wheels with 5.50 in. rims, 7.50x16 eight-ply all-service tread tube-type tires, heavy-duty hydraulic shocks on front only, one-quart oil bath air cleaner, side-mounted spare tire on right side, long running boards and rear fenders, two-speed transfer case, front bumper, 360 watt 45 amp generator, 100 amp battery, left-side rearview mirror, channel-type inside siderail frame reinforcements, velocity-type engine governor, replaceable-element one-quart oil filter, 3,750 lb. capacity front axle, 6,500 lb. capacity rear axle, 1,150 lb. front springs, 2,500 lb. capacity rear springs, 10 in. clutch, four-speed transmission with power takeoff openings, Deluxe Cab equipment consisting of dual vacuum windshield wipers, interior sun visor on left side, heavy-duty seat cushion and back, and ventilating wings on cab doors, and rear axle gear ratios of 4.89:1 with 7.50x16 eight-ply tires and 5.83:1 with 9.00x16 eight- or ten-ply tires.

Extra-cost optional equipment for the pickup model included vacuum brake booster, $42.50; directional signals, $30.50; draw bar, $23.10; generator for high charging at low engine speeds, $11.25; tinted windows, $19.80; mechanical governor for use with rear driveshaft assembly, includes carburetor with integral velocity-type engine speed governor, $85.60; heater and defroster, $40.80; long-arm adjustable rearview mirror, left side, $2.50, right side, $3; inside

A 1949 Power Wagon school bus. A number of Power Wagon chassis were mounted with school bus bodies in the early years. *They were often equipped with front-mounted winches to assist them in performing under the worst of conditions.*

rearview mirror, $3; replaceable-element oil filter, $12; front and rear fenders painted to match cab and body color any standard Dodge Truck color, $13.20; pintle hook, $12.50; power takeoff, $75.70; pulley drive unit, $85.60; combined fuel and vacuum pump, $9.90; radiator overflow tank, $9.90; three-ton hydraulic jack, $7.90; rear driveshaft assembly, $85.55; rear shock absorbers, $38.90; 1,600 lb. capacity front springs, $7.90; 3,000 lb. capacity rear springs, $15.20; auxiliary taillamp, $8.75; windshield washers, $11.90; pair front only tow hooks, $15.20; winch assembly with driveshaft, $251.40.

1968 Standard and optional equipment

Standard equipment for the pickup model included 251 ci engine, 6.50 in. five-stud disk wheels, 9.00x16 eight-ply tube-type, all-service tires, 3,750 lb. capacity front axle with 5.83:1 ratio, 6,500 lb. capacity rear axle with 5.83:1 ratio, 1,600 lb. capacity front springs, 3,000 lb. capacity rear springs, front heavy-duty shock absorbers, NP420 four-speed transmission, one-quart oil bath air cleaner, alternator, 60 amp battery, positive crankcase vent system, 11 in. clutch, turn signals, velocity-type engine governor, replaceable-element oil filter, two seatbelts, windshield washers, exterior rearview mirror, backup lights, traffic hazard warning switch, padded instrument panel, padded dual sun visors and recirculating heater with defroster.

Extra-cost optional equipment for the pickup model included 10 in. vacuum brake booster; 46 amp alternator, $20.15; 60 amp alternator, $27.90; 70 amp battery, $7.30; additional seatbelt, $8.60; manual front wheel locking hubs, $73.70; hydraulic jack, $13.20; interior rearview mirror, $2.60; long-arm exterior rearview mirror, left side, $2.70, right side, $9.60; power takeoff assembly, $138.20; combined fuel and vacuum pump, $9.90; radiator overflow tank, $29; rear hydraulic shock absorbers, $25; pintle hook, $26.40; front tow hooks, $25; undercoating, $11.90; winch with power takeoff and driveshaft, $387.50

Model numbers

1946–1947	WDX
1948–1949	B–1–PW
1950	B–2–PW
1951–1952	B–3–PW
1953	B–4–PW
1954	C–1–PW
1955–1956	C–3–PW
1957	W300
1958–1959	W300M
1960–1968	WM300

Pickup prices

1946	$1,627
1947	$1,764
1948	$2,045
1949	$2,045
1950	$2,045
1951	$2,170
1952	$2,353
1953	$2,307
1954	$2,307
1955	$2,449
1956	$2,449
1957	$2,636
1958	$2,850
1959	$3,197
1960	$3,239
1961	$3,515
1962	$3,515
1963	$3,531
1964	$3,531
1965	$3,555
1966	$3,587
1967	$4,295
1968	$4,634

Part II: Restoration

Chapter 10

Rebuilding and Restoration: First Steps

There are two ways to approach the repairs and cosmetic upgrading needed by most vintage vehicles. One is to leave the vehicle as intact as possible while making whatever repairs are required to various mechanical components such as the engine, brakes and steering, performing bodywork and refinishing, and redoing the bed and interior. This approach is called rebuilding. The other approach is to disassemble the vehicle, often to the last nut or bolt, and then overhaul virtually all mechanical assemblies, strip and repaint all metal, root out all traces of rust, and in effect return the vehicle to a condition as good as, or better than when it rolled out of the factory new. This is restoring.

The approach you take depends on several factors: your goal for the vehicle, your intended use for the vehicle, the investment you want to put into the vehicle, the amount of time you want to spend on the

refurbishing process, and your patience or endurance level.

Rebuilding

Although your truck will be inoperable for periods during the rebuilding process (while the engine is being overhauled, for example), taking this approach allows you to drive the truck during most of the time that you are upgrading its appearance and reliability. A major benefit of this approach is the ability to spread the cost of the upgrades over as long a period of time as is necessary, while still using and enjoying the vehicle. Rebuilding also takes less shop space than restoration because the truck is never completely apart. If this is your first experience reworking a vintage vehicle, you're not as likely to lose interest in the project if you take it one component at a time as you are if you scatter the truck all over your garage then have to muster the endurance to stick with the project for two or three years until every part is pristine, reassembled and working again. The rebuilding approach is most appropriate for well-preserved, original vehicles where it seems a travesty to dismantle the care the previous owner has lavished on the vehicle for so many years.

If you're fortunate enough to find or own a vehicle that has escaped the ravages of time and hard use, you'll impress far more people by keeping it as it is (with necessary cosmetic and mechanical repairs) than if you take it all apart and strip and paint every inch of metal so that it shines like a newborn. Any truck can be restored. But only an exceptionally well-cared for truck can demonstrate its original features.

A goal of rebuilding, especially if you are starting with a truck that's fairly well preserved, is to bring your truck back to what it looked like when it was three or four years old. It'll resemble the trucks you might have seen parked at the lumber yard or feed mill when you were a kid. And for many collectors, that's the desired look for an old truck.

Often an owner of a well-preserved older truck will leave the truck intact and perform cosmetic and mechanical upgrades. This is rebuilding. This Dodge W Series Panel is owned by Fred Lewis of Orangevale, California.

In rebuilding a typical older truck, you will remove and pound out the fenders, probably overhaul the engine (this is easier done with the engine removed), definitely redo the brakes, probably replace the wiring, upgrade the interior, and in nearly all cases, repaint at least the exterior. Of course, numerous other jobs may also be included, from replanking the box to replacing the window glass.

There's really just one drawback to the rebuilding approach, and that's the likelihood that there will always be something you wish you had done more thoroughly. For example, most bodywork will be done to visible panels, which could result in overlooking deteriorated cab supports, rusted inner body panels and the like. Repairing hidden damage is just as important in rebuilding as it is with restoration, but since the truck isn't taken apart, not all problems are likely to get noticed in any given phase of the work. Later, when you're hooking up an exhaust system, you may glance at the cab supports and suddenly realize that the body is supported by swiss cheese. Welding new metal into the support brackets at that stage will be a lot more difficult, especially if the nearby exterior surfaces have just been freshly painted.

Restoring

At best, restoring a vintage truck will take several months. In most cases, the time is likely to stretch into years. From one to three years is a realistic average if you do most of the restoration work yourself. During this period, the truck will be spread all over your shop or garage, perhaps with parts even sneaking into your living area. I have a speedometer for my truck sleeping in a desk drawer; a friend stored the headlights from his 1930s vintage truck behind the living room sofa as he was afraid they'd get banged up in the garage. The benefit of restoring is that every part of the truck needing attention gets it. When the restoration is finished, the truck should be better than new.

Before you start a frame-up restoration you should establish a plan that includes your projected (and fall-back) time schedule and budget. I advise that your schedule include a fall-back timetable because you're likely to run into unforeseen problems during the restoration process. For this reason, the budget should also include a healthy contingency— I'd advise thirty percent. If the extra isn't needed, you'll be money ahead when you're finished. But if you don't allow for unanticipated extras, you may fall short of resources to finish your truck—and just when the end is in sight.

Most first-time restorers begin by taking their vehicle apart. This is the wrong approach. It's true

The restoration approach strips a truck down to its basic components, all of which are then cleaned, rebuilt and refinished. Here a Dodge Power Wagon owned by Trucks Magazine *is entering the disassembly stage. Photos courtesy of Quality Truck Enterprises, Inc., Shippenburg, Pennsylvania.*

that the vehicle will have to be disassembled, but this is not the first step. You should begin by researching the vehicle as fully as possible; the research step should also be the starting point if you decide to take the rebuilding approach. Next, you should document your truck as thoroughly as possible. This means taking clear color photos from every conceivable angle. A quality camera, preferably 35 mm, should be used for the photos. If you're not a shutterbug and don't have a 35 mm adjustable lens camera, ask a friend whose hobby is photography to take the photos for you. You can buy the film and treat the photo-

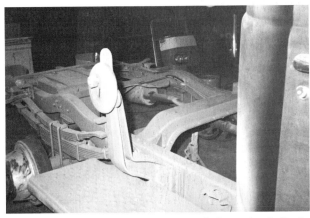

The chassis is sandblasted to bare metal then primed. In the process, spring hanger bushings should be replaced. Note the Power Wagon's heavy-duty two-stage rear springs.

All sheet metal is also stripped, straightened and repaired as needed. A thin skim-coat of body putty is acceptable to remove surface imperfections. Rear fenders on Power Wagons and Dodge B Series Pickups are of the so-called cycle style, which makes straightening and repair work quite easy.

grapher and spouse to a nice dinner out. Chances are they'll be delighted with the offer.

The photo session may take an hour or so. During this time, shoot every angle, front and back, top and bottom. Note such details as the location of the weatherstrip around the doors, any striping on the wheels or body reveals, the positioning of the upholstery panels lining the upper cab—everything you can think of. It's also a good idea to document the truck's condition with notes. Make a list of everything about the truck you find to be unoriginal (your research will inform you as to what's original and what isn't). Examples might be incorrect taillights (from a hardware or auto supply store), signal lights

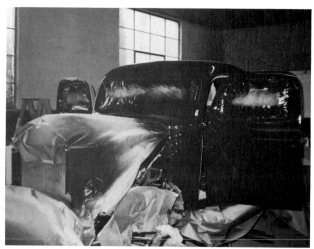

Once the chassis has been refinished, the cab is set in place and painted. Note the extensive masking of the chassis to prevent paint overspray on the chassis.

on trucks not originally so fitted, an incorrect engine, substituted sheet metal, missing hubcaps and so on.

Now make a list of items you know you'll be needing to replace, either because they're missing or damaged or are desirable accessories not found on your truck. Examples in the accessories category might include a radio, passenger seat if your truck is a sedan delivery model, or deluxe trim. Add to the list any upgrade you want to make to the truck. These could include conversion to a 12 volt electrical system and modern amenities such as air conditioning. With the list as complete as you can make it before taking the truck apart, you can begin to lay out the restoration time table and draw up a budget estimate.

Estimating costs

Costs for restoring or rebuilding your truck will include parts, labor, transportation and supplies. You can estimate parts costs by going through a catalog from a major Dodge parts vendor such as Roberts Motor Parts and listing all the items you think may be needed for your truck, then itemizing this list with prices. Most likely, you will shop around for parts, finding some at swap meets, others at auto supply stores, and some at salvage yards, so your actual parts cost may be less than the catalog estimate. However, your estimate is likely not to include all the items you will need, so the total parts bill will probably be close to, or may even exceed, your estimate. Labor costs you will pay others to do your truck's body, mechanical, or trim work can grow large, fast. For this reason, most collectors try to do as much work on their trucks as they can.

For many first-time rebuilders or restorers, the problem with doing much of the work yourself is that although you may be able to acquire the skills with some time and practice, you're still hamstrung without the tools. Bodywork is an example. You can't do much in the way of metal repair without a welder. As you estimate labor costs, you should decide which jobs you plan to do yourself and which jobs your current tool collection will enable you to do. For example, most of the mechanical repair on a vintage Dodge truck can be done using a ½ in. drive socket set, assorted wrenches, pliers and a few specialty tools like a ring compressor and micrometers if you're doing an engine overhaul. Most specialty tools you may need can be rented from a tool rental, or borrowed for the job from friends. For work that will require a tool investment (sandblasting, painting, welding body panels), your decision will be whether to buy the tools or have someone else do the work. If you see working on an older vehicle as a therapeutic pastime (and many do), then you may decide to buy the tools and do as much of the work as you can. The advantage here is that once you've made the initial investment, the tools are yours to use—probably for a lifetime.

For work that you plan to hire out, you'll need to get estimates. In many cases, shops will be reluctant to quote a price for mechanical or repair work on an older vehicle, not wanting to be held to the quote when unforeseen problems develop. You'll need to explain that for now, you're just looking for a ballpark figure. Some work will have to be farmed out. Chrome plating is the most obvious example. Other jobs better left to experts include gauge repair and windshield replacement. Here, too, you should get estimates.

There are other ways, besides doing the work yourself, to cut labor costs. One is to share work with friends. The times I've been able to do this have been among my most enjoyable old truck hobby experiences. As an example, a friend and I both needed to do steering and front-end rebuilds on our vehicles. We took the front ends on both our vehicles apart, determined the parts we needed, pooled our orders and got a small discount for doing so; then we set up an assembly line operation for cleaning, refinishing and rebuilding both front-end and steering assemblies. This approach was much more efficient than if we had overhauled each vehicle separately, but more importantly, we learned from each other and had a great time together in the process.

A cost-saving alternative, sometimes available, is to have major mechanical or bodywork done by students in a Vocational-Technical program. Admittedly, there are some risks here. Parts can be lost and the quality of the instruction will determine the outcome of the finished product. I teach at a technical college which trains students in engine rebuilding, bodywork, machining, and similar trades and have consigned my truck to these programs for all of its bodywork and painting, some engine and other mechanical work. The work is not speedy, and problems do arise, but any lower-quality work, such as some heavy orange peel texture in the paint near the bottom of the driver's door, has always been made right. The big plus to having a Vo-Tech program assist in a vehicle's rebuild or restoration is the nominal labor charges. A hoped-for offshoot is the students' appreciation of older vehicles.

The list of cost estimates should also include any transportation expenses. These may include hauling the cab to a chemical stripping facility, traveling to junkyards or swap meets, and UPS or freight charges for parts you may mail order. In one sense, you may see the travel expenses as part of the enjoyment of the hobby, but in a real way they are also part of the cost of restoring or rebuilding your truck, so you might as

Masking around the doors prevents scratches while the cab interior is redone. Upholstery work is performed after painting.

well project some figures and tally them in. Whether or not you will be using your truck in any business capacity, be sure to keep a log of travel, transportation and other expenses to use in calculating an accurate appreciation figure should you decide to sell your truck sometime in the future.

The last expense area is supplies. This includes miscellaneous packages of nuts and bolts, sandpaper, thinner, primer, paint, weatherstripping glue, as well as the reference literature you'll need, such as service and parts manuals and sales brochures. There's really no way to accurately project supply expenses in advance. The major cost items in this category are

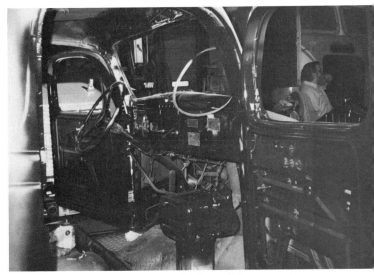

The refinished interior is now ready for upholstery and new door weatherstripping. New windshield rubber and glass are also typically installed after painting.

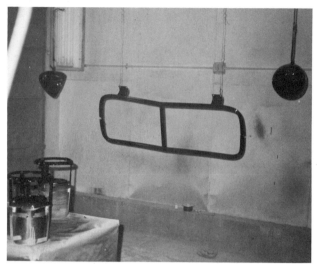

Parts, like the windshield frame and headlight buckets, are refinished separately. This way, all surfaces can be stripped of old paint and rust, and the parts completely refinished.

Gathering information

By now you're itching to get a wrench in hand and start taking things apart. Just a bit more patience is needed. Before you start scattering your truck all over the garage, you should make a list of parts you know you need and scout up a set of manuals. You will use the manuals to take the truck apart, as well as put it back together. That way, you're not so likely to create more damage during disassembly. Also, if you follow the disassembly steps in the manual, you'll find that things come apart easier. If you're buying just one manual, it should be the Dodge shop manual for your model truck. You'll find reprinted service manuals for the more popular W and B Series available from several parts vendors. For service manuals on the later and earlier models, you'll need to scout swap meets or contact a literature specialist. Besides the Dodge service manual, it's also advisable to have a copy of the *Motor's* or *Chilton's* manual covering your year and model truck. To gain full understanding of how a component operates, and to learn the assembly or disassembly sequence, it is often helpful to be able to read the instructions from more than one vantage point.

Disassembly

Now you can begin to take your truck apart. If you are following the restoration route, you will remove the bed, cab, fenders and running boards to expose the chassis. Then you will pull out the engine and drivetrain, keeping all these assemblies intact for now. Next, you will strip off the front end, steering and suspension, leaving just the bare frame. This is your starting point. You will clean, de-rust and repaint the frame, then begin to build up the chassis. Each component gets the same treatment, along with any further disassembly and repair work that's

likely to be paint and the reference resources. You should allow at least $100 for paint and an equivalent minimum amount for the manuals and other books that you will use in rebuilding or restoring your truck.

When you add up all the figures you may want to take a deep breath before you hit the total key on your calculator. Even rebuilding an older truck can be a more expensive undertaking than you would think—and restoring is likely to cost considerably more. But don't let the bottom line figure on your calculator sour you on sprucing up your old truck. You'll find that some of the costs can be trimmed and the expenses will be spread over the duration of the project. If restoration seems outside your budget, you might consider the rebuilding approach.

Rebuild or restore: which approach to take?

	Rebuilding	Restoration
Goal	To make a reliable running truck that looks as it might have when originally in use	To bring the truck to showroom or better-than-new condition
Approach	Start with a well-preserved truck	Start with any condition truck
Advantages/ disadvantages	Spread costs over as long a period of time as necessary	Lack of funds at any critical stage will delay completion of the project
	Can drive the truck most of the time while repairs are in progress	Truck will be inoperative through most of restoration period
	Takes less shop space than total disassembly	Requires space equivalent to two-car garage
	Less likely to lose interest	For average hobbyist, a frame-up restoration will take 1 to 3 years
Results	Likelihood there will be some things you wish you had done more thoroughly or overlooked	Every part needing attention will get it. When finished the truck will be better than new

needed. You'll find comprehensive instructions on how to clean and de-rust the chassis and other metal parts, as well as metal finishing, priming and painting in books such as *How to Restore Your Collector Car,* also available from Motorbooks International.

Although the service manual will provide detailed disassembly and rebuilding instructions for your truck's mechanical components, working on a twenty- to fifty-year-old vehicle is different than overhauling the same vehicle when new. For this reason, you will also find the instructions on rebuilding an older truck's hydraulic brake system, overhauling a straight axle front end, and replacing wiring, which are contained in Motorbooks' *Heavyweight Book of American Light-Duty Trucks,* to be a highly informative guide to these essential processes, whether your approach is restoration or repair.

When taking your truck apart, be careful not to throw things away. Even the old cardboard headliner can be used as a guide when installing its replacement. You should gather a collection of coffee cans, or cut the tops off plastic milk bottles and use these containers to hold nuts, bolts and other miscellaneous small parts. With coffee cans, you can paste a strip of masking tape on the outside to label the contents (left front fender bolts and washers, for example). The milk cartons can be labeled with a permanent marker. As you're disassembling your truck, make it a practice to label everything with tags and masking tape. Then place all the items in well organized storage. Otherwise, when you start reassembly, you'll waste lots of time looking for misplaced items.

Before starting rebuilding and reassembly, an important decision has to be made as to whether you want to redo your truck to original standards or make modifications for modern driving conditions. One of the most desirable modifications is installation of a higher-speed rear end. If your truck is a B Series, or earlier, it was designed for hauling loads down the highway at maybe 50 mph tops. You can coax these trucks a bit faster, but at the distraction of hearing the engine wind up like a street dragger at a red light. So a high-speed (lower gearing ratio) rear end is almost essential if you plan to drive the truck any distances. Another popular upgrade is converting the electrical system to 12 volts. If you opt for 12 volt electricals, you'll have extra electrical capacity for power-hungry accessories such as air conditioning, and the upgrade will improve engine starting—a factor of some significance on the early Dodge V–8s. You can modernize in these ways and still have a truck that looks stock. If you decide to mildly customize or rod the truck, chances are you're following your own blueprints. Our discussion here will take the stock approach.

Determining standards

Restoring or rebuilding a vintage truck to stock (or original) standards requires some research. If your truck has been repainted, and chances are it has, what was its original color? If you have a particular color in mind for your truck, was it offered for your model truck, and if not, what were the other color options? What was the original engine color, and was the engine that's in your truck now installed at the factory, or is it a later swap? These are questions you may want to research. An easy way to check the truck's original color is to look someplace that is not likely to have been repainted, such as on the firewall or underside of the hood.

Vintage Dodge parts suppliers ease the authenticity problem significantly by providing interior kits and other items that are as close to original materials and coloring as possible. If your goal is a show truck, you will use as many original parts as possible, and will need to be thorough in your research as to exactly what items actually belong on your truck. For example, today's plastic valve stem caps did not exist in the 1940s, so if you are restoring an early B Series, W Series or older Dodge truck for show, you will need to hunt up a set of the old-style, steel valve caps that had the prongs on top for unscrewing the valve stem. Likewise, spark plug bases were not plated until rather recently. This means that if you install modern spark plugs with plated bases in a 1940s or 1950s truck, you may lose judging points unless you paint the spark plug bases black. For show-quality authenticity, you may decide to clean and replate the original fender and chassis bolts; the other alternative is to grind the markings off modern bolts and replate them. As you'll discover if the trophy circuit is your aim, detail is the name of the game.

Meanwhile the box is also stripped, repaired and refinished. Like the rest of the truck, the Power Wagon box is an extra-rugged assembly.

181

Authenticity is important for personal satisfaction and to preserve a truck's value. There's no reason to invest in a new, but non-stock, interior that will be a detractor should you decide to sell or show the truck—unless you're just dead set on putting an interior of your own design in your truck. Original sales brochures can be helpful in showing you what your truck looked like when it left the factory. Most also illustrate or list accessories. Although trucks didn't have the long list of accessories that were offered on cars of the period, you might want to add some dress-up and convenience options that were available to your truck. For most models these included a radio, passenger-side sun visor and armrest, a heater, wheel trim rings, brake and clutch pedal pads (yes, pedal pads were accessories on Dodge trucks from 1930–53), spotlights, oil filters and other items. Since Dodge is well served by reproduction parts vendors, many accessories can be purchased "new" from parts dealers.

Shopping for parts

To learn what parts are readily available, and to do some price shopping, it's a good idea to gather catalogs from the parts dealers listed in the suppliers sources at the back of this book and others whose advertising you may see in publications such as *Hemmings Motor New*, *Cars & Parts* or *Old Cars Weekly*. For further price shopping, you should check the availability of mechanical parts for your truck at local auto parts stores. NAPA parts outlets (a nationwide network of independently owned stores linked by a massive warehousing system) have probably the most complete listing of parts for older vehicles. Not only are the items usually less expensive

The completed cab and chassis now awaits the refinished box. Benefits of the restoration approach can clearly be seen here. When the truck is finished, everything will have a fresh, factory-new appearance.

through a NAPA outlet than a restoration supplier, but there are no separate handling and shipping fees, and usually your local store can have the part within twenty-four hours after placing your order, if the part is not already on the store's shelves.

One of the reasons you're likely to have quite a bit of success finding mechanical parts for a forty- or fifty-year-old truck at an auto parts store is the extensive parts interchangeability throughout the Chrysler product line. Although the parts store catalogs will list the interchange applications for individual parts (a clutch, for example), there may be times when you need to know interchange information for a major assembly (the rear end, transmission or engine). For this data, you'll need access to the *Hollander* interchange manuals. These books are the mechanic's bible of parts substitution. General repair shops often subscribe to the *Hollander* series, but except for small towns, these businesses are nearly extinct. Fortunately, the vintage *Hollanders* are now being reproduced (see supplier's listing for publisher's information). Since a set of *Hollander* manuals is quite expensive, this would be a good investment for a club, or you might suggest to the community librarian that some of these manuals be purchased for the automotive section of your public library.

When you locate a *Hollander* manual covering your year vehicle, you can look up the range of components that will fit your truck. Of advantage here would be determining if a passenger-car rear end can be substituted for your truck's lower-geared third member. Even though the forward body metal of Dodge trucks in the mid 1930s looks as though it would interchange with similar vintage Dodge cars, it doesn't; these have to come off another truck. Besides, a *Hollander* manual doesn't show alternative sources of replacement sheet metal.

Working therapeutically, not in a frenzy

Working on your truck can be great therapy from the pressures of everyday life if you follow a few common sense guidelines. The first, of course, is don't let the truck become the driving compulsion of your life. If this happens, then daily life will become an escape from your truck, not the other way around. The simplest way to turn working on your truck from a relaxing pastime to a driving compulsion is to set deadlines on your work. Repair and restoration of an older vehicle never agree with deadlines. Sometimes jobs will go smoother than you expected (but not often). More commonly, the unexpected will throw your work off pace. Common causes of these contingencies are missing or incorrect parts, but sometimes setbacks seem to be absolutely uncanny tests of your patience. A friend, set on restoring his truck to na-

The box is positioned carefully using an overhead sling to prevent scratching either the box or chassis. The box on these trucks is heavy and would be difficult to lift into place manually.

The restoration approach results in a near-perfect show truck. Finishing touches will include signs on the doors advertising the owner's publication.

tional show-winner excellence (he has accomplished his goal), had placed the flawless, painted tailgate of his truck on sawhorses inside the open door of his shop to let the paint cure in the sun. Meanwhile, a batter for a ball team playing in a vacant lot across the street hit a fly ball that landed—you guess it—smack in the middle of the tailgate. Instead of simply mounting the tailgate on his truck, my friend now had to pound out the dent, prime and repaint the part. The heartache of that mis-hit ball could be an emotional disaster to a deadline-pressured restorer.

Breaking the work into manageable jobs

The second guideline to enjoying working on an old truck is to set your pace in manageable chunks. Although it's a good idea to keep an eye out for parts and information you may need for later jobs, even a frame-up restoration should be handled one job at a time. If the current stage of work is sandblasting, then give your attention to that step and deal with concerns about metal repair later. If while working on larger projects, such as rebuilding the drivetrain,

metal repair or refinishing, you sense frustration or impatience setting in, it's a good idea to break off and concentrate on a smaller, more manageable job that you can complete in several evenings or a couple of weekends. That way, you'll have the satisfaction of seeing something through to completion and you'll return to the larger project with renewed confidence in achieving your goal.

Any number of smaller jobs can be interspersed between the larger projects. If you live in a northern climate, rebuilding smaller assemblies like the starter, generator, or carburetor can be done in the house, keeping work on your truck progressing when it is too cold to work in the garage or shop. One of the more satisfying smaller jobs, that is needed on most older vehicles, is restoring the steering wheel. Redoing the steering wheel is somewhat messy work, so you won't want to do it inside the house, but it makes an ideal warmer weather project that can be completed in a couple of weekends and a few evenings in between, and will result in great satisfaction when you're finished.

Chapter 11

Wooden Pickup Box Replacement

Restoration of wooden bed floors in pickup trucks from the 1920s to 1960s can be accomplished in several ways, but when it comes to winning show trophies, care and professional quality are all-important. Cabinetmaker Bruce Horkey shows the step-by-step procedure he uses to restore wooden beds.

For ease while working on the restoration, remove the pickup box from the frame and set it up on sawhorses or stands. Remove the old bedwood, skid strips, bolts and cross-members.

The first step is to clean up the box and floor. Take pictures of all the details and make notes for reference at assembly time. Also make notes on the sequence and fit, and list all of the fasteners by size, type and location. This kind of detailed information will prove invaluable later on. Remove the fenders, lights and wiring harness.

Strip or sandblast all metal work, and refinish the box sides, front and tailgate. Clean the angle pieces along the sides of the bed and the area around them. These will be the first items replaced. Scribe a reference line above and below the angles on the box sides for replacement reference. Measure from the bottom of the boxside to the underside on the angle. Write down this measurement. Make notes on hole locations and angle location on boxside.

Center punch the spot welds attaching the angle to the box. The welds will be drilled out with a spotweld cutter. Set the depth of cutter to drill only through the angle. After drilling out the spotwelds, remove the old angle.

Set new angles in place, using notes, and mark hole locations onto the box side. If you are working with angles that have no holes on the shorter side, note fender and stake pocket locations and decide where to drill holes to attach the angles to the boxsides. Drill holes in the box side and attach angles. For originality, the angles should be spotwelded in place instead of bolting.

Set the edge boards in place, mark holes to attach angles to edge boards. Remove the boards and drill holes with ⅜ in. diameter drill bit.

Install the edge boards and drop bolts through the angles. Loosely install the cross-members.

Install one board and skid strip at a time. Install bolts, nuts and washers loosely from the inside of the box by reaching over and under boards. Install boards alternating them from one side of the box to the other.

Install the center board and the last two skid strips and bolts. Measure the box diagonally to assure squareness. Align the boards and adjust everything to fit.

From the underside, finish installing the remaining nuts and washers loosely. Make one final check for alignment and squareness, and then hand-tighten all nuts. After you're satis- *fied with the fit, set the box on the truck frame. Place a blanket over the front bed panel to protect it and the cab from bumping together and scratching the finish.*

Drop in the hold-down bolts and washers. Square up the box on the frame, make alignment adjustments and bolt the box in place. Don't overtighten the skid strip bolts.

Chapter 12

Replacing Rubber Components

Exposed to dampness and road salt, metal rusts. Exposed to sun and dryness, rubber dries out and rots. It seems like a no-win proposition. What may be good for a truck's body destroys its rubber moldings and other parts that are as important to a truck's appearance and structural integrity as the metal to which these rubber items are attached. In the process of restoring or just rehabilitating an older light truck, it's inevitable that weatherstrip and other rubber items will have to be replaced—quite possibly all of them.

Often when a vintage light truck is purchased, or earmarked for some upgrading, the thought may be that a little tinkering and some bodywork, plus repainting, are all that's needed to make it presentable. In compiling a list of jobs to be done, you may

On unrestored trucks the large rubber grommet around the gas tank filler neck is generally cracked or missing altogether. Fortunately, replacements are readily available. Once new rubber parts are installed on the truck, they can be kept looking fresh with periodic coatings of Armor-All. Shown here is the gas tank filler grommet on a Panel. Most of the rubber items for a pickup truck can be used on a Panel.

note the standard mechanical repairs such as overhauling the brakes, replacing worn steering parts, perhaps some engine work, and of course the obvious body and interior repair, but entirely overlook the truck's decayed rubber parts.

Actually, it's easy not to see deteriorated weatherstrip, a cracked rubber donut around the gas filler pipe, missing grommets at points where the wiring harness passes through body openings, and the generally dilapidated condition of original rubber parts—until the truck is repainted. Then cracked, chipped or missing rubber parts stand out like a Model T at a Packard convention.

If you're accustomed, as I am, to making your local auto parts store the first place to inquire about mechanical parts for your vintage truck, the need to find a source for replacement rubber parts may produce a thought of mild panic—are these items still available; is anyone making them? The answer is yes—and no. For newer trucks from the 1970s on, a dealer's parts counter is the starting point for your search for replacement rubber items. For older Dodge trucks, most rubber parts are being reproduced. In a few cases where replacements aren't available, generic parts can be used. In extreme cases, you may have to reproduce or repair the parts yourself. Unfortunately, there's really no way to renew a brittle and hardened rubber part. As Walter Vaughan of Lynn H. Steele Rubber Parts puts it, "Rubber is like toast. Once the substance turns crispy there's no way to make it soft again."

Before heading off in search of a supplier for the first rubber item that you see needs replacing (probably the windshield molding), it's a good idea to give your truck a close-up inspection and make an inventory of all the rubber parts that are needed. In most cases, your shopping list will grow to a respectable order.

The rubber inventory can start at the cab. If the weatherstrip on the doors is original, it's probably brittle, cracked and largely missing. Notice, too, the large rubber grommet (often called a donut) surrounding the gas tank filler pipe. Chances are it's hardened, cracked and maybe even chipped, torn or missing altogether. The rubber molding around the windshield, backlight and vent windows is also likely to be cracked and hardened. Looking inside you'll add brake and clutch pedal pads (on W Series and some other models, these pedal pads were accessories), accelerator linkage, floor shift and hand brake boots, and floor mat to the list. Since they're likely to be missing, you may overlook the clutch and brake draft seals that fit over the pedal's shafts and rest against the floorboards. Dodge used the same parts to keep drafts from blowing into the bottom of the cab on its trucks from 1928-1957, so these seals are readily available. Don't overlook the steering post pad, and check the firewall for missing grommets.

Back outside you may notice previously unseen rubber gaskets sandwiched between the headlight buckets and front fenders. Dodge trucks from 1937 to 1953 also used rubber pads under the doorhandle mounting plates. As you're walking around the front of the truck, note the condition of the rubber seal between the front fenders and cowl (1946 and 1947 models used welting in this area). If the seal or welting is original, chances are it is decayed, badly frayed, perhaps missing altogether. On the prewar V and W Series, Dodge also placed bead welt in the seam between the running boards and rear fenders and between the fenders and box. At the truck's business end, you may notice two important rubber parts, the tailgate chain covers, are missing. These will join the wanted list. If you trace the path of the wiring harness, you'll probably discover that grommets intended to protect the wiring harness as it passes through holes in the body have also disappeared. Replacement grommets are not supplied with new wiring harnesses, so these, too, need to be added to the list. Dodge trucks up to the late 1950s fed air into the cab through a cowl vent; chances are the rubber gasket under the vent flap needs replacing. The list is growing longer, but probably isn't complete yet. Have you inspected the shock absorber bushings? If the truck pre-dates airplane-style telescoping shocks, the lever shocks will probably be removed for cleaning and refilling, and possibly repair. When they're replaced, you'll also want to install new rubber bushings on the shock arms. When you looked inside the cab, did you notice the condition of the door bumpers (on trucks so-equipped)? And on 1930s vintage trucks, what about the condition of the hood pads, or are they missing altogether? Rubber items differ with the various model trucks. You may notice other items not mentioned here. In any event, make as complete a

list as possible of the rubber parts that need replacing on your truck. Then we'll go shopping.

Replacement rubber sources

For more recent models, mid 1970s and up, the place to start is your Dodge dealer. Many collectors overlook the manufacturer's dealer as a parts source thinking either that new car and truck dealers only carry parts for the latest models, or that manufacturer's prices will be higher than alternative parts sources. Most often neither is the case. Dealers can usually order parts for models built within the last decade, often earlier. It's also possible that a well-established dealer who has been on the same site for several decades may have accumulated a sizeable cache of parts for older models. As to price, the dealer's list is often lower than a specialty supplier and a dealer's wholesale price is likely to be substantially lower.

The next source for the rubber items on your list is vintage parts dealers specializing in your make vehicle. For Power Wagon collectors, the parts specialist is David Butler's Vintage Power Wagons (refer to supplier's listing in the appendix for the address). Collectors of regular light-duty Dodge trucks will find Roberts Motor Parts to be the largest one-stop outlet. Well stocked as both these suppliers are, it's

On the 1939-1947 series trucks, Dodge installed weatherstrip between the front fender and cowl. Except for exceptionally well-preserved original trucks, like the example shown here, this weatherstrip will be badly cracked and decayed. If the fenders are removed for dent work, new weatherstrip seals should be used when the fenders are replaced. If the fenders are not being removed, the bolts can be loosened and new weatherstrip slipped into place. Weatherstrip is used to fill the gap where the running board fits against the front fender and lower edge of the cab, too. If this weatherstrip is allowed to deteriorate, or is missing altogether, water will seep into this gap causing rust. Between the years 1939 and 1945 this seal is molded rubber. In 1946 this gap is filled with door-opening weatherstrip.

possible that you may still have to look elsewhere to find all the rubber items on your list.

Two suppliers that should also be consulted in filling your truck's rubber parts order are Metro Moulded Parts, Inc. and Steele Rubber Parts. These suppliers specialize in manufacturing rubber parts for a wide range of vintage cars and trucks. If their catalogs don't list exact items for your truck, take measurements (or in the case of weatherstripping, examine the profile of original parts) and compare these with the universal items shown in the catalog. Manufacturers often used the same rubber parts on many vehicles.

Don't fall into the trap of ordering a universal floor mat, however. Reproduction floor mats meeting OEM standards are available for most year Dodge trucks at a reasonable price. While it's usually possible to trim a universal floor mat to match your truck (they're molded oversized to fit the widest possible range of vehicles), problems arise in trying to match any pre-cut holes with the actual location of the clutch and brake pedals, floor shift lever, accelerator and starter linkage. In addition, universal mats usually aren't molded to the contour of the transmission hump, so they won't lie flat. If a proper reproduction floor mat isn't available, it's always possible to have a trim shop cut carpeting to fit the cab floor.

If you want to dress up your vintage Dodge truck with carpeting, you'll also find floor covering kits available. This approach has two drawbacks, however. First, no one put carpet in a truck until

Lacing is used on the radiator shell and cowl to prevent the hood from squeaking or rattling. The lacing is held in place with rivets. New lacing is available from vintage Dodge truck parts suppliers.

recent years when we started to confuse the purposes of a light truck with those of a car, so this approach is definitely not original. Second, if you intend to use your truck for hauling a boat to the lake and toting occasional supplies home from the lumber yard—not especially dirty work, but jobs where you will track some grit inside the cab—you'll find it easier to sweep a floor mat than vacuum a carpet.

Occasionally, it's possible to find original rubber parts at swap meets. To be sure you've found the right part, look the part number up in advance, or better yet, bring along a cross section or the complete original part. If you buy any new-old-stock (NOS) rubber parts, make sure they are still pliable, and don't listen to a vendor's story that a stiff rubber part can be softened with a couple of coatings of Armor-All.

As a last alternative, small rubber parts can be molded or cut from rubber blocks, and larger rubber parts, such as window moldings, can be repaired at least temporarily. Molding your own rubber parts is time-consuming and most rubber parts needing repair are better discarded and replaced, so neither of these approaches is really a solution. Sometimes, though, there seems to be no other way.

Whenever you're working on an older vehicle, you should always keep your eyes open to simple alternatives for hard-to-find parts. I discovered a perfect source for rubber tailgate chain sleeves while talking to a fellow pickup truck owner at the Hershey, Pennsylvania, Fall meet. As I admired his truck, which had been in his family since new, I noted the shiny black tailgate chain covers. "Where did you find new rubber covers for the tailgate chains?" I asked. The owner chuckled, "I cut those from ten-speed bike inner tubes." Bike tire inner tubes do make ideal tailgate chain covers. Just cut the inner tube to the length you need, stretch the tube over the hook at the end of the chain, and pull it over the links. Snip off any extra, and give the rubber a shiny new look with a coating of Armor-All.

Signs that rubber needs replacing

Dryness, cracking and chunks of missing rubber are not the only reasons for replacing a truck's rubber parts. A Mustang convertible I owned a few years back would collect water in the trunk every time the car sat outside in the rain. With the deck lid open, the weatherstrip appeared to be resilient and in good condition, but when the lid pressed shut, a portion of the rubber would collapse, letting water runoff seep into the trunk. The same condition may be occurring with the door weatherstrip on your pickup. Windshield rubber can also dry out causing water to seep past the glass and drip onto the dashboard and into the cab. If you are disassembling the truck for a major restoration, you will want to replace all possible rubber parts so this job doesn't have to be done later, and so that everything will have a consistent, like-new appearance. But even if a full-scale restoration isn't planned, you may still have occasion to replace welting (fenders only need to be loosened) and many other rubber parts.

Trucks that have been partially or completely disassembled, or have received an amateur restoration, often lack many original rubber parts. Here the question becomes, what's missing? One way to determine what rubber items belong on the truck, and their locations, is to order Roberts Motor Parts Dodge truck catalog and compare the inventory of rubber items shown in the catalog with those on hand (if your truck is disassembled for restoration) or those on the truck (if it has been through the restoration process). Likely to be missing are draft seals for the clutch, brake, starter pedal, and floor shift, hood bumpers and corner pads, grommets, and other small parts.

While not rubber parts, per se, you should check the condition (and presence or absence) of the hood and cowl lacing and door window channels and glass sweepers. If your truck has experienced a lot of use or abuse, the lacing that forms a pad for the hood at the cowl and radiator may have been torn off and discarded. To check the lacing's condition, just open the hood and look for a thin strip of woven fabric running up the sides and over the top of the cowl and nose assembly. If the original lacing is still in place, most likely it will be worn, compressed and generally look its age. Window channels (the U-shaped, whisker-lined grooves in which the window glass slides) may likewise be missing. Since these channels prevent drafts and keep the window glass from rattling against the door, replacements should be installed if the originals are absent or badly worn. In most cases, the sweepers at the bottom of the window openings will also need to be replaced. These sweepers attach to the door at the base of the window frame and keep water from dripping down inside the door. They also clean the window as it is rolled up and down.

The condition and completeness of the rubber parts make a great difference in a restored or otherwise spruced-up truck's appearance. They probably won't catch your eye before repainting, but the same shabby rubber items on a freshly painted truck tell a story of a job half done.

Buying replacement rubber

The guideline here is to purchase replacement rubber only from parts vendors who carry quality Dodge reproduction parts, such as Roberts Motor Parts, or from specialty rubber parts vendors, such as

Lynn H. Steele and Metro Moulded. Avoid dealing with discount mail-order parts outlets that may carry older car parts as a sideline. Although these catalogs may show a lower price for the few rubber parts they may list as fitting Dodge trucks, the discount parts are likely to be of inferior quality, and worse yet, may not fit. Often these suppliers list so-called universal rubber parts as fitting specific makes and models. Universal door weatherstrip or window rubber may "fit" in the broadest sense of the word—that is, you could glue it onto your truck—but universal parts seldom look like originals and may have the wrong contours to make a proper seal.

After you have completed your inventory of rubber, window channels and related parts for your truck, the next step is to order parts catalogs from Roberts, Steele, and Metro Moulded, or other rubber parts vendors. When you have located the needed parts from your inventory list in the catalogs, you can compare prices and place your orders.

Installing replacement rubber

Rubber parts are typically installed as part of a larger process—while replacing a windshield—or as a detailing step *after* repainting the exterior or repainting and reupholstering the interior. Usually the only difficult part of installing rubber parts is making sure they're not forgotten and in some cases recalling exactly where they fit. If your truck is still intact (awaiting a mechanical and cosmetic upgrade, or thorough restoration), be sure to take photos and

Special weatherstrip, called fender welt, is used to fill the seam between the front fenders and grille flaring. Note the anti-rattle pad on the front corner of the hood. As can also be seen, the rivets on the hood-locking mechanism are not painted.

make notes of where the rubber parts go before taking the truck apart. If the truck is already apart, take photos and note the locations of the rubber parts on other original or restored trucks you may see at club events or shows. You may be surprised at how easily it is to be confused on the exact location of a part as familiar as the door weatherstrip.

As a case in point, on a warm August afternoon, I gathered my teenaged sons as helpers and announced that we were going to replace the door rubber on my pickup. I sent one son to the auto parts store to buy a tube of special glue used to hold weatherstrip in place and a roll of masking tape to position the rubber while the glue set. My other son and I headed for the barn where my truck is stored to plan who'd do what. Suddenly, I couldn't remember whether the rubber glued against the body or the door—both seemed suitable locations. After some thinking, I recalled peeling the weatherstrip off the bottoms of the doors and my son said he had seen rubber on the doors of a junkyard truck we'd combed for parts. Still, I couldn't recall whether the rubber followed the contour near the door's edge, or another ridge further in. Clips at the bottom of the door further confused the issue. Had they held on the original weatherstrip, or had the rubber been glued nearer the lip? We wound up gluing the weatherstrip in the location that seemed logical—not an advised approach, particularly for those who are trying to

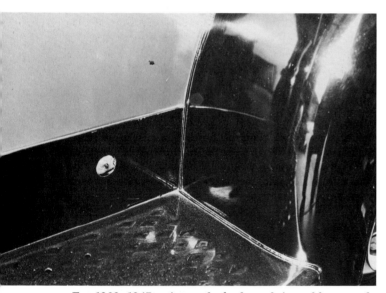

For 1939–1947 series trucks fender welt is used between the rear fender and box, and to seal the gap between the edge of running board and rear fender. This fender welting is not painted, which means that the fenders and running boards should be painted before installing them on the truck. Care will be required to avoid scratching these parts as they are bolted in place.

make their trucks factory-authentic. If I'd thought to take a few photos of the doors before they were stripped for painting, or made a drawing of the door, showing the weatherstrip's path, I'd have known exactly where the new rubber was supposed to have been attached.

In almost every instance, install rubber parts after painting. This is the sequence in which they were originally attached, with the result that rubber items left the factory unpainted. Since some disassembly is usually required to remove old rubber parts and install new, just plan to do any required painting while whatever assembly the rubber items adjoin is apart. Hood lacing should also be attached after painting, and the same sequence applies to door window channel and sweepers. In some cases, as with fender welting, the rubber items will be replaced as part of an assembly step. This means that on the older models, where welting is used to prevent squeaks at the seams, the front fenders would be painted separately, then installed. You'll discover that this approach requires great care to avoid nicking or scratching the paint in the process of bolting the fenders in place. On T and W Series, welting also seals the seam between the rear fenders and the box. The B, C and later Series do not use welting on the rear fenders; however, a bead of suitable sealer (liquid anti-squeak or rubber caulk) should be applied to the fender lip where it contacts the box to prevent moisture from penetrating this seam.

Rubber parts that are installed as part of mechanical repair, such as shock absorber bushings, are fitted in place during the reassembly step. If you're replacing the steering post pad, it'll be necessary to remove the steering column from the truck and disassemble the tube from the steering box. This effort is warranted on a full-scale restoration where you'll be overhauling the steering box and applying a high-gloss finish to the column, but if you're only doing needed mechanical and cosmetic work, pulling the steering column to replace the post pad probably isn't worth the effort, unless the original pad is completely deteriorated or missing, and then you may want to slit the replacement pad so as to fit it onto the post. The slit can be mended with glue.

Many rubber items, both inside the cab and on the truck's exterior, are replaced during the detailing process. Examples inside the cab include the pedal pads, draft seals, and glovebox bumpers; examples on the exterior would be doorhandle mounting pads, the gas tank filler pipe grommet and tailgate chain rubbers. Most of these items just fit into place. If the fit is snug, as will most likely be the case with the filler pipe grommet and tailgate chain rubbers, a light coating of liquid dish soap to the rubber surface will allow the items to slide easily into place.

As stated earlier, door weatherstripping attaches with special glues. The process is relatively simple, but does involve several steps. At some point, the old rubber has to be removed. Usually this is done in preparation for rust repair and repainting. Although the old weatherstrip can often be pulled loose by hand, usually some of the rubber and glue sticks to the metal and has to be scraped clean with a putty knife. If you just want to replace the rubber and aren't planning on repainting, you will need to scrape cautiously to avoid scratching the paint. Prep solvent, used to remove wax and tar from a finish in preparation for painting, can be used to soften the old glue and should be used to clean the surface before gluing new weatherstrip in place. If the old rubber has hardened and is difficult to remove, you can soften it by removing the door insert or upholstery panel and applying a low flame from a torch against the backside of the metal. This method should not be used if the inside of the door is undercoated since the flame could ignite the petroleum-based undercoating.

The metal around the old weatherstrip may look solid, but you're likely to find rust scale behind hardened or decayed rubber. If so, it's essential to clean away the rust before proceeding. When metal work isn't planned, you can clean surface rust with a wire-brush or spot sandblaster, then prepare the metal with Naval Jelly, a phosphoric acid gel available in hardware stores. The white residue left by the gel should be wiped off with a damp cloth before painting. The metal can then be primed and touch-up painted. If refinishing is planned, the weatherstrip channel can be sandblasted and any rustout (which typically occurs at the bottom of the doors) repaired.

Weatherstrip cement is available at auto parts stores. This glue comes in two types. One is applied to the metal and the weatherstrip is pressed in place while the glue is still fresh. With the other, a bead of glue is applied to both the metal and weatherstrip. When both glue surfaces have become tacky the weatherstrip is pressed in place. With either type, you should be careful not to dab the glue outside the weatherstrip channel. Extra glue can be cleaned up with prep solvent, but it doesn't come off easily. If necessary, the rubber can be held in place on curves and the bottom of the doors with strips of masking tape. Normally, though, the glue is sticky enough to hold the rubber snugly in place. The doors should not be closed for several hours to give the glue time to set. The rubber cowl vent seal is attached following the same method.

In most cases, weatherstrip can be replaced with the doors on the truck. If it is necessary to remove the

Welting is also used between the rear fenders and body, and at the running board on 1939–1947 Panel trucks. Owners who enter their trucks in show competition will clean wax residue from the seams around the welting with a toothbrush.

doors to place the weatherstrip along the fronts of the doors, be sure to mark the hinge locations so that the doors can be reinstalled with a minimum of fitting. If you take the doors off for refinishing, it's wise to apply the finish and glue on the weatherseal before refitting the doors. The only difficulty with this approach is avoiding scratching the freshly painted doors as they're being jockeyed into place.

On some trucks, window channel simply press-fits into the U-shaped channel on the door frame. On others, it glues in place against blocks, or is held by screws. If you removed the old channel, then the attaching method should be clear. If you didn't, ask the vendor which attaching method applies to your truck when you buy the replacement channel. To install new window channel, first measure the channel distance (sides and upper window frame area), then cut and bend the channel to fit the contour of the window frame. Weatherstripping glue can be used to hold the channel to the window frame.

Installing door glass sweepers is a bit trickier. On older trucks, the sweeper strips are held in place with clips. On newer models, the sweepers are secured with staples, but clips can be used if holes are drilled. When installing the sweeper, make sure the glass is rolled down as far as it will go. If you need even more glass clearance, you can detach the glass frame from the roll-up mechanism and let it rest against the bottom of the door. The sweeper has to be installed after the glass is in the door, and the problem here is the risk of breaking the glass while squeezing the clips to secure the sweeper. If the window is

Rubber grommets seal the bumper brace hole in the body of 1939–1947 Dodge Panel trucks. Also notice how the taillight wiring enters the rear panel door below the door hinge. When restoring a truck, it is a good idea to take photographs of details like these so that you will be sure to recapture the original look when the restoration is completed.

plain automotive glass (found on some older trucks or often used as replacement), it will crack easily.

Window channel and glass sweeper material are supplied in 8 ft. strips. These items can be purchased by mail order from vendors such as Roberts Motor Parts or Restoration Specialties and Supply, or others who frequent most large swap meets. It's advantageous to buy these long items at swap meets because they have to be cut or folded to meet postal or UPS regulations if being mailed.

Replacing glass

Unless you have experience replacing windshield glass, it's best to leave this job to professionals. Besides making glass installation look easy, the professionals will also make sure that the rubber is sealed to the window channel to prevent future seepage. On an older truck, window glass should be removed for painting so that any rust which may have developed from water seeping past the dried out window rubber can be cleaned off and the window frame area repainted. If the glass has discolored (likely on an older vehicle) you can purchase new flat safety glass from GLASCO, and other vendors.

On models through the B Series that used flat glass exclusively, and for flat door glass on later years, you can also have replacement windows cut by a local automotive glass sales office. Unless you specify otherwise, the glass shop will cut the replacement windows from standard automotive safety glass. This glass cracks easily and you will find door glass prone to breakage if the doors are slammed shut. A recommended alternative is tempered safety glass, the type used in modern vehicles. This glass is resistant to cracking. If struck a hard, sharp blow, tempered glass will fracture (but not shatter) like an ice cube. Your local glass shop probably can't cut tempered glass, but the shop should be able to send templates (cardboard patterns) of your truck's flat windows to the distributor or manufacturer where the glass will be cut. If you order tempered replacement glass, be sure to cut the template exactly to the contour of your truck's window. Tempered glass is hard and nearly impossible to recontour once the shape has been cut.

Rubber preservation

Rubber deteriorates (dulls, hardens and cracks) when exposed to sunlight, so to keep rubber parts soft and pliable, and to preserve their freshly-installed, glossy look, it's a good idea to treat the rubber each time you wash your truck. The product to use is Armor-All, a rubber moisturizer and protectorant, available at any discount mart's automotive department. Armor-All can be sprayed directly onto the rubber, or applied to a rag and wiped on, where it freshens the rubber and leaves a glossy sheen. This protective and rejuvenating coating should be applied to the tires as well.

Unless you hear wind whistling past the doors, or see telltale water marks on the dash, the condition of your truck's rubber parts can be easy to overlook. Nonetheless, you should plan on replacing most, if not all, of the rubber parts on an older light truck, especially if the vehicle has spent most of its life in warm, sunny climates. When estimating restoration and refinishing expenses, plan to allow between $300 and $500 for the replacement rubber parts (not including tires). It's wise to order the complete rubber inventory early so you will be able to install new rubber items whenever they're called for in the rebuilding process.

Chapter 13

Interior Restoration

Although truck interiors are designed for utility, ruggedness and durability, a vintage truck would have to be extremely well cared for not to show wear, tears, a sagging headliner and other signs that the interior needs repair or replacement. Fortunately, redoing a truck interior is a much simpler and less expensive process than replacing the upholstery in a car. Until recently, truck interiors were outfitted in plain, durable Naugahyde or vinyl, with a cardboard headliner, door and kick panels. Through the 1950s, even the color of the interior was durable. Typically, the seats and cardboard trim were a sort of moose brown color that withstood soiling because dirt and grease blended right in. But that's not to say that a worn, soiled interior will look good in a refinished truck. One of the most dramatic upgrades you can make is repadding and recovering the seats and installing new interior panels.

Thanks to interior kits, which are available for all Dodge light trucks from 1936 to 1960, redoing your truck's upholstery can be an easy, highly satisfying, weekend undertaking. If you're not the do-it-yourself type and plan to have an upholstery shop install the interior, you're still ahead to start with a kit for two important reasons. First, with the kit you'll get as close to the original color and materials as it is possible to come. Second, the headliner is almost impossible to fabricate, even by an experienced trimmer. An interior kit (available from Roberts Motor Parts) provides the headliner and other interior panels, all precision-cut and trimmed to fit in your truck just like the items an assembly worker would have installed when the truck rolled down the line.

When you tell an upholsterer that you want him to install an interior kit in your truck, he may at first be skeptical about quality. Some interior kits for older cars are of inferior materials and shoddily cut. If the upholsterer has had a bad experience with one of these kits, he will be understandably leery of kit interiors. You can assure him that this is not the case with a Dodge truck interior kit purchased from a reputable supplier such as Dave Butler's Vintage Power Wagons or Roberts Motor Parts. If you order the kit in advance, you can show it to the trimmer to relax his fears about quality. Besides keeping your truck as close to original looking as possible, a kit enables a professional upholsterer to replace the seat coverings and install the interior panels in a fraction of the time that would be required to fabricate these items.

It's a good idea to make contact with an experienced interior man even if you are planning to redo

Hog-ring pliers are the basic tool needed to replace seat coverings. The jaws on these special pliers are grooved to hold the rings. When pliers are used to pinch the rings closed, the rings are likely to slip, possibly causing you to pinch your fingers and turning what could be an easy job into a frustrating experience. The Eastwood Company

Using a special tool called a stretching plier to pull seat covering over the springs assures a uniform pull on the fabric and prevents tearing or stretching. The wide jaw on the stretching plier gives a much better grip on the fabric than you can get by hand. The Eastwood Company.

your truck's interior yourself. Then, if you run into trouble, you will have someone to call on for advice—or rescue.

A complete interior kit is purchased in three packages: a seat kit containing the upper and lower spring coverings and clips for securing these coverings; a spring pad kit containing burlap to recover the springs, plus cotton and foam padding; and the headliner kit which also includes the cardboard door and kick panels (except for Power Wagons where only the headliner is needed). Dodge trucks back to the mid 1930s also contain three other interior trim items: a firewall pad, an armrest and a sun visor. Authentic firewall pads with all holes cut in the correct locations, and properly covered, and ready-to-install armrests are also available. Sun visors also typically need recovering.

Recovering seat cushions

Before starting to redo your truck interior, you will need the proper tools. These include heavy-duty scissors, hog ring pliers, a utility or X-Acto knife, and a pair of heavy wire cutters. Since the seats will be removed from the truck during body repair and painting, they can be recovered anytime. Installing the headliner and panel kit will wait until after exterior and interior painting. If your truck still has its original headliner and cardboard panels, you should

take detailed photos or make drawings of exactly how these pieces fit in place. It's also a good idea to keep the original pieces to use in checking the fit of the new panels. In addition, the sharp, original coloring on the edges of the original headliner will show where one piece overlapped another.

Several preparation steps come before actually recovering the seats. First, the cushions are removed from the truck and stripped of old covering, padding and spring wrapping. With the old upholstery material removed, you can now inspect the springs for damage to the frame and broken coils. If the coils are sagging or broken, you should look for a better set. It is possible to replace the broken coils, but in most cases you'd be ahead just to find another set of springs. If the springs and frame are rusted, you should clean the metal with a wirebrush and spray on a protective coating of rust-resistant paint. This is also the time to place the order for the seat covering and interior kits.

One person can recover a set of seat springs fairly easily, but it helps to have an extra pair of hands when pulling on the covering. When you come to that step, it's a good idea to invite a friend to help. Starting with the bare springs, the first step is to wrap the springs with burlap. The covering anchors to the seat and backrest frames with hog rings that are supplied with the kit. The purpose of the burlap is to keep the padding from settling into the coils. Next you will lay the padding over the top and around the sides of the springs. In most cases, kits supply the right amount of fabric and padding, so don't cut any excess until you are sure everything is installed right. Now you can place the foam rubber over the padding on the top of the cushion. The padding and foam are held in place by the cover, which is now fitted over the top and sides of the springs.

As you fit the cover over the cushion, your three aims are to align the seam with the outline of the frame, work out all wrinkles in the covering, and pull the fabric tightly enough so that it won't sag when you sit on the cushion, but not so tight that seats have no give. Once you have the cover in place, with the seam forming an even outline around the contour frame, turn the cushion over and pull the fabric tight. Now you can begin to attach the covering to the spring frame using hog rings. If these small wire clips are not supplied with the kit, they can be purchased from most any upholstery shop, auto dealers, local hardware stores or ordered through a restoration supplier such as The Eastwood Company. The hog rings have sharp ends that can be pressed through the cover fabric and are squeezed around the seat frame using hog ring pliers available from specialty tool suppliers such as Eastwood.

Attach the hog rings at the seatfront first, then pull the fabric snug and attach a few hog rings at the rear. If the covering has too much, or not enough, give, you can remove the clips at the rear of the frame and give it a little more slack or pull the covering tighter. By adjusting the tension from the back of the seat, any extra holes punched by refitting the hog rings won't be noticed. When the covering has the desired snugness, it should be pulled slightly tighter to allow for future stretching, then secured to the frame with hog rings spaced about 2–3 in. apart.

Installing interior panels

On a vintage truck, the headliner, door and kick panels are made of cardboard. When these panels are purchased in a kit, they are cut to fit and the headliner may be pre-bent to the roof contour, so installation is quite simple. On some Dodge truck models, the interior panels are held in place with screws. On others, a combination of screws and snaps do the job. Above the doors and at the door edge of the kick panels, the cardboard may be secured behind metal strips. As with the seat cushions, a helper should be on hand when you set out to install the headliner. One person can easily install the door and kick panels, but if you also have help with this job, it will be done in half the time.

As you fit the headliner panels around the rear window(s), you'll find it helpful to look at the original interior, or your notes on the assembly sequence. In most cases, the lower panels are installed first, with the headliner panel overlapping slightly. If you've kept the original panels, you can easily see where the overlaps occur by looking at the edges. Areas that have been covered by another panel will be darker colored than the exposed surface which has been faded by the sun. On a quality kit, the panel edges will be trimmed out with Naugahyde.

If the headliner contours are not pre-formed, or if you need to increase the bend, moisten the backside of the cardboard in the areas where the bends will occur with a mixture of 80 percent household ammonia and 20 percent water. This mixture can be sprayed onto the cardboard; remember to spray the backside so that stains will not show on the good side. The cardboard should not be soaked, just moistened. You will then find that it bends easily without crinkling. The ammonia will smell for a day or so until it dries, but this is a small inconvenience compared to the ease with which the mixture enables you to bend the cardboard. You'll find that installing a headliner

Door upholstery on B Series Dodges consists of an embossed panel that attaches to the door skin with sheet metal screws. This straightforward approach makes upholstering a truck much easier than a car. The metal panel below the door upholstery can be removed to reach the window mechanism.

Door upholstery on 1939–1947 Dodge Pickups also consists of an embossed panel. For 1939 and 1940, this panel was colored Royal Blue. Note the position of the window crank and doorhandle.

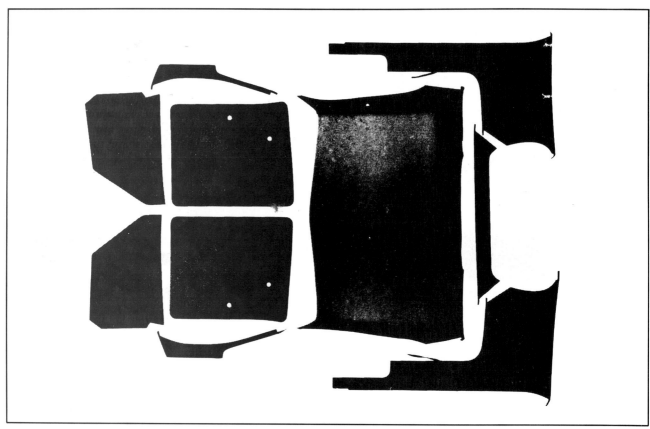

Replacement headliner and interior kits for 1936–1959 Dodge trucks are available in kit form from suppliers such as Robert Motor Parts. With a little care and patience, reupholstering a truck can be a successful do-it-yourself project. A Power Wagon interior kit is shown here.

is a two-person job, so plan to have an assistant on hand when you tackle this project.

While the basic interior panel design applies to most vintage Dodge trucks, you may encounter some variations. Power Wagon interiors differ from standard pickups in that the military-based Power Wagon dispensed with the cardboard door and kick

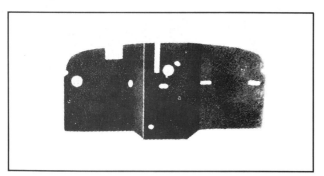

Firewall pads typically need replacing as well. When installing the firewall pad, you'll need a helper to hold the bolts on the opposite side of the firewall. Reproduction pads are available from Dodge parts suppliers like Roberts Motor Parts.

panels. A Panel truck's interior will also be different in that you probably won't find upholstery kits for the bucket seats. However, the covering and seat design are straightforward enough for any upholsterer to easily redo these seats. Owners of W Series Panel trucks may be interested to know that Dodge offered real leather seat coverings as a deluxe option. If you'd rather sit on leather, you can have an upholsterer recover the driver's and optional passenger's bucket seats in genuine hides and be fully authentic. The door and kick panels from a pickup interior kit will also fit on a panel truck, as may part of the headlining.

Armrests and sun visors

Shabby armrests and sun visor will certainly stand out in a restored interior unless these items are also recovered or replaced. If you've had an upholsterer make up the seat coverings, the armrests can also be recovered in leftover seat material. If you ordered a seat covering kit, you may also want to order replacement armrests.

The cardboard lining in the glovebox may also be tattered, or missing. Replacements for this item

Lower cab interior coverings consist of the kick panels on the sides of the cab, the firewall pad and floor mat. This photo shows these items on a 1940 Dodge Pickup. Avoid purchasing a universal floor mat as holes for the shift lever and pedals are unlikely to be cut in the correct locations.

On 1939–1947 series Dodge trucks the forward edge of the headliner is also held in place by retaining moldings that attach above the windshield header. Note that these retaining moldings are painted to match the interior cab color.

are available from Roberts and other Dodge truck parts suppliers.

Even though it isn't seen unless you are cleaning your truck's floor, the firewall pad is also likely to be a candidate for replacement. If you decide to install a new firewall pad, you'll need a partner on one side of the cowl while you remove fasteners and linkages or wiring that passes through the firewall on the other.

The best time to replace a firewall pad is while the truck is disassembled for restoration.

Steering wheel restoration

If your truck dates to the 1950s or earlier, it's likely that the original plastic steering wheel is cracked, possibly gouged and chipped as well, and is a candidate for the discard pile. If your thought has

The headliner on 1939–1947 Dodge Pickups had no seam above the door and was of one-piece, molded design. On replacements, the bends are pre-stamped making this piece quite easy to install. Note the retaining strip above the door that holds the sides of the headliner in place.

The headliner in Dodge Panel trucks covers only the driver's area. Note the moldings and retaining screws that hold the headliner in place. The body framing is left exposed on the Panel's cargo area.

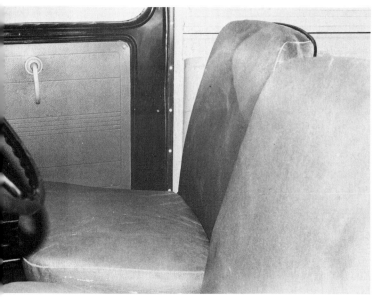

Seat upholstery in 1939–1947 series Dodge Panel trucks consists of simple Naugahyde coverings. Leather seat coverings could be ordered for these trucks as an option. This truck is fitted with the optional passenger seat.

The domelight is set into the headliner at the rear of the cab on 1939–1947 Dodge Pickups. Note the retaining molding that surrounds the rear window. This molding serves the double purpose of holding the cardboard panels in place as well as giving a finished look in this area.

been to buy a replacement steering wheel, you're in for a disappointment. Reproduction steering wheels aren't being made for vintage Dodge trucks, new-old-stock wheels are extremely scarce, and used wheels without cracks are no more plentiful. Sending the wheel to a restoration service is one solution, but you can quite easily restore a cracked, deteriorated steering wheel yourself for the cost of some inexpen-

sive supplies. The main ingredients are time and patience, and if you like to tinker and putter at your hobby, the time spent restoring a vintage car or truck steering wheel can be a therapeutic diversion from daily concerns.

Steering wheel removal

The first step is to remove the steering wheel from the vehicle. For this job, a puller will be used.

This rear view of the Panel truck shows the unfinished cargo area. Operators of these trucks often hung tool or supply racks from the metal bracing.

The domelight also appeared in the rear of the cab on B Series trucks. Note the buttons holding the headliner in place as opposed to screws used on W Series trucks. Here, too, moldings give a finished look around the rear windows.

First, you'll have to access the nut holding the steering wheel to the shaft. This nut is located under the horn button, which can't just be pried loose. On most Dodge trucks pushing in on the button and turning it clockwise will move the ears past their slots, allowing the button to pop free. Still, its a good idea to refer to the service manual for your model truck to check on the exact procedure for removing the horn button.

Now the nut holding the steering wheel to the end of the steering shaft should be visible. This nut may be crowded by the spring-mounted ring that held the horn button in place. The ring can generally be removed by loosening a few screws. To avoid rounding the edges of the steering shaft nut, use a socket wrench, not an adjustable wrench or pliers, to remove the nut. A breaker bar should provide ample torque. The next step, pulling the wheel loose from the shaft, will typically be harder.

Unless the steering wheel shows signs of sliding off the shaft easily, don't try to free it by pulling on the spokes. Although the service manual may show a special steering wheel puller, a push-type puller and attachment for removing gears that will fit under the base of the steering wheel hub can be used as well. This type of puller and gear attachment may be purchased from an auto parts store that carries a professional tool line. Also, it may be possible to rent this tool combination from a rental store. The push-style puller should be used to free the steering wheel because the gear attachment will anchor the puller against the base of the steering wheel hub so that all force is exerted against the shaft, not on the soft

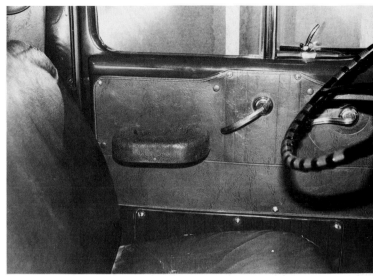

Dodge DeLuxe cab Pickups featured one armrest, which was placed on the driver's side. The lack of this amenity and a sun shade on the passenger side give the impression that the manufacturer thought its trucks would typically be operated without passengers. Also, leaving off these extras helped keep truck prices low.

steering wheel. A grip-type puller (this style has two or three arms called jaws) should not be used. The problem with a grip puller is that the jaws exert uneven force on the steering wheel hub, raising the possibility of cracking the hub if the steering wheel is rusted to the shaft. Also, the jaws may slip, cracking or gouging the plastic.

Dodge Pickups through the 1950s typically carried one sun shade on the driver's side. Many restorers install the passenger-side sun shade, which was available on Pickups as an option.

To fill the cracks in the rim and hub of your Dodge truck's steering wheel, you'll need a file to open up the cracks and Flexible Bumper & Plastic Patch, Martin Senour product 6352 available from NAPA auto parts stores nationwide. The patching product is designed for repairing rubber fascia on modern cars.

The filler material is a two-part epoxy that is mixed in equal proportions. The two tubes contain material in contrasting colors (black and white) so a consistent gray coloring shows when the two parts have been thoroughly mixed. The filler dries in about 15 minutes, so only a portion of the wheel is repaired at a time.

Crack repair

Once the wheel is removed, its restoration can begin. This process, which is really very simple, begins by opening the cracks with a V-shaped file then filling the enlarged channels, along with any chips, with two-part epoxy. Don't worry about the look of the steering wheel at this point. What's important is that the filler penetrates to the bottom of the cracks.

To fill the cracks you will use a special epoxy patching compound formulated to repair plastic fascia on modern automobiles. Several companies produce this patch epoxy which is available from auto supply stores. Evercoat, the trade name of a line of automotive refinishing and body repair products, markets a two-part epoxy called Flex Patch, product

The filler is applied in sufficient quantity to completely fill the cracks. A small finishing nail or toothpick works well as an applicator to apply the filler. Since the filler is of a thick consistency, it can be applied all the way around the wheel.

number 385, which is specifically formulated for automotive use. Martin-Senour sells a similar product called Flexible Bumper and Plastic Patch, number 6352. The Martin-Senour product has a rubber consistency and appearance. These patch epoxies make an extremely strong bond, yet remain flexible, thereby lessening the possibility of the filler's cracking loose in temperature fluctuations.

The patch epoxy is activated by squeezing equal amounts from each tube onto a scrap of cardboard. The two puddles are mixed together and the epoxy is dabbed into the cracks using a slender applicator such as a small nail or toothpick. You'll want to build up the filler so that it flows over the top of the cracks. The same applies if you are filling chips and gouges. The extra filler will make a messy-looking job, but overdoing things a bit now will make the next steps easier. If you're filling deep chips and cracks, you'll have to wait for the filler to set—usually just a few minutes—before turning the steering wheel over and working on the other side.

When the epoxy has cured thoroughly (the time varies with temperature and humidity, check the box for recommended curing times), file the overflow nearly smooth with the adjacent contours. For this step you'll use a medium-coarse metal file, rounded on one side. You'll need to tap the file frequently to clean the teeth of build-up, and it may be necessary to run a wirebrush over the file occasionally to grate away the extra filler.

The file will cut through the epoxy with ease and into the steering wheel with equal ease. To avoid making new gouges that will also have to be filled, work the file only over the filler. The rounded side is used to level excess filler in cracks around the ends of the spokes and in the finger grips.

After you've grated away most of the filler, sand the epoxy so that the filled spots are perfectly smooth with the surface of the wheel. Coarse sandpaper will make this step go faster, but can also cut into the steering wheel's soft plastic. Instead use a medium-coarse, 80 grit paper and proceed cautiously. I wrap the sandpaper around a small stick, slightly wider than the filler (such as a Popsicle handle) so that I can sand the epoxy without risking cutting into the wheel. For rounded spots, such as the finger grips, I roll the paper around a small dowel to make sure the cutting action is focused on the filler, not the steering wheel's soft plastic.

Once all excess filler has been removed, the entire steering wheel should be sanded to erase the glaze from its original finish. For this step, I use 220 grit automotive sandpaper and wet sand the hub, rim and spokes. Wet sanding requires special wet-and-dry sandpaper, available at automotive supply stores.

Dip the sandpaper in a bucket of water prior to sanding, and then frequently dunk the sandpaper in water while sanding. The advantage of wet sanding is that the water acts as a lubricant to carry off used abrasive and surface residue, which in turn keeps the sandpaper clean. After sanding, the plastic will be substantially duller. Depending on the product used, the filler may stand out as glossier spots.

Now you can carefully inspect all the places you've filled and sanded, making sure that each is smooth with the adjacent surface. Give the entire steering wheel a close inspection at this point to make sure you didn't overlook any cracks, nicks or gouges. If imperfections remain, mix more filler, dab it on, wait for it to dry, then file away the excess and sand these touch-up areas smooth. You may have to repeat this patching, filing and sanding process several times before the entire surface of the steering wheel is free from imperfections and ready to paint.

Before coating the steering wheel with a shiny layer of paint, a primer coating needs to be applied. You can spray the primer from an aerosol can if you wish since you will be wet sanding the primer before you finish painting. Whether you use an aerosol can or spray gun, build up a fairly heavy primer layer by applying several thin coatings. Let the primer dry thoroughly, then wet sand to a smooth finish using 360 grit paper.

To make sure every imperfection has been eliminated, you can spray on a coating of red primer, let it dry, then go over the red with another coating of gray primer. Now, as you sand away the gray coating, spots of red will show low areas that need to be filled. To raise deep nicks, you'll need to sand to the plastic and fill with epoxy. Minor cavities can be filled with a build-up of primer. When the surface is smooth, spray on a light primer coat and wet sand with fine 600 grit paper. Now the steering wheel is ready for finish painting, but don't be impatient. The primer coat should be given 24–36 hours to dry.

Painting

For the finish coat you should position the steering wheel so that its major surfaces, the spokes and rim, are flat and both the top and underside are easily accessible. To access both the top and underside for painting, I placed my wheel on a tall stand. An alternative is to drill a hole near the end of a ½ in. diameter wooden dowel (the dowel must fit through the hole in the center of the steering wheel hub), then run a short nail through the hole you've drilled. This dowel can now be inserted up through the steering wheel and suspended from the ceiling of your shop to hold the wheel while painting.

There are a couple of options for applying the finish coat. The first is a lacquer finish to which a

After the filler has hardened, the excess is pared off using a sharp X-Acto or utility knife. As an alternative method, the excess filler can be sanded off. When sanding, be careful not to cut into the soft surface of the steering wheel.

flexible catalyst has been added. A flexible catalyst is a painting additive (available from any automotive paint store) that is typically mixed with paint sprayed over rubber fascia on modern cars to keep the paint from cracking. The flex agent would be added to the steering wheel finish coat for the same reason.

The second option is to apply a finish coat of enamel. If you primed the steering wheel with an aerosol primer from a discount mart, chances are the base coating is enamel. This means that the finish

When all excess filler has been removed, the steering wheel is primed. An aerosol spray automotive primer works fine for this step. Your main goal is a good build-up of primer. It is not essential to avoid runs at this step because they will be sanded out.

After priming, the wheel is sanded using 360 wet-and-dry automotive sandpaper. Imperfections are filled by applying more primer and resanding. This process is repeated until the surface of the wheel is perfectly smooth and ready for final finishing.

Black epoxy enamel, also available in spray cans, produces a glossy, durable finish. The repaired steering wheel will really dress up the truck's interior.

coat must also be enamel. An epoxy enamel, such as DuPont's Imron, gives a durable, high-gloss finish. Imron, or its equivalent from other paint manufacturers, must be sprayed using a spray paint gun and air compressor, and also requires that stringent safety precautions be taken. These include wearing a charcoal-activated breathing mask to protect against inhaling the toxic fumes, and full clothing to prevent the paint overspray from contacting the skin.

Another easy way to apply a high-gloss finish to your steering wheel is with an aerosol epoxy used to touch up appliances. This finish will look every bit as good as sprayed lacquer or enamel and doesn't require an air compressor and spray gun. You'll find epoxy paints in aerosol cans at appliance stores and most discount marts.

Both lacquer and epoxy paints dry quickly, so as long as you keep the spray gun or aerosol nozzle moving around the wheel to avoid building up any one spot you should have little problem with runs. Usually several thin coats are applied, waiting 10–15 minutes between coats. The last coat needs to be thin and wet for high gloss. If a run develops, don't stop. Complete the coating, then let the paint dry thoroughly. The run can be sanded, the spot re-primed if needed and the entire wheel finish painted again.

If dust settles in the paint, a lacquer finish can still be smoothed to a mirror surface with polishing compound. Let the paint cure several days before polishing. Epoxy isn't as forgiving. When spraying epoxy, wait for a warm, still day and paint in a clean shop or spray booth.

Remounting

Before replacing the steering wheel on the vehicle, spray a liberal coating of light lubricant such as WD–40 or CRC 5–56 on the steering shaft splines and on the splined hub in the center of the wheel. This way, if you want to remove the wheel later on, it will come off much easier than most likely was the case at the start of the steering wheel restoration process. The steering wheel should slide easily onto the shaft. If it doesn't, don't force it by pressing your weight against the rim or the spokes. Instead, clean the end of the steering shaft with a wirebrush or steel wool, then coat the splines with WD–40 and a dab of light grease (petroleum jelly works well). If the steering wheel is still tight on the splines, place a short piece of pipe over the threaded end of the steering shaft and tap against the metal collar in the center of the steering wheel hub.

When the steering wheel is seated on the shaft, you can replace the nut and horn button apparatus. The job is now finished. Admirers will think you found a new-old-stock steering wheel, but you'll have the satisfaction of knowing that you've rescued yet another part for your vehicle from the discard pile. Steering wheel restoration is a job that requires no special skills and is a putterer's delight, offering a perfect break from the tensions of the day and providing visible progress at each stage.

Chapter 14

L-6 Engine Rebuild

by David Pollock

In addition to passenger car and truck applications, Chrysler L-6 engines can be found running pumps, sawmills, boats, forklifts, generating plants and tractors. They were available new up to about 1970 and are still listed by many rebuilders, including your local Chrysler agency, if they have a sharp parts manager. Since so many were built, and because of their wide application, Chrysler-built sixes are not hard to find, even today. This is a big advantage to the restorer of a truck powered by one of these engines. Replacement parts are relatively easy to get, and parts interchangeability is truly amazing. If you are the owner of such a car, you owe it to yourself to have

your engine running as well as possible, be it in stock or modified form.

Several names have been given to these engines over the years. The polite ones include Gold Seal, Getaway, Ace, Crown, Spitfire and the formidable T-120, which was a heavy-duty 251 used in truck and industrial applications. They were widely known for economy and long life, but those of us who tried to run them too fast and too hard often called them names which cannot be printed here.

Many of us have discovered this engine's limitations. Despite its faults, however, it's a lovely piece of engineering. About 90 percent of my mileage has been behind these engines; we're suspicious about "them-there overheads" around my place. Compare

The first step in overhauling a Dodge L-6 is to remove the engine from the truck. In doing so, be sure to follow the instructions in the service manual, and label all wiring leads. It also helps to have containers ready to store all washers, nuts and other small parts. After the engine is removed it can be cleaned by power washing at a car wash.

This engine from a B Series truck is attached to a Fluid Drive transmission. Note the fluid coupling and friction clutch. Fluid Drive was a semi-automatic transmission that used a clutch for starting and reverse.

the Dodge-Chrysler six with the competition back in the 1930s and 1940s and you'll see what it had to offer as things that are taken for granted today: precision insert bearings, aluminum-alloy pistons, fully drilled crankshaft, hardened valve seats, floating power

The transmission may be removed with the engine out or left in the truck. Here the Fluid Drive is removed from the clutch housing for inspection and repair as needed. Note that the engine and transmission have been cleaned prior to disassembly. Work proceeds easier when time is taken for a thorough cleaning.

For rebuilding the engine will be completely disassembled. An engine stand supports the engine block at a convenient working height, and prevents parts from becoming damaged as might occur if the engine is worked on while resting on the shop floor.

mounts, a block which was not prone to crack, bypass thermostats, controlled water distribution, vacuum and centrifugal spark advance, oil filtration and more.

That's the good news; now for the bad. Head gaskets may fail between siamesed cylinders; upper cylinders wear, causing top-ring failure; crankshafts tend to get out of round, causing rod bearing failure; and timing chains stretch, reducing power. These problems are common to all aging engines and need not be chronic or terminal. Their onset depends on how the engine is used and maintained, rather than on age or mileage. I have seen engines with more than 100,000 miles running well, and others totally worn out at 40,000. An average, pre-overhaul life, in my experience, is about 70,000 miles in passenger-car service.

Outlined are several approaches to engine repair, from patch-up to the complete rebuild. It is not my intent to give how-to lessons. These engines require the same overhaul techniques as any other, and specifications are available in technical publications, but perhaps my experiences may benefit those of you who are new to the game.

Three approaches to engine rebuilding are outlined. It is rare nowadays to find an engine that will respond to a quick, in-car overhaul, so it might be wise to do as complete a job as required while parts are still available at reasonable prices.

Budget overhaul

A low cost patch-up is never a cure-all, but if well done, it may last for years. This can be done in or out of the chassis, and involves replacing bearing inserts, timing chain, seals, rings and grinding valves. It is feasible if the engine is running smoothly with good oil pressure and has no horrible knocks and clunks.

Flush the cooling system before disassembly to ascertain general condition. It is important that the water distribution tube behind the water pump is clear and in good condition. Some of these are brass, but many are steel and subject to corrosion. Sediment tends to collect in the lower region of the block. Be wary if the block drain is plugged; I've found sediment more than 2 in. deep there.

Remove cylinder ridges with a reamer before attempting to remove pistons. If the top rings are broken, it would be wise to check cylinders for taper. Badly tapered cylinders will greatly reduce the life expectancy of your overhaul. Mark number 2 and 3 mains to avoid confusion; on postwar engines, they look the same.

After all parts are cleaned, the top grooves of the pistons should be machined and Hastings G.L. spacers installed. This brings the top groove back to specs, preventing up and down slapping of the ring. In cylinders that are slightly tapered, the top ring has a lot of flexing to do and it needs all the help it can get.

Other points to check are the cylinder head; a good straight surface checked from end to end is a must! The oil pump and pickup should be checked as well as the tube that lubricates the timing chain. Standard assembly procedures should then be followed.

Plastigage all bearings and don't forget to seat the bearing against its journal before gauging; tap gently on the top of the piston and suport the weight of the crankshaft when checking the mains if the engine is still in the car, otherwise you will not get a true reading. Bearings are available in 0.001 and 0.002 in. undersize for slightly worn shafts; shim stock may also be placed under the shell. Special feathered stock is made especially for this purpose; follow the directions on the package. I would be careful with this approach and would not recommend it for an engine which is going to be used hard. Never file bearing caps.

Valve tappets should be set hot, but I have found 0.011 in. cold is a good initial setting. The cylinder head must be tightened according to sequence and should be retightened as soon as the engine is warm. Although the book says not to, I usually apply a good gasket sealer to the head gasket. I have never had a gasket that has been sealed fail in normal service, including some that have been used two or three times!

At this point, you may wish to have a priest bless your work, but if you have used care and common sense, the engine will run better than before.

Stock rebuild

This is a straightforward job of returning all wearing and gasket surfaces to factory specifications. Done correctly, a rebuilt engine should be as good or better than new—no green castings, that's for sure! The services of a machine shop specializing in engine work will be required. If you are prepared to do the dirty work and reassembly, a rebuild can be done for about $600, but don't be surprised if it runs to twice that amount.

Most people will want to use the engine block that is in their truck. Check the block for signs of trouble before you are totally committed. While cleaning, look for the cracks that are most likely to occur on either side of the distributor due to a frozen water jacket or through the fuel pump opening from careless handling or a collision. Check the area around exhaust valve guides, looking down into the block after removing valves. Chrysler L-6 blocks

were not prone to cracking, but it pays to check. A careful visual inspection is usually sufficient. If you suspect a crack, fill the water jacket with kerosene and the crack will show up for sure.

If the engine has unusual wear or damage to the crankshaft, check the alignment of the main bearing seats. A problem here can be corrected by align-boring. Do not reuse a connecting rod that has spun a bearing shell. Check all rods for alignment and true-ness of the bearing seat. A simple test for rod alignment is to swing two rods on one wrist pin and see if any light shows between the big-end flanges.

Chemical cleaning of the block is a good idea. Bear in mind that the cam bearings will be destroyed

As the pistons and connecting rods are removed, they are marked as to their position in the engine. Note that the rod caps have been bolted to the ends of the rods. It is important that these parts not be mixed up.

The crankshaft is checked and machined if necessary to eliminate any scoring on the journals. This work is done at a machine shop. You will want to inquire of the shop's reputation as poor machining can ruin hard-to-find parts.

in the process so have a new set on hand before you start. Replace all core plugs with new ones.

Before boring, choose an oversize piston that will compensate for cylinder wear and have these on hand.

If the engine has had a history of head gasket failure, it would be wise to deck the block. This is the same process as cylinder head resurfacing. It's a lot easier to do this now than later, and has the added bonus of narrowing the valve seats a little.

The rest of the rebuild follows standard procedure. You would be wise to use the later, rotor-type oil pump as it pumps a higher volume of oil. Watch for oil pipe on prewar engines; the way that looks right, isn't! The counterweight next to the number 3 main bearing will hit. I learned this the hard way and even then I almost installed it backwards a second time. Follow tightening specs carefully.

A low-budget balancing job can be done right at home with an ordinary balance-beam scale. Find the lightest piston and pin assembly, and remove material from the others until they are all the same. Do the same for the rods. If you really want a smooth runner, a professional, dynamic-balance job, including flywheel and clutch, is in order. That's a job for a pro, but may be worth it if your engine has been built using parts from many other engines.

There is little left to luck in this approach to engine repair. Retighten the cylinder head and break it in carefully. With routine maintenance it should last as long as you can afford gas to run it.

Incidentally, there is no reason why these engines will not run well on unleaded gas. The stellite seats on the exhaust valves were meant for long, trouble-free service. I ran one engine for years on no-lead propane without any problems at all.

Parts interchange

On all sixes, except certain industrial and truck engines, valve guides are interchangeable, as are exhaust seats, wrist pin bushings and oil pumps. Rear oil seals are of two or three designs and are sometimes interchangeable, but watch out for a slight space if you are using a later seal on the 201. This space is between the metal seal holder and the block, and can be filled with silicone. Gasket sets are of two sizes for the two different-size blocks. There is an extra water passage at the front of the head on 1951 and newer engines; this is part of the later bypass system and eliminates the need for extra plumbing.

Crankshaft bearings are the same for all 3¼ in. bore blocks. The 3⅜ and 3⁷⁄₁₆ in. bore blocks share slightly larger bearings. Crankshafts within each block size can be interchanged, but you must use the rods that match the crankshaft. I have often put a Dodge crankshaft into a Plymouth block for an extra 13 cubic inches.

A simple but effective check for connecting rod alignment can be done by standing two rods side by side on a flat surface. The wrist pin holes should line up and the forks at the bearing end should touch. Bent rods will bind on the crankshaft, possibly seizing the engine and quickly tearing out the bearings.

The top groove clearance on the pistons should be on specs to prevent the ring from slapping up and down. As an alternative to buying new pistons, spacers can be installed to take up wear.

Performance modifications

The Mopar sixes will respond to all the traditional hot-rod tricks and they needn't spit their insides all over the street, either. As you read on, you may think that I have a trophy room full of bent and broken con rods. Not so! I blew my one and only rod bearing on a cold January day in 1959 while driving a 1935 Plymouth coach on farm roads. I was not old enough to have a license, nor did I recognize that clunking noise. I learned fast and have gone straight ever since.

If you're going to boost the horsepower and performance of your Dodge truck L-6 engine, you'll need to improve the oiling. This is done in several ways. The first is to increase the size of the groove in the main bearing shells. The technique here is to clamp the bearing shells in a four-jawed lathe chuck by bolting two surplus center main caps together. Make the groove in the bearing shell approximately three times as wide and twice as deep as that cut by the factory. It will then match the diameter of the oil hole in the block. This should be done to all four mains.

With a greater volume of oil coming from the larger grooves in the main bearing shells you can plug the squirt holes in the rods. This little hole tends to deflate the oil cushion around the bearing, especially during the power stroke. With the added oiling there will be plenty of throw-off for cylinder walls.

It is also prudent to install a new rotor type pump. Putting a ¼ in. spacer behind the relief valve spring gives an additional boost in oil pressure.

With these modifications, the oil pressure gauge will show about 40 lb. at idle and between 60 and 70 lb. at 30 mph. If your block has a full-flow filter as later Chrysler and DeSoto blocks (to 1954) do, great! If it has the bypass type, make sure it is correctly hooked up. The drain goes from the bottom of the cannister through the pressure relief valve (hole faces straight up). Be satisfied that it is not reducing pressure.

If you are choosing a crankshaft, use one from 1955 or newer. If it is still standard, so much the better. Don't forget you can interchange shafts in the 217 and 230 engines as long as you use the rods that go with the crankshaft. Same with all 3⅜ and 3⁷⁄₁₆ engines. Early shafts have 4 bolts in the flange, later have eight, but all flywheels fit, with the exception of some Plymouth Hydrive models. There is a ring-gear-starter change between 1956 and 1957. They do not interchange. Select components that match the bell housing you are using.

Compression

Compression on these engines can be raised as high as 10.5:1. In one case, I planed an Edmunds aluminum head as far as possible. Unfortunately, head gasket failure was chronic, but it was fun while it lasted!

You will probably wish to be conservative—say, an 8.0:1 compression ratio, which was stock for 1959. It helps to polish the chamber in the head before starting out. Compression can be raised by three methods: first, by milling the stock head 0.060 to 0.125 in.; second, by installing a head from a later engine; finally, by installing an aftermarket head such

A simple tray made by drilling holes in a length of 2x4 board keeps the valves in correct order. When original engine components are reused it is important that they go back in the same place they were removed from.

To improve the engine's breathing efficiency, the ports should be cleaned and opened up to match the manifold passages. This work does not require great skill, but does require patience and care.

as Edmunds or Fenton. If you use a later head, watch for the extra water passage on engines from 1951 and later. When installing a later head on an earlier engine the later gasket must also be used. On heads from 1956–1959, the temperature gauge fitting is smaller, but it can be drilled out and retapped to use the fitting for your truck.

Aftermarket heads are rare, but not impossible to find. I purchased a brand new Fenton for $75 within ten miles of home and found a good used Edmunds at a swap meet for $80. Unfortunately, these vintage speed parts are not being remanufactured. With these heads use AC44FF spark plugs.

Watch out if you are swapping a head from an engine with a different bore size or you may wind up reducing compression. For example, a 3$\frac{7}{16}$ bore engine has a larger chamber than a 3$\frac{3}{8}$ bore engine. On the other hand, you can raise compression this way by reversing the operation. If in doubt, "C.C." the chambers.

Good gasket surfaces are an absolute must!

Years ago, I carried a spark plug wrench so I could open up the gap of number six spark plug after every 5500+ rpm run. It is hard to look cool doing this on the side of the road, so check valve clearances.

Don't forget the tightening sequence and re-tighten the head as soon as it's warm and again after 500 miles.

Induction

Better induction really wakes these engines up—even a two-barrel carburetor as used on 1957–1959 Dodge cars helps. Edmunds and Fenton both made manifolds for both sizes of blocks, or you can make a manifold using your stock cast-iron one as a base. Three-ton trucks used a dual carburetor manifold which also had dual-exhaust headers. It works well, but is bulky and heavy.

Carburetors are a cut-and-try proposition as big is not always better. I would recommend the Zenith carburetor as found on International trucks of the 1940s. They are beautifully made with a brass-piston accelerator pump and have replaceable venturis,

---

Dodge Truck engines

With few exceptions, Dodge Truck engines through the years were based on corporate car engines. Still, Dodge Truck engines were not the *same* as car engines.

Truck engines were always upgraded to make them suitable for severe service. The extent to which an engine was upgraded depended upon expected use. For example, an engine designated for service in a half-ton pickup would be only mildly upgraded and limited to something as simple as chrome rings in place of steel rings. On the other hand, an engine built for service in a four- or five-ton truck would be fitted with heavy-duty components such as stellite-faced sodium-filled valves, a shot-peened crankshaft, timing chains instead of gears and valve rotators. Truck engines were built on an exclusive engine line separate from car engines.

The early Dodge Truck engines were identified as upgraded engines as Premium engines.

Truck engines beginning in the 1960s were designated by dash numbers as 225-1 and 225-2. The same engine in a car was simply a 225. The 225-1 was used in light-duty models from the A100 to the D300. The 225-2 was built for use in medium-duty trucks. The premium components on the 225-2 were roller timing chain, bi-metal connecting rod bearings, stellite-faced exhaust valves, roto-caps on exhaust valves and polyacrylic valve stem seals. Jack Poehler, manager and editor of the Slant 6 Club of America states that all slant six truck engines were equipped with truck crankshafts that were shot-peened and heavy-duty oil pumps.

The origin of 1960–1980 S-6 engines can also often be determined by its color. The original 1960

slant sixes were painted silver and had a turquoise valve cover. From 1963–1969, all truck engines were painted yellow, while car engines were red. From 1970–1980, all slant six engines, truck and car, were painted blue.

There were two truck engines which were used as is, without any changes from those in passenger cars. The first shared volume-production engine was the 383 V-8 used in D100, D200, D300, W100 and W200 models beginning in 1967. Until 1967, the old polyspherical-head 318 was the only V-8 available in light-duty trucks. Dodge Engineering reasoned that the sheer displacement and power output of the 383 made it suitable for light-duty use without upgrading internal components. Pressure for a larger V-8 to improve light-duty truck performance came from Dodge Truck Marketing via dealers. Engineering was asked to move fast on this request, so dropping the 383 in without modification or testing seemed to be the way to go, especially after the Service Department agreed to pick up all additional costs resulting from engine warranty claims. Fortunately, the 383 worked superbly and warranty costs were negligible.

The other V-8 used unmodified from the car line was the 426 Wedge engine in the Custom Sports Special in 1964 and 1965. Because the High Performance Package for the Custom Sports Special was expected to be a low-volume item and due to the outrageous size and power of the 426, upgrades seemed superfluous.

To the great advantage of the restorer, there are no external differences between light-duty truck and car engines. As long as you don't care whether the numbers match up, either one will bolt right into your truck.

which come in a number of sizes. Jets also come in several sizes, assuming you can find a source. Studebaker used a slightly smaller version of the Carter Ball and Ball which would work well on a dual-carburetor system.

Exhaust

Any improvements will help. A simple split manifold is good. Fenton headers are nice to look at and work well, too. Headers can be made from two stock manifolds or from tubing. The fact that the engines have six exhaust ports is a plus there. Put on nonrestrictive mufflers (remember the Blue Bottle), and a good, clean exhaust system and this part of the job is done.

Porting

The most significant improvement to be made here is the matching of the ports with the manifold passages. Careful use of templates and a rotory file will do this job. This is a simple, but exacting, operation as carelessness can ruin your block. Even a stock rebuild will benefit from port matching.

There is no advantage in relieving the block, since the area between the valves and the cylinders is flat. Instead, polish the combustion chamber in the head.

Clearances

Slightly greater clearances are desirable in a performance engine to insure good lubrication and allow for expansion due to greater heat. Allow 0.004 in. for piston skirt clearance and between 0.0015 and 0.002 in. for bearings. Set valve tappets at 0.002 in. over factory specs.

Camshafts

I have found the stock camshaft to be adequate and the ones used between 1957–1959 are supposed

Besides cleaning and repainting, the head should be checked for warpage. If the head is warped, the head gasket won't seal properly, possibly causing water to leak into the cylinders. If this happens, the engine could be ruined by corrosion and the caustic reaction of antifreeze on the piston rings.

to be the best. A mild street grind would probably help. Iskendarian and Howard Cams used to offer camshafts for these engines, and most cam grinders have performance specs in their files.

Spark

Use a 1951 or later distributor. Try to get a vacuum-advance unit which has a removable plug,

In most cases, cylinder wall taper will require reboring the block and installing slightly oversize pistons. When machining work is being done to the block, it is also wise to have hardened valve seats installed so that the engine can be operated on unleaded gasoline without damage.

An Edmunds aluminum head and dual intake manifold will increase compression and carburetion for better all-around performance. In addition, these speed parts give the engine a dressier appearance.

allowing adjustment of the amount of tension against the diaphragm. Road testing and adjustment will eliminate pre-ignition. Quality of fuel, humidity and altitude as well as compression and driving habits all enter into this adjustment. It's another cut-and-try operation, but worth every minute spent. Four degrees initial advance to 36 degrees total works for a 251 ci engine that a friend runs in his 1958 Dodge coupe.

I used to love to watch a B-Modified circle track racer powered by a 1954 Chrysler six beat the ohv competition. I have always admired the spirit of someone who dares to be different, especially if he's a winner.

At this present time, I am running a 1957 Canadian Plymouth engine; originally a 215, it now displaces 260 ci due to a $3\frac{7}{16}$ in. plus 0.060 in. overbore. It has been ported and polished, but runs stock carburetion and exhaust. Performance and mileage are impressive, and the modified oiling system adds a degree of reliability.

So there it is, you don't need a Hemi to keep up with traffic. Enjoy that Dodge L-6. Overhead valves are just a passing fad.

L–6 Engines

Bore and stroke (in.)	Displacement (ci)	Typical application
$3\frac{1}{8}$x$4\frac{3}{8}$	201	Plymouth 1935–1941
$3\frac{1}{4}$x$4\frac{3}{8}$	217	Dodge and Plymouth
$3\frac{1}{4}$x$4\frac{5}{8}$	230	Dodge and Plymouth 1954–1959
$3\frac{3}{8}$x$3\frac{3}{4}$	201	Canadian Plymouth and Dodge 1938–1939
$3\frac{3}{8}$x$4\frac{1}{16}$	218	Canadian Plymouth and Dodge to 1954
$3\frac{3}{8}$x$4\frac{1}{4}$	228	Fluid Drive Dodge, Plymouth with Powerflite in 1954 (Canada)
$3\frac{7}{16}$x$4\frac{1}{4}$	236	DeSoto
$3\frac{3}{8}$x$4\frac{1}{2}$	241	Chrysler early 1940s
$3\frac{7}{16}$x$4\frac{1}{2}$	251	Chrysler 1946–1951 T-120 and Dodge truck
$3\frac{7}{16}$x$4\frac{3}{4}$	264	Chrysler 1952–1954, Crown Marine

Appendices

Paint Colors

Dodge Truck paint colors are listed here by years and alphabetically for cross-referencing. A couple words of warning are in order, however. Dodge Truck sales literature occasionally described certain colors by visual appearance instead of by actual name. Paint supplier data sometimes differed regarding model-year applications and color names.

In the detailed alphabetical listing, several matching colors, which had different names when used by other Chrysler divisions, are listed to help in cross-referencing paint chip charts. Alternate color names are followed in parenthesis, by the names most commonly used by Dodge. Slightly different colors were frequently given the same name in different years. Ditzler paint codes are included as an aid in cataloging colors.

As you examine your paint chip charts, terms you may find are Poly and Irid. These are abbreviations for polychromatic and iridescent, better known as metallic finishes. Syn. stands for synthetic. Bleeders are colors containing pigments which tend to come to the surface of lighter finishes painted over them.

We hope this appendix will be of value to all those interested in Dodge trucks. Many hours of research have made this listing as complete and accurate as possible. However, sources do not agree in every case so no responsibility can be accepted for errors or omissions.

Dodge Truck Paint Colors: Annual Listing
1933–1934
Black (fenders and sheet metal)

Dodge Brothers Blue (lacquer) (standard on Commercial Sedan)

Gray Olive Green (lacquer) (optional on Commercial Sedan)

Kiltie Green (enamel) (optional on all except Commercial Sedan)

Maroon (enamel) (optional on all except Commercial Sedan)

Monarch Maroon (lacquer) (optional on Commercial Sedan)

Oakbrook Brown (enamel) (optional on all except Commercial Sedan)

Ripley Brown (enamel) (standard on three-quarter- to one-ton, optional on all except Commercial Sedan)

Shaw Yellow (enamel) (optional on all except Commercial Sedan)

Smoke Gray (lacquer) (optional on Commercial Sedan)

Suburban Blue (enamel) (standard except on Commercial Sedan, optional on all except Sedan)

Twentieth Century Red (enamel) (optional on all except Commercial Sedan)
1935–1936
Black

Gray Olive Green

Kiltie Green No. 4

Prairie Gray

State Maroon

Suburban Blue

Twentieth Century Red
1937–1939
Atlanta Orange

Black

Kiltie Green No. 4

Maxim Red (1939)

Milori Green

Silver Wing Gray No. 3

Suburban Blue

Twentieth Century Red (1937–38)
1940–1942
Black

Dodge Truck Dark Blue

Dodge Truck Gray

Dodge Truck Green

Dodge Truck Light Blue

Dodge Truck Orange (1941–42)

Dodge Truck Red

Dodge Truck Yellow (orange tint) (1940)
1946–1947
Black

Dodge Truck Dark Blue (discontinued July 15, 1946)

Dodge Truck Dark Blue No. 2 (introduced July 15, 1946)

Dodge Truck Dark Green

Dodge Truck Red
1948–1953
Armour Yellow

Black (also optional wheel color, 1950–53)

Charlotte Ivory (Route-Van only)
Deep Blue (introduced July 1, 1949)
Dodge Truck Cream (1951–53 wheel color)
Dodge Truck Dark Blue No. 2 (discontinued July 1, 1949)
Dodge Truck Dark Green
Dodge Truck Red
Ecuador Blue (Route-Van only)
Granite Gray (1950–52)
Judson Green (Route-Van only)
Rio Maroon (two-tone color, 1950–52)
Sun Lemon Yellow (1950 wheel color, same as Dodge Truck Cream)
Waterway Blue (discontinued July 1, 1949)

1954–1955 (C-1 Series)

Armour Yellow
Banner Green
Black
Chrome Metallic (wheel color)
Dodge Truck Red
Ecuador Blue (Route-Van only)
Judson Green (Route-Van only)
Panama Sand (previously Charlotte Ivory) (Route-Van only)
Ponchartrain Green
Sonora Blue

1955–1956 (C-3 Series)

Armour Yellow
Banner Green
Canyon Coral
Chilean Beige (two-tone upper color and wheels)
Dodge Truck Red
Ecuador Blue
Ponchartrain Green
Rackham Blue
Terra Cotta

1957

Bayview Green
Bermuda Coral
Dodge Truck Red
Ecuador Blue
Mojave Beige (also two-tone upper color)
Omaha Orange
Pacific Blue
Ponchartrain Green
Stone Gray

1958–1960

Alaska White (1958–59)
Angus Black
Arctic Blue
Bell Green
Buckskin Tan (1959)
Dodge Truck Red
Heron Gray (1959)
Indian Turquoise (1960)
Klondike Yellow
Marlin Blue

Mustang Gray (1960)
Nile Green (1960)
Omaha Orange
Pine Green (1960, previously Ponchartrain Green)
Ponchartrain Green (1958–59)
Ranch Brown (1958)
Sahara Beige (1958) (also two-tone upper color)
Sand Dune White (1959–60)
Stone Gray (1958)
Toreador Red (1960)
Valley Green (1958)
Vista Green (1959)

1961–1968

Angus Black
Arctic Blue
Bell Green (1961)
Bell Green No. 2 (1962–66)
Bermuda Turquoise Metallic (1964–68) (A-100 Custom Sportsman only)
Buckskin Tan (1967–68) (not available on A-100)
Desert Turquoise
Dodge Truck Red (not available on A-100)
Dodge Truck White (1965–68)
Fawn Beige (1967–68)
Golden Tan Metallic (1964–68) (A-100 Custom Sportsman only)
Marlin Blue
Mojave Yellow (1967–68) (not available on A-100)
Mustang Gray
Omaha Orange (1961–66) (not available on A-100)
Pine Green
Sand Dune White (1961–64)
Sunset Yellow (1961–66) (not available on A-100)
Toreador Red
Turf Green

1969–1971

Angus Black
Arctic Blue
Beige
Bright Green (introduced February 2, 1970)
Bright Red (1971, previously Toreador Red)
Bright Turquoise (1971, previously Desert Turquoise)
Bright Yellow (introduced February 2, 1970)
Burnt Orange (introduced February 2, 1970)
Desert Turquoise (1969–70)
Dodge Truck Red (discontinued February 2, 1970)
Dodge Truck White
Light Green Metallic
Light Tan Metallic
Lime Green (introduced Spring 1970)
Maroon (introduced February 2, 1970)
Medium Blue
Medium Blue Metallic
Medium Green
Medium Tan
Mustang Gray (discontinued February 2, 1970)
Mojave Yellow (discontinued February 2, 1970)
Pine Green
Toreador Red (1969–70)

Dodge Truck Paint Colors: Alphabetical Listing

Paint color	Years	Ditzler codes
Alaska White	1958–59	8131
Angus Black	1958–71	9000
Arctic Blue	1958–71	11666 or 2229
Argent Silver (interior color)	1969–71	DX-8555
Armour Yellow	1948–56	80346
Army Scarlet (Maxim Red)	1939	70077
Atlanta Orange (or Mountain Orange)	1937–39	60004
Bahama Yellow (Motor Home color)	1970–71	81877
Banner Green	1954–56	41480
Bay Green (Milori Green)	1937–39	40001
Bayview Green	1957	41276
Beige (Motor Home color)	1964–71	22421
Beige	1969–71	23057 or 2218
Bell Green	1958–61	40648
Bell Green No. 2	1962–66	42801
Bermuda Coral	1957	70719
Bermuda Turquoise Metallic (A–100 Custom Sportsman only)	1964–68	12647
Black	1933–42	NA
Black (or Angus Black)	1946–57	9000
Black (interior color)	1968–71	9346
Black (interior color)	1969	9324
Blue (interior color)	1968	13466
Blue (Motor Home color)	1964–71	12882
Boatswain Blue (Dodge Truck Light Blue No. 2)	1941–42	10157
Boeing Orange (Dodge Truck Orange)	1941–42	60000
Boulder Blue (Suburban Blue)	1933–46	10000
Bright Green (introduced February 2, 1970)	1970–71	2224
Bright Red (previously Toreador Red)	1971	70773 or 2227
Bright Turquoise (previously Desert Turquoise)	1971	42687 or 2221
Bright Yellow (introduced February 2, 1970)	1970–71	2211
Buckskin Tan	1959	21631
Buckskin Tan	1967–68	22817
Burgundy Red (State Maroon)	1935–36	50006
Burnt Orange (introduced February 2, 1970)	1970–71	2226
Canyon Coral (or Geranium) (C–3 Series)	1955–56	70578
Carnival Red No. 1 (Twentieth Century Red No. 1)	1933–36	70072
Carnival Red No. 2 (Twentieth Century Red No. 2)	1937–38	70076
Cataract Green (Milori Green)	1937–39	40001
Charcoal (interior color)	1968	32656
Charlotte Ivory (or Panama Sand) (Route-Van only)	1949–53	80001
Chevron Blue (Dodge Truck Light Blue No. 1)	1940–41	10038
Chilean Beige (two-tone upper color and wheels) (C–3 Series)	1955–56	20873
Chrome Metallic (Silver Wheel Enamel) (wheels) (C–1 Series)	1954–55	31256
Chrysler Blue (Suburban Blue)	1933–46	10000
Cinema Gray (Dodge Truck Gray No. 1)	1940	30057
City Green (Dodge Truck Green)	1940–53	40028
Cruiser Gray (Silver Wing Gray No. 3)	1937–39	30015
Dark Blue (or Dodge Truck Blue No. 2, Dodge Truck Dark Blue No. 2) (introduced July 15, 1946, discontinued July 1, 1949)	1946–49	10349
Dark Green Metallic (interior color)	1968–69	43721
Dark Green Metallic Suede (interior color)	1970–71	43435
Deep Blue (or Dodge Truck Blue No. 3, Dodge Truck Deep Purple Blue) (introduced July 1, 1949)	1949–53	10629
Desert Turquoise (or Bright Turquoise)	1961–70	42687 or 2221
Dodge Brothers Blue	1933–34	NA
Dodge Truck Blue No. 1 (Suburban Blue)	1933–46	10000
Dodge Truck Blue No. 2 (Dark Blue)	1946–49	10349

Paint color	Years	Ditzler codes
Dodge Truck Blue No. 3 (Deep Blue)	1949–53	10629
Dodge Truck Cream (previously Sun Lemon Yellow) (wheel color)	1951–53	80485
Dodge Truck Dark Blue No. 1 (Suburban Blue)	1933–46	10000
Dodge Truck Dark Blue No. 2 (Dark Blue)	1946–49	10349
Dodge Truck Dark Green (Dodge Truck Green)	1940–53	40028
Dodge Truck Deep Purple Blue (Deep Blue)	1949–53	10629
Dodge Truck Gray No. 1 (or Cinema Gray, Palace Gray)	1940	30057
Dodge Truck Gray	1941	30063
Dodge Truck Gray	1942	30000
Dodge Truck Green (or City Green, Dodge Truck Dark Green)	1940–53	40028
Dodge Truck Light Blue No. 1 (or Chevron Blue, Washington Blue)	1940–41	10038
Dodge Truck Light Blue No. 2 (or Boatswain Blue)	1941–42	10157
Dodge Truck Orange (or Boeing Orange, Shalimar Orange)	1941–42	60000
Dodge Truck Prairie Gray (Prairie Gray)	1935–36	30014
Dodge Truck Red No. 1 (Maxim Red)	1939	70077
Dodge Truck Red	1940–50	70002
Dodge Truck Red	1951–56	70339
Dodge Truck Red (discontinued February 2, 1970)	1957–70	70458 or 2242
Dodge Truck Silver Gray Metallic (Panel only)	1950	30827
Dodge Truck White (grayish tint) (exterior and interior color)	1965–71	8358
Dodge Truck Yellow (or Sioux Yellow) (orange tint)	1940	60003
Ecuador Blue (Route-Van only, 1949–55)	1949–57	10506
Fawn Beige	1967–68	22541
Firechief Red (Maxim Red)	1939	70077
Geranium (Canyon Coral) (C–3 Series)	1955–56	70578
Golden Bronze Metallic (interior color)	1957	21313
Golden Tan Metallic (A–100 Custom Sportsman Only)	1964–68	22296
Granite Gray	1950–52	30575
Gray Olive Green (or Gray Green, Rockwood Green, Sea Spray Green)	1933–36	40228
Green (Motor Home color)	1964–71	43268
Heron Gray	1959	31738
Horizon Gray (Prairie Gray)	1935–36	30014
Huntsman Green (Kiltie Green No. 4)	1933–39	40003
Indian Turquoise	1960	12102
Judson Green (Route-Van only)	1949–55	40627
Kiltie Green No. 4 (or Huntsman Green, Meadow Green)	1933–39	40003
Klondike Yellow	1958–60	80942
Lake Green (Valley Green)	1958	42122
Light Beige (Motor Home color)	1969–71	23207
Light Buff (interior color)	1957	21341
Light Green Metallic	1969–71	43807 or 2222
Light Tan Metallic	1969–71	23039 or 2217
Lime Green (introduced Spring 1970)	1970–71	2236
Limousine Blue No. 3 (Suburban Blue)	1933–46	10000
Marlin Blue	1958–68	11653
Maroon (introduced February 2, 1970)	1970–71	2225
Maxim Red (or Army Scarlet, Dodge Truck Red No. 1, Firechief Red, Signal Red)	1939	70077
Meadow Green (Kiltie Green No. 4)	1933–39	40003
Medium Blue	1969–71	13748 or 2216
Medium Blue Metallic	1969–71	13668 or 2215
Medium Blue Metallic Suede (interior color)	1969–71	13449
Medium Blue Metallic (interior color)	1970–71	13668
Medium Green	1969–71	43913 or 2223
Medium Green Metallic (interior color)	1970–71	43807
Medium Tan	1969–71	23137 or 2219
Medium Tan Metallic (interior color)	1970–71	23039
Medium Tan Metallic Suede (interior color)	1969–71	81600
Milori Green (or Bay Green, Cataract Green, Milori Light Green)	1937–39	40001
Mojave Beige (also two-tone upper color)	1957	21275

Paint color	Years	Ditzler codes
Mojave Yellow (discontinued February 2, 1970)	1967–70	81579 or 2243
Monarch Maroon	1933–34	NA
Mountain Orange (Atlanta Orange)	1937–39	60004
Mustang Gray (discontinued February 2, 1970)	1960–70	31892 or 2241
Nile Green	1960	42586
Oakbrook Brown	1933–34	NA
Off White (Motor Home color)	1964–71	8384
Olive Green (Motor Home color)	1970–71	44379
Omaha Orange	1957–66	60242
Pacific Blue	1957	11559
Palace Gray (Dodge Truck Gray No. 1)	1940	30057
Panama Sand (previously Charlotte Ivory) (Route-Van only)	1954–55	80001
Pine Green (previously Ponchartrain Green)	1960–71	41256 or 2220
Plymouth Blue (Suburban Blue)	1933–46	10000
Polar White (Motor Home color)	1970–71	8860
Ponchartrain Green (or Pine Green)	1954–59	41256
Prairie Gray (or Dodge Truck Prairie Gray, Horizon Gray)	1935–36	30014
Rackham Blue (C–3 Series)	1955–56	10142
Ranch Brown	1958	21427
Red (Motor Home color)	1964–71	71420
Rio Maroon (two-tone color)	1950–52	50105
Ripley Brown	1933–34	NA
Rockwood Green (Gray Olive Green)	1933–36	40228
Sahara Beige (also two-tone upper color)	1958	21428
Sand Dune White (tannish tint)	1959–64	80624
Sand Dune White (Dodge Truck white) (exterior and interior)	1965–71	8358
Sandlewood (interior color)	1958	21429
San Leandro Ivory (West Coast color)	1954	80640
Santa Rosa Coral (West Coast color)	1954	70454
Sea Spray Green (Gray Olive Green)	1933–36	40228
Sea Wolf Green (Power Wagon only)	1946–50	40284
Shalimar Orange (Dodge Truck Orange)	1941–42	60000
Shaw Yellow	1933–34	NA
Shorebeige (Smoke Gray)	1933–34	20015
Signal Red (Maxim Red)	1939	70077
Silver (Argent Silver) (interior color)	1969–71	DX-8555
Silver Wheel Enamel (or Chrome Metallic) (wheels) (C–1 Series)	1954–55	31256
Silver Wing Gray No. 3 (or Cruiser Gray)	1937–39	30015
Sioux Yellow (Dodge Truck Yellow) (orange tint)	1940	60003
Smoke Gray (or Shorebeige)	1933–34	20015
Sonora Blue (C–1 Series)	1954–55	11075
State Maroon (or Burgundy Red)	1935–36	50006
Stone Gray	1957–58	30966
Suburban Blue (or Boulder Blue, Chrysler Blue, Dodge Truck Blue No. 1, Dodge Truck Dark Blue No. 1, Limousine Blue No. 3, Plymouth Blue) (discontinued July 15, 1946)	1933–46	10000
Sun Lemon Yellow (or Dodge Truck Cream, Sun Yellow) (wheels)	1950	80485
Sunset Yellow	1961–66	81184
Terra Cotta (C–3 Series)	1955–56	21169
Topaz Metallic (interior color)	1958	21483
Toreador Red (or Bright Red)	1960–70	70773 or 2227
Turf Green	1961–68	42770
Turquoise (Motor Home color)	1964–71	43269
Turquoise No. 2 (Motor Home color)	1969–71	44051
Twentieth Century Red No. 1 (or Carnival Red No. 1)	1933–36	70072
Twentieth Century Red No. 2 (or Carnival Red No. 2)	1937–38	70076
Valley Green (or Lake Green)	1958	42122
Vista Green	1959	41586
Washington Blue (Dodge Truck Light Blue No. 1)	1940–41	10038
Waterway Blue (discontinued July 1, 1949)	1948–49	10450
White (Dodge Truck White) (exterior and interior color)	1965–71	8358
White (Motor Home color)	1968–71	8725

Clubs and Parts Sources

If you have recently acquired a vintage Dodge truck, you may have questions about sources or parts, or may want to make contact with others who enjoy preserving and driving an older truck as much as you do. The listing that follows provides answers to those questions. First, you'll find the addresses and brief descriptions of clubs for owners of Dodge light trucks and their Plymouth cousins. Of possible interest, too, are special model registries. A registry is not a club in the sense that information is shared by frequent newsletters and other activities. It is simply a listing of all known vehicles of this type. This listing may be published periodically, or you may have to request a listing from the keeper of the registry. Since registries are maintained only for low-production vehicles, their primary benefit is providing a way to get in touch with other owners of similar trucks. Otherwise, if you own a low-production 1957–1959 Dodge Sweptside, for example, you might wait a long time to meet another owner at a show, or see another listed in an ad.

In addition to providing addresses of well-stocked vendors of Dodge parts, the suppliers listing puts you in touch with sources of replacement wood and other items needed to rebuild your pickup's bed, quality wiring harness manufacturers and other specialty items. These are followed by service listings, helpful literature, and a discussion of other Dodge collectibles.

Even if you are prepared to overhaul your truck yourself, chances are you'll need an expert's help for specialized jobs such as cleaning and rekeying the locks or refacing or recalibrating the gauges. A literature listing puts you in touch with further restoration and Dodge history information, and the collectible section takes you into the realm of models and memorabilia. Part of the appeal of collectibles is their novelty. A friend constructed a truly unique coffee table for his living room from an engine block standing on chromed connecting rods and covered with a sheet of plate glass. Needless to say, the table not only served its function well, but made a great conversation starter. The world of Dodge doesn't have to start and end with your truck.

Clubs and publications

Dodge Bros. Club
  c/o Carl Roebuck
4 Willow Street
Milford, NH 03055
  Publishes a newsletter

Light Commercial Vehicle Association
Rt. 14, Box 468
Jonesboro, TN 37659
  Addresses all makes and models of light trucks; bi-monthly newsletter has Dodge column, parts column, free member ads and Dodge technical advisors

Military Vehicle Collector's Club
P.O. Box 33697
Thornton, CO 80233
  Promotes preservation and display of all makes and models of military vehicles; provides technical and authenticity information; holds regional, national and international meets

Plymouth Owner's Club
4407 Richmond Road SW
Calgary, Alberta
CANADA T3E 4P5
  Encourages collection and preservation of Plymouth cars and light trucks; publishes informative bi-monthly newsletter; holds regional and national meets, and has technical advisors

Powell Registry
Box 345
Walhalla, ND 58282
  Maintains listing of all known Powell Plymouth-based pickups.

Power Wagon Advertiser
RR 1, Box 59
Norway, IA 52318
  Monthly publication addressing Dodge four-wheel-drive trucks 1940–71

Slant Six Club of America
P.O. Box 4414
Salem, OR 97302
  Addresses all Slant Six powered cars, trucks and vans; publishes a quarterly newsletter. Holds regional and local meets, and has technical advisors

Sweptside Registry
5109 W 105th Street
Bloomington, MN 55437
  Maintains listing of all known Dodge Sweptside pickups

WPC Club
P.O. Box 3504
Kalamazoo, MI 49003
   Addresses Chrysler products generally and distributes
an excellent monthly magazine

Dodge parts

Andy Birnbaum Auto Parts
321 Lake Avenue
Newton, MA 02161
   Large inventory of new-old-stock parts

Arizona MoPar
320 East Pebble Beach
Tempe, AZ 85282
   Extensive new-old-stock parts inventory

Len Dawson
1557 Yokeko Drive
Anacortes, WA 98221
   Large inventory of new-old-stock parts

Dan Kirchner
404 North Franklin
Dearborn, MI 48128
   Complete line of original factory Dodge truck parts
manuals, shop manuals, original literature, including drivers manuals and sales brochures

John McMahon
6272 Athena Drive
Huntington Beach, CA 92647
   Extensive inventory of new-old-stock parts

Mitchell Motor Parts
2467 Jackson Pike
Columbus, OH 43223
   Large Dodge parts inventory

Older Cars Parts
3481 South 152nd Street
Seattle, WA 98188
   Good new-old-stock parts source

Roberts Motor Parts
17 Prospect Street
West Newbury, MA 01985
   Largest line of reproduction parts for Dodge trucks

Vintage Power Wagons
302 South 7th Street
Fairfield, IA 52556
   Specializes in parts and information for military and
civilian Dodge 4x4s

Suppliers

Bruce Horkey Cabinetry
RR 4, Box 188
Windom, MN 56101
   Stock or custom pickup bed floors and complete boxes

The Eastwood Company
580 Lancaster Avenue
Malvern, PA 19355
   Extensive line of specialty tools and literature for automotive and light truck restorers

GLASCO
85 James Street
East Hartford, CT 06108
   Replacement flat windshield and door glass

Lynn Steele Inc.
1601 Highway 150 East
Denver, NC 28037
   Large inventory of reproduction rubber parts

Metro Moulded Parts
11610 Jay Street
P.O. Box 33130
Minneapolis, MN 55433
   Large inventory of reproduction rubber parts

MikeCo.
c/o Michael Anthony Varosky
1901 Colonia Place #B
Camarillo, CA 93010
   Pre 1975 auto and truck lens replacement specialists

NAPA
Auto parts stores nationwide
   Large parts inventory for modern and vintage vehicles
available overnight from regional warehouses

Neil Riddle
452 Newton
Seattle, WA 98109
   Mopar signs, clocks and memorabilia

Restoration Specialties
P.O. Box 328, RD 2
Windber, PA 15963
   Weatherstrip, fasteners and hardware

Rhode Island Wiring Service
P.O. Box 3737
Peace Dale, RI 02883
   Wiring harnesses

Y n Z's Yesterday Parts
333 East Stuart Avenue
Unit A
Redlands, CA 92374
   High-quality replacement wiring harnesses for Dodge
and Plymouth trucks

David F. Lodge
RD#1, Box 290B
Saylorsbury, PA 18353
  Reproduction data plates

Photo Card Specialists, Inc.
1726 Westgate Road
Eau Claire, WI 54703
  Makes high-quality color business cards based on a photo of your truck, also color postcards and calendars

The Horn Shop
7129 Rome-Oriskany Road
Rome, NY 13440
  Repairs for most models

The Key Shop
144 Crescent Drive
Akron, OH 44301
  Repairs and rekeys all locks

Darren DeSantis
67 Lou Ann Drive
Depew, NY 14043
  Recovers and reupholsters sun visors

Literature

Classic Motorbooks (Motorbooks International)
P.O. Box 1
Osceola, WI 54020
  Distributors and publishers of wide range of motoring books including *Heavyweight Book of American Light Trucks 1939–1966* and *How to Restore Your Collector Car*

Dan Kirchner
404 North Franklin
Dearborn, MI 48128
  Complete line of original factory Dodge truck parts manuals, shop manuals, original literature, including drivers manuals and sales brochures

Walter Miller
6710 Brooklawn Parkway
Syracuse, NY 13211
  Huge assortment of original 1910–1980 sales literature, repair and owners manuals for Dodge trucks and other vehicles

Index